Mean Lives, Mean Laws

CRITICAL ISSUES IN CRIME AND SOCIETY

RAYMOND J. MICHALOWSKI, SERIES EDITOR

Critical Issues in Crime and Society is oriented toward critical analysis of contemporary problems in crime and justice. The series is open to a broad range of topics including specific types of crime, wrongful behavior by economically or politically powerful actors, controversies over justice system practices, and issues related to the intersection of identity, crime, and justice. It is committed to offering thoughtful works that will be accessible to scholars and professional criminologists, general readers, and students.

For a list of titles in the series, see the last page of the book.

Mean Lives, Mean Laws

OKLAHOMA'S WOMEN PRISONERS

SUSAN F. SHARP

RUTGERS UNIVERSITY PRESS
New Brunswick, New Jersey, and London

Library of Congress Cataloging-in-Publication Data

Sharp, Susan F., 1951
    Mean lives, mean laws : Oklahoma's women prisoners / Susan F. Sharp
        pages cm.—(Critical issues in crime and society)
    Includes bibliographical references and index.
    ISBN 978-0-8135-6276-6 (hardcover : alk. paper)—ISBN 978-0-8135-6275-9
    (pbk. : alk. paper)—ISBN 978-0-8135-6277-3 (e-book) (print)
    1. Women prisoners—Oklahoma. 2. Female offenders—Rehabilitation—Oklahoma
    3. Reformatories for women—Oklahoma. 4. Corrections—Oklahoma. 5. Children
    of prisoners—Oklahoma. I. Title.

    HV9475.05S53 2014
    365'.608209766—dc23
                                                        2013042858

        A British Cataloging-in-Publication record for this book is available
                            from the British Library.

            Visit our website: http://rutgerspress.rutgers.edu

        Manufactured in the United States of America.

This work is dedicated to Gwen, Karen, and Tracy, three wonderful women whose lives have intersected with mine, and in memory of Aline. You have taught me so much. My life is far richer because of you.

Contents

ILLUSTRATIONS

PREFACE

As I was finishing my doctorate, I hoped to teach and conduct research in the area of deviance and gender, bringing a feminist perspective to my work. I was initially more interested in demonstrating gender differences in deviance and less interested in focusing on crime and the criminal justice system. However, three separate but related events led to the research agenda that has culminated in this book, changing the direction of my career.

The first event occurred in February 1996, when I interviewed at the University of Oklahoma for an assistant professor position in the Department of Sociology. My dissertation focused on female injecting-drug users (IDUs), and I was being considered as someone who would specialize in issues related to gender, crime, and deviance. As I was being driven around the Oklahoma City metropolitan area, something occurred which has had a lasting impact on my work. My guide, in an effort to convince me that I would really like being at the University of Oklahoma, proudly announced that Oklahoma had the highest female incarceration rate in the nation. I asked him why, expecting to hear a sociological explanation such as poverty level, lower educational attainment, high rate of drug use, or the lower status of women in the state. Instead, he commented, "Oklahoma has mean women." I was appalled and speechless, but as I returned to Austin, I kept thinking about that statement and what it meant. Having worked as a drug counselor for years prior to obtaining my doctorate, I had firsthand experience, though little data, that suggested that the pathways into addiction and crime were often very different for women and men. Indeed, one of my reasons for wanting to study gender and deviance was to gather hard data that would support (or not support) my real-life experiences. I reached the conclusion that a feminist criminologist was needed in the state of Oklahoma if even academics saw the high female incarceration rate as solely the fault of the women. Therefore, I ended up taking the position at the University of Oklahoma, where I have remained. That incident, juxtaposed with the subsequent years of research, led to the title of this book.

The second event occurred during my first semester on campus. I was contacted by a professor in the Department of Human Relations, Dr. Susan Marcus-Mendoza. She had seen my areas of specialization in a list of incoming faculty, and she realized we had overlapping interests. At our initial meeting, she suggested that we apply for a small grant from the Oklahoma Criminal Justice Research Consortium, a now defunct association of academics and criminal justice professionals. They wanted a study conducted on the effects of incarceration on families of drug offenders in the state. My suggestion was that we title our proposal, "Gender Differences in the Effects of Incarceration on Families of Drug Offenders," and this proposal was funded. This led to data collection in both men's and women's prisons, a few publications, and a clearer understanding of the issues of women prisoners. I will always be indebted to Susan for reaching out to me. Not only has it led to long-term collaboration and friendship, but it has led to a deep passion for female offenders and their families.

The third event resulted from a report that Susan Marcus-Mendoza and I made to the Oklahoma Sentencing Commission on the effects of incarceration on families of offenders. Representatives of a victim's advocate group protested the focus of our study, arguing that the state should not waste money on the families of offenders but should reserve that money for the families of victims. Again, I was disturbed at the willingness to reject those affected by the incarceration of a family member, particularly the children. The assumption appeared to be that these family members were guilty by association or relationship (and therefore, unworthy). As a result, I began emerging as an advocate for the families of offenders, an "accidental activist." As I learned more about the histories of the women prisoners themselves, I expanded my scholarship and advocacy towards helping improve their situations, as well.

Those three events helped shape my research agenda. Several years later, the Oklahoma Commission on Children and Youth (OCCY) contacted me to replicate and extend the portion of that project that focused on women prisoners and their families. An Oklahoma State Representative, Barbara Staggs, and a State Senator, Debbe Leftwich, had put forth a Joint Resolution (SJR 48, 2004) directing OCCY to conduct a study on the impact of maternal incarceration on the children. OCCY wanted me to conduct the research, and had no issue with my obtaining additional data on the women themselves. This led to several years of research surveying the women prisoners and interviewing caregivers of their children. The research has been life-changing for me, and I became a spokesperson for women prisoners and their children in Oklahoma. Finally, a number of my graduate students have developed an interest in women prisoners, leading to several theses and dissertations and numerous presentations. One former student, Dr. Juanita Ortiz, developed her own project, interviewing women who were incarcerated for a second or subsequent time, and some of her findings are included as a chapter in this book.

The book is grounded in a feminist strain approach. Elements of general strain theory as well as the Adverse Childhood Experiences (ACE) study have been incorporated to further elaborate the pathways model. Additionally, I have tried to locate the high incarceration rate of women in Oklahoma in the legal and social climates of the state and nation. Clearly, to truly understand why Oklahoma imprisons women at such a high rate, we must look beyond the women themselves. Legislators and average citizens, often acting on a fear of crime, are at least as responsible as the incarcerated women for Oklahoma's exorbitant imprisonment rate.

The journey to this stage of my research has involved many people. The Oklahoma Department of Corrections has some incredible administrators, and several have played an enormous role not only in my research but in my understanding of the issues involved. Justin Jones, Director, and Dr. Laura Pitman, Deputy Director for Female Offender Operations (recently renamed Division I), have made access to prisoners available and helped shape my understanding of the women prisoners as well as of policies and laws. Dr. Michael Connelly, former administrator of the Evaluation and Analysis Unit of the Department of Corrections, facilitated both the administration of surveys to the women and locating related data. Lisa Smith, Director of the Oklahoma Commission on Children and Youth, has worked tirelessly with me on producing the annual studies and disseminating our findings. Finally, and most importantly, as a result of showing up at the women's prisons year after year, many women prisoners have found me after their release back into society. Their insights and stories have been invaluable in shaping this book and my research in general. To protect their anonymity, I have used pseudonyms and have not disclosed their names, but I hope they know they have touched my life in indescribable ways. These women are courageous and committed, to improving not only their own lives but the lives of the women still in prison and their families. It is in their honor that I have undertaken this project.

I would like to thank the Oklahoma Department of Corrections, especially Justin Jones, Dr. Laura Pitman, and the Evaluation and Analysis Unit, for allowing me access to the prisons to conduct this research and providing me with additional data. I am indebted as well to the Oklahoma Commission on Children on Youth for their partnership in the research—in the form of material support through grants—that is the foundation of this book.

Mean Lives, Mean Laws

Introduction

OKLAHOMA HAS long led the nation in the rate of female imprisonment. At the time of the writing of this book, the per capita incarceration rate in Oklahoma (135 per 100,000) was double the national rate (67 per 100,000) (Guerino, Harrison, and Sabol 2011). This is not surprising, as Oklahoma also ranks low in indicators related to the well-being of women. For example, Oklahoma ranks 48th in the United States in the percentage of women with health insurance and first in poor mental health among women (Institute for Women's Policy Research 2010). Overall, it ranks 45th out of the states in social and economic autonomy (Institute for Women's Policy Research 2010). Indeed, the status of women in Oklahoma is low enough to motivate a young student in Oklahoma to create a website entitled, Oklahoma Hates Women (n.d.). While Oklahoma does not fare well in the well-being of women, over the past two decades it has dominated the nation in the per capita incarceration of women. Understanding this phenomenon is a major purpose of this book, the culmination of nearly fifteen years of research on Oklahoma's women prisoners and their children.

A few important lessons have emerged from my work. First, most of the women prisoners report childhoods fraught with poverty, abuse, and neglect. One woman talked about growing up with no running water in her home and ongoing sexual abuse at the hands of various male relatives. Not surprisingly, by the time she was in her mid-teens, she was on her own and supported herself through prostitution. She also frequently hooked up with men involved in various criminal activities. That led to her first incarceration, as the get-away driver at a convenience store robbery. She has spent the majority of her adult life in prison, and thus has never acquired the tools that would allow her to live successfully outside of prison, so she does not last long outside of institutions. She recently returned to prison on a parole violation after only eleven months on the outside. Her story, unfortunately, is not unique.

Second, most of the women described lives centered on drugs. Many are addicts, and some were involved in drug manufacturing or distribution. Not surprisingly, many of the women had run away in their teens and become addicted to drugs. However, others reported drug use that began or escalated following a divorce. One woman, a former teacher, became addicted to pain pills following a back injury. Because she was upset about her divorce and loss of custody of two small children, she began using her prescribed medication to deal with painful emotions. As her drug use escalated, her doctor refused to refill her prescription. She eventually was caught passing a fraudulent prescription, written on a prescription pad she had stolen from her sister, a nurse. Now her children live with their father in another state, she can no longer teach, and she is wondering what she will do upon her release. Other women, upon divorcing, said they began hanging out in bars. They eventually met men involved in the manufacture of methamphetamine. While few of these women became very involved in the methamphetamine trade, many of them found themselves convicted of manufacturing or conspiring to manufacture a controlled substance as a result of their association with men involved in the drug trade. This has often resulted in excessive sentences, including several with life without the possibility of parole. Some have still not received any form of drug treatment.

Third, most of the women in Oklahoma prisons are mothers. For them, imprisonment means separation from their children, often the most important relationships in their lives. More disturbingly, many of the women may not be able to reunite with their children. Their parental rights are often terminated while they are in prison. Those who have not permanently lost their children still face obstacles. Many of the women lack resources to provide for their children once they are released. The children themselves also suffer, and the stories of these children and those who care for them are an important part of this work.

When I first began studying women prisoners, I often met with distrust. Many women did not want to participate in the research, voicing doubts about how the studies could possibly benefit them. However, over the years, policies started changing, in part as a result of research around the country, including my own. The women began writing to me, and the last time I administered a survey, over sixty percent were willing to participate. While this may not seem like a particularly high percentage, it is important to note that this is sixty percent of the entire sample. Some of those who did not participate had been moved or discharged, while others could not participate due to work assignments or restrictions. One year, the women were so glad to see me that I received an ovation at one of the facilities when my students and I arrived to administer the survey. Furthermore, former prisoners began showing up in my office once they were released, and several have become involved in efforts to change laws and policies. I introduced one woman to a progressive state legislator, who hired her as her executive administrative aide. This led to other women working in the legislator's office as part of their community service. Another former prisoner has gone to work in the field of substance abuse treatment and is working on obtaining funding for a program to assist women transitioning back into the community after incarceration. A number of former women prisoners also formed an informal group they refer to as "Just Us Girls," a play on words, providing support to women returning home from Oklahoma's prisons.

Over time, it became apparent to me that there were both individual and societal reasons for the high incarceration rate. At the individual level, these women have experienced mean lives of abuse and poverty: an important explanation of why so many of them become imprisoned. At the societal level, the state is impoverished, with women and children often faring poorly. Additionally, Oklahoma focuses on harsh punishments for those who offend the collective morality. Women who use drugs and commit crimes are viewed with distrust and disdain.

Drug crimes account for at least half of the new receptions each year, and almost two-thirds of the women in Oklahoma prisons need substance abuse treatment. The high level of drug use among the women can be at least partially explained by their abuse histories. Questions drawn from the Adverse Childhood Experiences (ACE) study help provide a more clear understanding of the relationships between their dysfunctional childhoods, mental health problems, substance abuse, and crime (Felitti et al. 1998). Put simply, most of these women have been abused in many ways and have grown up in households characterized by instability, addiction, mental illness, and violence. As adults, many have re-created the same conditions in their own families. As a result of abuse they have suffered, many have experienced mental health problems and have used drugs to self-medicate.

Additionally, Oklahoma is a poor state. The educational achievement of women is one of the lowest in the nation. Not surprisingly, poverty-induced property crimes account for the majority of the women who are not incarcerated for drug crimes. Chapter 1 focuses on the theoretical foundations that provide the framework for examining the lives of Oklahoma's women prisoners and how their histories of abuse and poverty help explain the high incarceration rate.

However, individual explanations of why these women use drugs and engage in other crimes can only partially explain the high imprisonment rate. Despite the American emphasis on individual responsibility for behaviors, it would be remiss to exclude an examination of the social climate in which this mass incarceration occurs. Oklahoma takes great pride in being tough on crime. While the War on Drugs provides a broader framework for understanding how policies around the country led to mass incarceration, specific laws and policies in Oklahoma—mean laws—have created an atmosphere that has made the state number one in the incarceration of women. Thus, in chapter 2, I examine these laws, Oklahoma laws and policies embedded in an examination of the broader movement to a more punitive approach in the United States.

Chapter 3 briefly describes the methods used to gather the data on the women prisoners themselves, as well as the caregivers of their children. I conducted several studies over the years. The first studies, in 1997 and 1998, were on gender differences in the effects of incarceration on families of drug offenders. Then in 2004, the Oklahoma State Legislature passed SJR 48, requiring the Oklahoma Commission on Children and Youth to conduct a study showing the effects on children of incarcerating their mothers. Data were collected in 2004, 2005, 2007, 2008, and 2009. The survey instruments included extensive questionnaires about the family histories of the women, with questions on the composition of the households in which they grew up; drug and alcohol use in those households; violence, abuse and neglect in their homes; and their education. The next part of the questionnaires focused on their legal, mental health, and substance abuse histories. The women were also asked about rapes and domestic violence that occurred during adulthood. Additionally, a portion of the studies focused on the children themselves, including placement in foster homes and problems the children experienced both before and during the mother's incarceration. Finally, the women were asked open-ended questions about what they saw as their biggest challenges and needs. Over the course of several years, I also conducted in-depth interviews with the caregivers of the minor children of women prisoners. After this in-depth description of the study, I then focus on the childhood experiences of the women, with attention paid not only to their abuse but also to the dysfunction in their childhood homes. In addition to an emphasis on childhood experiences, the chapter also examines their adult experiences, including abuse and rape, intimate relationships, and their legal histories.

Chapter 4 turns to institutional responses and how the women experience imprisonment. The focus is on what the women experience in prison as well as what programs are available to them. For years, the state utilized Moral Reconation Therapy (Brame et al. 1996), a program developed for work with antisocial personality disorders. It is better suited for more hardcore offenders than most women prisoners. In the past few years, there has been a shift towards woman-sensitive programming to deal with women's past traumas as well as to plan for their reintegration into mainstream society. The chapter will include both the women's experiences and the administrators' perspectives.

Chapters 5 and 6 give two different views of what happens when the women are released from prison. Chapter 5 was written by my former doctoral student, Juanita Ortiz. Dr. Ortiz interviewed women who were serving their second or subsequent incarceration. It is a poignant examination of the problems women face between incarcerations. In contrast, chapter 6 focuses on interviews of women who have successfully stayed out of prison. It explores problems these women faced on release, followed by descriptions of what they did to minimize the impact of those problems.

In Chapter 7, the focus shifts to the children of the women prisoners and the people who care for those children. When a mother is incarcerated, she is not the only one punished. Her children may suffer, and their care often places emotional and economic burdens on those who care for them. This chapter illuminates the experiences of the children, both from the mothers' perspectives and those of the people caring for their children.

While much of the book has focused on the problems implicit in mass incarceration of women, change is starting to occur, largely due to the scholarship of feminist researchers who have documented the need for woman-sensitive programming and a fresh look at policies. Chapter 8 focuses on some of the positive changes occurring in Oklahoma, many of them mirroring changes around the country. In late 2008, the Oklahoma Department of Corrections (DOC) established the Division on Female Offenders (now renamed Division 1), placing all assessment, treatment, and custody of women offenders under a new deputy director. In addition to the changes within the DOC, many new programs are being provided by private and non-profit agencies as a result of grant money made available for faith-based initiatives and other programming.

Finally, Chapter 9 summarizes the lessons learned from studying Oklahoma's women prisoners and prisons, and examines both theoretical implications and policy implications. While this text focuses on Oklahoma's women prisoners, they are not unique. Instead, this book may hopefully serve as a case study of women prisoners, their problems and their needs. In addition, the goal is to approach the study of female incarceration from a micro/individual level as well as a macro/societal level. Unless we begin to address the problem of over-incarceration of women at both levels, long-term change is unlikely.

CHAPTER 1

Mean Lives

A THEORETICAL FRAMEWORK

ALTHOUGH THE public attitude is often that women offenders are mean or bad, the real stories are far more complex. It is impossible to understand the choices of women who offend without placing those choices in the context of the women's lives and social placement. Today there is an evolving understanding of women who offend, but that has not always been the case. Historically, women offenders have either been ignored or seen as abnormal, because they not only violated the laws but also gender norms.

EARLY THEORETICAL APPROACHES TO WOMEN OFFENDERS

Forty years ago, there was little information on women who offended or on women's imprisonment. Since women constituted only a small proportion of all prisoners, they were deemed as being of only marginal interest to criminologists. Most of the theories of crime that were developed in the first half of the twentieth century ignored women, and thus little information was available to be incorporated into correctional programming. When attention was paid to women offenders, the attitude was that they were somehow both criminal and unlike other women, or "doubly deviant."

In theories developed during that period, women who committed crimes were usually portrayed as sexually deviant. Indeed, female criminals were in some ways viewed as more deviant than male criminals, since they not only violated criminal laws but also violated the norms of "ideal womanhood," and thus were a threat to dominant patriarchal ideas regarding acceptable female roles (Schur 1984). While much has changed since then, much has remained the same, at least in the eyes of the general public. While feminist criminologists have developed far better explanations of why women offend, female prisoners are still viewed by the average person as doubly deviant women.

The tendency to overlook female offenders was long-standing. However, even during the early days of criminology, a few theorists attempted to explain women's crime. These explanations tended to be based in devaluation

of women in general, with a focus on "inappropriate" sexuality as the explanation. For example, in the nineteenth century, Cesare Lombroso sought
to explain the crimes of both men and women. Lombroso considered criminality to be the result of being a biological throwback, or atavist, someone
less evolved. Lombroso and his son-in-law Guglielmo Ferrero argued that
women were less evolved than men, but women criminals offended because
they were more like men (Lombroso and Ferrero 2004; Rafter 2005). They
linked female offending to female sexuality, arguing that increased sexuality was
a way that "female born criminals" were more masculine than other women.
Lombroso also sought to explain why women offended less often than men,
which created a dilemma for him. He believed that crime was the result of being
less evolved but also that women were less evolved than men. However, he
knew that women were also less criminal than men. Thus, he attempted to
resolve this inherent conflict by postulating that criminal women were more
masculine than other women, as evidenced by their sexual conduct, and thus
they were more like atavistic men than like other women. In other words,
women who committed crime did so because they were masculine, especially in their sexuality (Smart 1976; Lombroso and Ferrero 2004; Rafter 2005;
Belknap 2007).

A few decades later, W.I. Thomas (1923) focused more on social explanations and less on biological explanations than Lombroso, but his work still
barely scratched the surface in its examination of the causes of female offending. Like Lombroso, Thomas linked female criminality to female sexuality.
He argued that girls became delinquent due to a desire to have compan-
ionship and be loved. Unlike males, whom he believed committed crimes
for economic reasons, Thomas suggested that females became promiscuous in
order to manipulate males (Thomas 1923; Belknap 2007). Two weaknesses
in his approach stand out. First, he equated female sexual behavior with female
criminal behavior. Second and even more importantly, he ignored the social
and economic forces which contributed to women's crime.

The works of these early criminologists have had a long-standing impact
on the American penal system. Ignoring the ways in which lack of opportunity and power shape women's crime has had a serious effect on how women
prisoners have been treated or—more often—not treated. It was not until the
middle of the twentieth century that more in-depth studies of women, crime,
and the criminal justice system emerged. At the forefront of this change, Otto
Pollak did acknowledge that there could be structural reasons, such as poverty,
for women's crimes. And yet he also continued the theme of blaming women's
biology for their offending, albeit from a slightly different perspective. Pollak
focused more on the argument that women's hormonal fluctuations contributed to their criminal behavior. He further argued that women were as

criminal as men, but their behavior was more hidden, devious, and secretive. He postulated that both their own deceitful natures and a chivalrous system kept the public from being aware of the true extent of crimes committed by women (Pollak 1950, 1961; Smart 1976). Again, the blame was placed squarely on the women themselves, with little thought about how social conditions and unequal power might shape their lives.

More recent research has called Pollak's suppositions about the level of female crime into question. In their influential work, Darrell Steffensmeier and Emilie Allan (1996) observed that while both male and female offenders were much more likely to engage in less serious types of crime, males committed less serious offenses at much higher rates than females as well as more serious offenses. Their study of arrest records pointed out that over a three decade period, females constituted 15 percent or less of the arrests in all crime categories, with one notable exception: The increase in women's participation in minor property crimes such as larceny and fraud had risen to over 30 percent by 1990. This increased representation of women in larceny and fraud crimes pointed to the feminization of poverty during the shift to a post-industrial society (Chesney-Lind 1989; Steffensmeier and Allan 1996; Belknap 2007). These trends were substantiated by other data sources such as the National Crime Victimization Survey and self-report data. However, research continued to demonstrate that not only did fewer women than men offend, but they offended at lower rates. Steffensmeier's work has challenged Pollak's argument that the chivalrous nature of the criminal justice system and women's devious natures combine to keep their crimes hidden. Indeed, it is clear that males offend more than women. Not only do more males offend, but they offend more often and more seriously. Therefore, it should be no surprise that women are less likely to be incarcerated.

EMERGENCE OF FEMINIST APPROACHES

Other explanations of women's crime began to emerge. Feminist criminological theories began arising during the 1970s, largely due to the women's movement of the late 1960s and early 1970s. However, prior to the emergence of clearly feminist explanations of crime, Freda Adler and Rita Simon set forth the argument that female crime would begin to increase as a society moved toward gender equality. This approach, often known as the liberation/emancipation hypothesis, was based on the idea that as women's positions in society improved, they would have increased opportunities to engage in illegitimate as well as legitimate activities (Adler 1975; Simon 1975). John Hagan took this argument a step further with the power-control theory, suggesting that growing up in more egalitarian families would also increase female delinquency (Hagan, Gillis and Simpson 1987, 1993).

While these theories are by and large refuted by today's feminist criminologists, one point made by Simon is noteworthy, and in some ways
foreshadowed the explosion of female imprisonment in the latter part of the
twentieth century. Simon reflected that the idea of gender equality might
impact the criminal justice system. She was concerned that there might be
a punitive reaction to more gender equality, increasing the rate of incarceration for women (Simon 1975; Daly and Chesney-Lind 1988). Clearly, policies
and laws put into place during the 1980s and 1990s have demonstrated that
women who offend have been disproportionately impacted by the changes
(Chesney-Lind 1991; Chesney-Lind and Pollock-Byrne 1995; Chesney-Lind
2003). One has only to look at the words of Maricopa County Sheriff Joe
Arpaio to see evidence of the backlash against women who offend (Faludi
1991). "If women can fight for their country, and bless them for that, if they
can walk a beat, if they can protect the people and arrest violators of the law,
then they should have no problem with picking up trash in 120 degrees"
(Chesney-Lind 2003). Feminist criminologists have responded to these arguments. In an early feminist treatise, Meda Chesney-Lind pointed out that the
behavior of girls received a different response than that of boys, and that girls
were far more likely than boys to enter the juvenile justice system through
the commission of status offenses such as truancy, running away, and curfew
violations (Chesney-Lind 1973, 1974, 1977, 1986, 1989, 1997; Belknap 2004;
Chesney-Lind and Shelden 2004). The regulation of female sexuality was at
the core of responses to these offenses. Her later work brought recognition
of what is perhaps the most important precursor of female offending: childhood abuse, particularly sexual abuse (Chesney Lind 1977, 1986; Chesney-
Lind and Shelden 2004). In her own words, "Ever since I met Michele [Alvey]
in the first class I taught in prison, I knew the place to locate the story was
almost always in the victimization" (Belknap 2004, 18). Although her voice
is perhaps the best known, Chesney-Lind is not alone in speaking out about
women offenders and their treatment. Dana Britton views the publication of
Carol Smart's critique as the beginning of feminist criminology as a distinct
approach (Britton 2000). However, I would place the commencement more
with the work of Frances Heidensohn, whose first publication raised important questions about women's crime and their imprisonment (1968). Although
not openly feminist in her initial approach, Heidensohn's early work laid the
groundwork for other scholars to follow.

Feminist criminology received a boost with the publication of Smart's
treatise in 1976. Her work not only pointed out the false impressions of women
offenders found in earlier works but also began developing theories based on
the unique issues of women offenders (Naffine 1996). Feminist criminologists
have also focused on the treatment of female offenders by institutions of social

control. For example, a 1980s study found that while family was considered a stabilizing factor by the courts for both men and women who offended, legal decisions appeared to be based on a traditional view of gender roles (Eaton 1986). Women who were "proper housewives" were seen as less of a risk than other women (Kruttschnitt 1982; Eaton 1986). Motherhood, especially by middle class standards, was found to be a protection against imprisonment (Carlen 1983).

But perhaps the most important development in feminist criminology has been the incorporation of advocacy and the voices of the subjects into the research. Feminist standpoint theory takes into account the social placement of both the researchers and the subjects (Carlen 1983; Harding 1991; Ngaire 1996; Flavin 2001). It is through works like Pat Carlen's edited volume of autobiographies that we have learned much about the nature of life within women's prisons and about the women themselves (1985). Standpoint feminist criminology is not without its critics, however, including those who point out that it is dangerous to view women as a unidimensional whole, that race and class must also be part of the discussion (Cain 1990).

CURRENT APPROACH:
FEMINIST STRAIN THEORY

This book is framed in a feminist strain approach, drawing from feminist pathways approaches (Simpson 1989; Daly 1992; Owen 1998; Moffitt et al. 2001; Reisig, Holtfreter, and Morash 2006; Simpson, Yahner, and Dugan 2008; Salisbury and Van Voorhis 2009; Salisbury, Van Voorhis, and Spiropoulos 2009; Brennan 2012; Burgess-Proctor 2012), general strain theory (Agnew 1992), and research from the Adverse Childhood Experiences (ACE) study (Felitti et al. 1998). By incorporating the major elements of general strain theory into a feminist pathways approach, our understanding of women's crime can be enhanced.

Feminist pathways models have some relationship to life-course and developmental theories that focus on transitional points which place individuals on different trajectories (Sampson and Laub 1993). However, because Rob Sampson and John Laub based their work on the Glueck data, their version of life-course theory was developed to explain the behavior of males. It focuses on social bonds during childhood and adulthood and how weakening or strengthening of these bonds can explain the onset as well as either persistence or desistance of delinquent and criminal behavior. The argument is that childhood experiences may place an individual on a delinquent or criminal trajectory, but salient relationships such as entering into a meaningful job or a strong marriage can change the trajectory of a youthful offender into a more conforming path (Sampson and Laub 1993; Laub and Sampson 1993, 2006).

It does not, however, focus on ways in which the very structure of society may place certain individuals and groups, such as women and minorities, in tenuous and often painful positions, including remaining in abusive relationships. Nor does life-course theory examine how the system as a whole responds to those who react to strain with nonconforming and often criminal behaviors. Finally, it fails to take into consideration that marriage and career may be less important for many women, while motherhood instead may serve as a turning point (Sharp 1998; Hope, Wilder, and Terling-Watt 2003). Thus, mainstream life-course theory cannot provide a true feminist framework. Indeed, the trauma and lack of power experienced by women may serve as turning points that funnel them into crime. Limited choice of intimate partners further insures they will be exposed to crime and drug use. The social placement of women, especially poor women, is an integral part of women's pathways into crime.

In feminist pathways approaches, the focus is on how the abuse and oppression of women and girls narrows their options and may place them on a trajectory where crime may be the most logical response. Most pathways approaches describe multiple pathways of women into crime.

For example, in her examination of the lives of female heroin addicts, Marsha Rosenbaum (1981) found that the pre-addiction social worlds inhabited by the women shaped their entry into the world of heroin addiction. In her research, middle-class white women sometimes retreated into the "hippie trip." While they did not experience poverty growing up, they often were the products of emotionally (and sometimes physically or sexually) abusive homes and felt socially isolated in school. They often began running away during their teens, living on the streets, and being arrested. Arrest then led to either detention or return to their homes, followed by running away again. On the streets, they were often preyed upon by older males who introduced them to drugs and crime as a way of life.

In contrast, lower- and working-class girls who associated with male gangs often dropped out of school to party with these males, limiting their options as they became adults. These women tended to be subservient to the males in their circle, often carrying drugs or weapons for them or committing petty thefts to bring in money. They viewed themselves and the males with whom they associated as outlaws. They were introduced to drugs by the males in the gang and became involved with the justice system when arrested for either carrying drugs weapons or for petty theft (Rosenbaum 1981).

Among lower-class women of color, particularly black women, limited opportunities and substandard schools often led to involvement with men who were successful as drug dealers, deemed the "fast life" by Rosenbaum (1981). Often coming from chaotic families rife with poverty and violence, these

women sought refuge by attaching themselves with men who were successful in the underground economy. Unfortunately, this often led to prostitution
when they were pimped out by their male partners.

Rosenbaum (1979) also found that many of these women became mothers at an early age, and their drug use led to difficulty meeting their parental
obligations and then to extreme guilt, which in turn led to further drug use.
While the popular view of drug-using mothers is that they do not care about
their children, other research has documented that, in reality, they care a lot
about being good mothers. When possible, they try to manage both addiction
and motherhood. If that becomes untenable, they may place their children
with other family members. However, involuntary loss of their children can
create further strain and lead to further drug use and other self-destructive
behaviors (Kearney, Murphy, and Rosenbaum 1994; Sharp 1996, 1998).

Throughout these pathways into addiction and crime, the role of strains
in the lives of these women is readily apparent. For those following the
hippie pathway, childhood abuse and poor relationships with peers was evident, while the women following the outlaw pathway experienced strain
from limited options due to low educational attainment. Those entering
addiction (and crime) via the fast life experienced multiple strains due to
poverty and abuse in their childhoods. Furthermore, many women became
mothers at an early age, creating still more strain. Regardless of the initial
pathway, all the women who had children faced additional strains resulting from difficulties juggling their drug-using and criminal lifestyle with
motherhood.

In one of the better known pathways models, Kathleen Daly (1992) delineated five pathways into crime. Women who ran away or were turned out of
their home at an early age developed survival skills that often were criminal,
such as prostitution or theft. Those who had been the victims of childhood
abuse began using drugs to cope with their abuse and often acted out vio-
lently. In contrast, battered women who had not been involved in crime or
drug abuse early in their lives sometimes became violent, especially toward
their abusive partners. Additionally, some women became involved with
drugs through relationships with males. Daly's final group of women became
involved in crime through the commission of economic crimes, often motivated by poverty (see also Morash and Schram 2002).

In one of the most in-depth analyses of women's pathways into crime,
Barbara Owen (1998) documented not only the life histories of women prisoners, but how those histories contributed to how the women served their time.
Through data and in-depth interviews, she described not only their extensive
abuse histories but also their economic marginalization. Owen cited childhood family life, children and life on the streets, and a "multiplicity of abuse,"

stressing how these contributed to a "spiraling marginality," placing these women on the outer fringes of American society (1998, 41).

Pathways approaches often incorporate Cathy Widom's "cycle of violence." (Widom 1989; Widom and Rivera 1990; Widom 1995; Widom and Maxfield 2001). The focus is on how those who are abused are more likely to become offenders themselves. The fundamental concept of Widom's work is that abuse and trauma during childhood are linked to offending during adulthood, much as general strain theory and the ACE study argue. In one study, she found that abused girls were 73 percent more likely those without a history of abuse to engage in nonviolent offending later in life (Widom and Maxfield 2001). Abuse has also been linked to girls running away (Kaufmann and Widom 1999; Kempf-Leonard and Johansson 2007). Running away puts girls on the streets, often forcing them to turn to prostitution, theft and drug-dealing to survive.

Joanne Belknap (2007) cites research on prostitutes to emphasize the link between sexual abuse and later prostitution, pointing out, however, that some early studies failed to delineate the coercive nature of prostitution. The young woman or girl who is living on the streets is often forced into prostitution to survive or to gain protection, and she often remains in prostitution due to a lack of other options. Other early work has emphasized not only childhood sexual abuse but also neglect and severe physical abuse in the childhoods of women prisoners, emphasizing the link to drug addiction (Chesney-Lind and Rodriguez 1983). Finally, additional research notes that abuse does not stop at the end of adolescence but continues into adult battering relationships, further marginalizing women (Richie 1996).

Recently, Chesney-Lind has added to our understanding, refuting the argument that female incarceration is increasing because girls and women are more criminally violent. Her focus is less on the histories of the girls and women and more on the social climate in which they exist. In other words, society punishes those females who do not live up to the standard of behavior that is acceptable for girls and women (Chesney-Lind and Irwin 2007).

To understand how general strain theory can help inform pathways approaches, a clear understanding of the theory is needed. Robert Agnew originally argued that a strain is an occurrence disliked by the individual, and noted three major sources of strain: (1) the presence of negatively valued stimuli, (2) the loss of positively valued stimuli, and (3) the failure to achieve positively valued goals. The latter involves a gap between what an individual expects and actually receives or aspires to versus the actual outcome. The degree of strain is also increased when the outcome is seen as unjust or unfair. Finally, the magnitude, duration, recency, and incidence (Agnew calls this "clustering") increase the likelihood that strain will result in criminal behavior (Agnew 1992, 2006). In the lives of women offenders, it is clear that all three sources of strain are frequently present. Furthermore, the theory provides guidelines for examining the impacts of different strains.

However, it is the complexity of the theory that lends itself to feminist analysis. According to general strain theory, strain in and of itself does not create delinquency. Instead, it is the negative emotional response to strain that is the culprit. General strain theory argues that some negative emotions, like anger, are more likely to produce crime that is directed against others, such as robbery or assault. In contrast, depression, guilt, and anxiety contribute to the likelihood the individual will abuse drugs (Jang and Johnson 2003; Agnew 2006). These latter emotions are particularly relevant with women offenders. The number one reason for female incarceration is drug offending, and women offenders also report higher rates of depression than their male counterparts. Thus, exploring the relationship between different types of strain in their lives, with both depression and drug use, seems logical. Additionally, gender differences are common in the types of strain, responses to strain, coping strategies, resources, and deviant behaviors (Broidy 2001; Jang and Johnson 2003; Agnew 2006).

Equally important, general strain theory also provides an explanation for why not all women who experience the types of strain we see in pathways approaches engage in crime or drug use. Having resources and other coping strategies decreases the likelihood of deviance. Social support, self-esteem, and self-efficacy can all reduce the possibility that the individual will engage in deviance. Likewise, some have learned legitimate coping strategies that decrease the likelihood of choosing a deviant coping strategy. These become important in developing strategies to help women successfully disengage from crime and drug use. While the women who end up in prison may not originally have these assets, many can be learned through appropriate gender-responsive programming.

In short, individuals use various coping strategies, both legitimate and illegitimate, to reduce negative emotional states resulting from strain (Agnew 1992). Those who have developed legitimate coping strategies to deal with the strain in their lives (talking out problems, physical activity, cognitive reframing, etc.) will be less likely to engage in deviance to reduce the impact of negative emotions. Traits and skills the individual possesses may also help reduce the impact of the strain on negative emotionality, "including temperament, intelligence, creativity, problem-solving skills, interpersonal skills, self-efficacy, and self-esteem" (Agnew 2006, 71).

Additionally, the environment in which the individual is raised may constrain or enhance the ability to develop healthy coping strategies (Agnew 1992, 2006; Heimer 1997). This is quite relevant to female offenders, who often come from homes rife with conflict and chaos. Indeed, prior research indicates that specific types of strain are common in female offenders, who often experience unstable and chaotic childhoods, are victims of multiple types of abuse, and are single parents. This can lead them to involvement in street life and with men in the criminal and drug underworld, leading to even more marginality (Bloom, Owen, and Covington 2003).

Because most women offenders come from highly stressful home environments and continue to be involved in stressful situations and relationships in adulthood, it is no surprise that they have high levels of depression and anxiety, which often lead to substance abuse. Furthermore, because they tend to be marginalized in the work sphere, they frequently find themselves unable to earn an adequate living for themselves and their children. This can lead to further pathways to prison, especially through forming relationships with deviant males to help support their families, selling drugs, or engaging in low-level property crimes such as writing hot checks.

General strain theory alone lacks the capacity to fully explain female offending (Belknap and Holsinger 2006). However, it does point to the importance of looking at what types of strain may impact the lives of women and how these may differ from the strains in the lives of men. Thus it is important to incorporate what we have learned from feminist pathways approaches into our explanation. In our patriarchal society, women have less power, and this is even more problematic for women in marginalized communities. Additionally, women are far more likely than men to have experienced sexual abuse (Gaarder and Belknap 2002). This may be abuse during childhood, it may occur in adulthood or, most commonly, it may occur in both periods.

With long-term or chronic strains, the ability to respond in a legitimate manner is reduced, sources of legitimate response are exhausted, and the individual begins to see her efforts as futile (Agnew 2006). The young girl may respond to the strain in her home by running away, which can lead to a host of new problems. Once on the streets, she is exposed to other types of violence, to delinquent peers, and to drugs (Chesney-Lind and Shelden 2004). A patriarchal juvenile justice system often adjudicates her as delinquent, and either returns her to the abusive home that she fled or places her in a juvenile detention facility (Chesney-Lind 1989). Either is likely to exacerbate her problems.

Additionally, negative emotions become traits rather than transient emotional states as she grows up, and she becomes more likely to normally respond to strain with anger, depression, or frustration. She then becomes caught up in a cycle of illegitimate responses to adverse events. The woman experiencing chronic strain may also find herself more often in association with others who are also responding to strain in socially unacceptable ways. She may also experience gender discrimination and resultant monetary strain. This is particularly true among marginalized groups such as racial minorities and the lower classes (Agnew 2006). Eventually, she may develop a belief system that supports criminal and deviant behavior, a sort of outlaw mentality, where crime is seen as not only justifiable but actually desirable (Agnew 2006). Furthermore, her constrained social network, embedded in a society dominated by males, often places her in the position to experience more abuse. As her negative emotionality and low constraint lead her to self-select into abusive situations and relationships, this creates a downward spiral.

Finally, recent scholarship has examined the relationship of childhood strains to adult criminal and deviant behaviors delineated by the ACE study. This can help us further understand the relationships between abuse, mental illness, substance abuse, and incarceration among women offenders.

Recent research by Kaiser Permanente and the Centers for Disease Control (CDC) provides additional insight into female pathways to offending and further illuminates how childhood strains occur in clusters. Additionally, the ACE study points out the increased likelihood of negative outcomes in adulthood when there is no effective intervention. This study involved individuals enrolled in the Kaiser Health Plan who utilized the Health Appraisal Clinic in San Diego. The purpose of the study was to examine the relationship between life experiences, risk behaviors, and health problems. However, the ACE study can be easily applied to incarcerated women because of the focus on negative or adverse experiences in childhood and the subsequent relationship to risky behaviors such as drug use (Felitti et al. 1998; Sharp, Peck, and Hartsfield 2012).

Findings from the ACE study can help us understand incarcerated women and their histories. One of the most striking things about the study is that it was conducted with a population that was integrated into the fabric of society, as evidenced by having health insurance. Yet the researchers found similar outcomes to those seen in women offenders when several adverse childhood experiences were present. Additionally, rather than simply examining the discrete relationships between individual negative childhood experiences, the focus was on the cumulative impact of growing up in a dysfunctional household.

Essentially, the ACE study argues that adverse experiences during childhood—such as abuse or living in a home with multiple problems—lead to social, emotional and cognitive impairments. These in turn increase the likelihood of engaging in risky behaviors, which then leads to both health and social problems (Anda n.d.). It is the cumulative impact of these childhood experiences, however, that may be the most relevant to the study of women who offend. Stated simply, the more adverse experiences a woman has during her formative years, the more social problems, mental health problems, and physical health problems she is likely to experience as an adult. Furthermore, the ACE study researchers have cast this clearly as a public health problem rather than as a moral issue, providing neurobiological data to demonstrate why childhood trauma results in adult maladjustment. It is also important to note the finding that there is a biological basis for abuse being underreported: The human brain may shield the victim from the effects of the trauma by selective forgetting (ACE Reporter 2007).

While many negative health outcomes have been examined in the ACE study, the reported relationship between adverse childhood experiences and both substance abuse and mental health problems is most germane to a theory that explains female offending. Growing up in a home with parental substance abuse has been clearly linked to both adult depression and adult substance abuse. It is also strongly linked to experiencing many other types of adversity and abuse as a child, each of which further increases the likelihood of mental health or substance abuse problems in adulthood (Anda et al. 2002; Dube et al. 2002; Dong et al. 2004). While adverse childhood experiences in general contribute to alcohol abuse in adulthood, one of the most striking findings of the study is the relationship between parental alcohol abuse and the likelihood the individual will grow up to abuse alcohol as well, creating an intergenerational cycle of alcohol abuse (Dube at al. 2002; ACE Reporter 2003b). There are limited data examining the link between parental drug abuse and adult drug abuse, but the findings concerning parental alcoholism suggest there may be a similar pattern.

Likewise, depression has been clearly linked to adverse childhood experiences (Anda et al. 2002). In one study, almost 40 percent of those who experienced four or more adverse childhood experiences reported a history of depression, and a stunning 54 percent of the depression in women was related to having experienced the types of adverse childhood experiences documented in the ACE study (Felitti and Anda 2010). The ACE team of researchers stressed the importance of determining the presence of parental alcohol abuse in developing both effective interventions and effective treatment for depression.

> [Data] strongly suggest that prevention and treatment of alcohol abuse and depression, especially among adult children of alcoholics, will depend on clinicians' inquiring about parental alcohol abuse and the long-term effects of adverse childhood experiences, with which both alcohol abuse and depression are strongly associated (Anda et al. 2002, 1007).

Additionally, illegal drug use has been highly correlated with adverse childhood experiences. In the words of the ACE co-investigators, that relationship was "an exponential progression" (Felitti and Anda 2010). In other words, with more adverse childhood experiences, the likelihood of becoming an injecting drug user increased at a phenomenal rate. This was further supported in another ACE report, where those who reported five or more adverse childhood experiences were seven to ten times more likely to use illegal drugs than those who reported fewer adverse childhood experiences.

In addition, the adverse childhood experiences measured in this study were linked to early onset of drug use (Dube et al. 2003).

Because drug abuse is the primary reason women go to prison, these findings underscore the link between traumatic childhoods and incarceration. Felitti and Anda further emphasized that drug use was temporarily a *solution* for the person who had experienced multiple types of childhood trauma. Rather than demonizing the drugs (or their users), the ACE study illuminates the pathways for women into drugs and ultimately prison. It also demonstrates the importance of addressing addiction and other deviant behaviors as public health issues. Both prevention and treatment are sorely needed.

The ACE study calls for an integrated approach to early intervention for children growing up abused, neglected, witnessing domestic violence, or with substance-abusing, mentally ill, or criminal household members. All of these childhood stressors are interrelated and usually co-occur in these homes (Anda n.d., 3). This is an apt description of the childhoods of many women prisoners.

In the most recent analyses, the number of adverse childhood experiences has been expanded to ten, divided into three different areas: abuse, neglect, and dysfunctional household. While the majority of those participating in the ACE study reported at least one adverse childhood experience, only one in ten reported five or more. This is in stark contrast to the incarcerated women in this book, about half of whom report five or more adverse childhood experiences.

In Table 1.1, I compare the percentage of each adverse childhood experience in the ACE study population and in my 2009 study of incarcerated women. Because the women in Oklahoma's prisons have a much higher incidence of adverse childhood experiences than the Kaiser Permanente subjects, we can surmise that mental health problems and substance abuse problems would occur at very high rates in the incarcerated population. The contrast of the two groups brings home the degree of trauma experienced by women prisoners as children, and why their offending is evidence more of a public health crisis than a moral crisis. This is particularly true for those factors that reflect overall household dysfunction. For example, 13 percent of the subjects in the Kaiser study reported their mother was battered in the home, compared to nearly 35 percent of the women prisoners. Likewise, 27 percent of the Kaiser subjects reported growing up in a home with alcohol or substance abuse, compared to more than 66 percent of the women prisoners. Also noteworthy is the incidence of sexual abuse. In the Kaiser study, 21 percent reported sexual abuse compared to 56 percent of the women prisoners.

When an ACE score was computed for the women in prison, over half (59.3 percent) reported a score of 5 or higher, indicating they had experienced 5 or more adverse childhood experiences. Even more disturbingly, 19 percent reported a score of 8 or higher (Sharp 2009a). This is in comparison to about

Table 1.1

Percentage Reporting Adverse Childhood Experiences,
Kaiser Health Plan Enrollees and Women Prisoners in Oklahoma

Adverse Childhood Experiences	Percentage of Kaiser Health Plan Enrollees (1997–2005)	Percentage of Oklahoma Women Prisoners (2009)
Childhood Abuse		
Emotional	11	64.5
Physical	28	49.8
Sexual	21	56.1
Childhood Neglect		
Emotional	15	69.4
Physical	10	46.5
Dysfunctional Household		
Battered mother	13	34.6
Substance abuse in home	27	69.8
Mental illness in home	17	47.2
Parental divorce	23	61.1
Crime in home	6	26.2

Source: Kaiser Health Plan enrollees (Anda n.d., 6); Oklahoma Study of Incarcerated Women and Their Children: Phase I data (Sharp 2009).

12.5 percent of female Kaiser subjects reporting a score of 5 or higher (Anda n.d., 9). So few of the Kaiser subjects scored higher than 5 that the study does not even report scores of 8 to 10 (Anda, n.d.)!

In the current study, three common pathways into drug use and crime emerged, although they are not necessarily discrete. First, those from poor, high-crime communities and families with multigenerational drug use and offending may see the world as unfair and believe their opportunities for success in legitimate activities are minimal, if not nonexistent. In the Oklahoma Study of Incarcerated Women (2007; Sharp and Pain 2010), I found that many of the women, particularly women of color, came from very disadvantaged backgrounds with multigenerational incarceration. More than 15 percent of the black women, almost 12 percent of the Hispanic women, and almost 10 percent of the Native American women reported that their mother had gone to prison, compared to only 5 percent of the white women. Furthermore, 5 percent of the black women compared to only 2 percent of the white women reported a grandparent had gone to prison.

Not only did the women report intergenerational patterns of incarceration, but they also reported other characteristics indicative of poverty. For example, about one in six of the women of color and one in ten of the white women reported often not having enough to eat as a child. More than half of the women of color had less than a high school education, many with less than an eighth-grade education. White women fared slightly better, but even so, 40 percent had not graduated from high school. Furthermore, only one in eight black women and one in twelve Hispanic women had any college education, while white and Native American women were slightly more likely to have attended some college. Self-reports of behavior during adolescence provide further evidence of strained childhoods. Almost two-thirds of the Hispanic and Native American women reported running away from home before age 18. White women were only slightly less likely to report running away from home, and more than half said they had. Black women were the least likely at 40 percent.

Relationships with criminal men were the second common pathway reported by the women. Not only did the women become involved in crime and drugs through their association with men in the criminal underworld, but they often ended up in prison because of these relationships. There were significant racial and ethnic differences in this, however. More than one-fourth of the black women reported that they had committed the crime for which they were in prison with their boyfriend or husband. Native American women reported similar levels of males involved in the crimes they had committed. In contrast, about forty percent of Hispanic and white women reported that a male was involved with them in the crime, again usually a husband or boyfriend.

The final pathway was the most common. Very simply, the women imprisoned in the Oklahoma Department of Corrections facilities had extensive histories of abuse, both as children and as adults. It is the intersection of economic disadvantage with childhood abuse that lends itself to incorporating elements of a blended pathways/strain approach into the analyses presented in this book. While the cycle of violence and feminist pathways approaches describe factors relevant to female offending, incorporating general strain theory can put those together into a larger, single framework. The complexity of general strain theory helps not only explain why some women offend but also why others with equally bad histories do not, something missing from most pathways approaches. Furthermore, the exemplary work of Kaiser Permanente and the CDC in the ACE study can further inform our understanding of how the women in the current study ended up as offenders who were ultimately imprisoned (Sharp, Peck, and Hartsfield 2012).

Summary

By incorporating some of the concepts derived from the ACE study as well concepts derived from general strain theory and feminist pathways approaches, our understanding of female offending can be further advanced. Thus, in recent years I added measures derived from the ACE study into my annual research on incarcerated women and their children, and began developing a feminist version of general strain theory that would take into account women's placement in the social system, their lesser power, and how that plays out as abuse and neglect. Additionally, I incorporated measures of personal characteristics such as mastery and self-esteem that might mediate some of the effects of abusive childhoods (Agnew 1992, 2006; Agnew and White 1992). Theoretically, this book explores the pathways of women prisoners into crime, incorporating measures of strain, particularly adverse childhood experiences from the ACE study. Although I cannot compare women prisoners to women who are not incarcerated, the ACE study allows for some *ad hoc* comparisons.

The mental health and substance abuse histories of these women will also be examined in subsequent chapters, and differences in their personal resources such as self-efficacy and self-esteem may help explain why some of these women have more severe mental health problems than others. Feminist research has brought to light the importance of developing a clearer understanding of how the life histories of female offenders may, to paraphrase Agnew (2006), "pressure" them into crime. From a feminist perspective, it is important to understand that the pressures and pathways of girls and women are often very different from those of boys and men, producing different outcomes.

Finally, recent medical research has highlighted what criminologists already know: adverse childhood experiences lead to risky behaviors in adults, especially substance abuse. By considering the contributions of feminist pathways theory, general strain theory, and the ACE study, a clearer picture of the channeling of abused women into mental illness, drug use, and ultimately prison emerges.

It is also imperative to understand that the high rate of female incarceration (particularly in Oklahoma, the location of this research) cannot be explained simply by focusing on the women and their characteristics. Their experiences with the criminal justice system must be examined within the social and legal context of the state. Consequently, in chapter 2 I seek to contextualize the experiences of women prisoners in a clearer understanding of the changes in laws that have had tremendous impact on incarceration, especially of women.

CHAPTER 2

Mean Laws

THE RISE IN FEMALE IMPRISONMENT

THE INCREASE in the population of Oklahoma's women's prisons is not unique, but reflective of a trend throughout the United States, where overall prison populations grew during the late 1980s and early 1990s. By 2005 the United States had more than two million people in prison, the highest incarceration rate in the world (Jacobson 2005; Shelden 2010). Before we can examine the laws and policies in Oklahoma, we need an overview of the changing laws that affected the rate of imprisonment in this country. Many of these changing laws targeted less serious offenders and drug offenders. Women offenders are more likely than men offenders to have serious drug problems, and they are also more likely to be near the bottom of drug-dealing enterprises. Essentially they are low-hanging fruit easily targeted by law enforcement. Because of this, the changes in drug laws have affected women disproportionately. In Oklahoma, the effects have been devastating.

CHANGES IN THE U.S. PRISON POPULATION

Imprisonment as punishment has a long history in the United States. Initially formed with an ostensible goal of rehabilitation, prisons have undergone numerous shifts in purpose and policy over the past two hundred years. From reformatory to warehousing and back to rehabilitation, prisons have long been a part of the fabric of American society (Austin and Irwin 2001). Following a period of attempts to rehabilitate offenders during the mid-twentieth century, the United States entered a period of excessive punitiveness. Exponential prison growth occurred during the last two decades of the twentieth century, with prison populations increasing fivefold (Irwin 2005; Kruttschnitt et al. 2013).

Several reasons have been given for this incredible growth. The fear of street crime and street criminals has been an extremely important factor (Irwin 2005). With its roots in the late 1960s, American politicians first launched a war on crime, followed by a war on drugs, both fueled by public perceptions of personal risk. According to Austin and Irwin, powerful interest groups used concerns about crime to deflect attention from the economy and the rising gaps in income between the wealthy and everyone else (Austin and Irwin 2001). This public perception bore little resemblance to the truth, with more than half of U.S. prisoners incarcerated for crimes that are generally perceived as petty offenses, such as marijuana possession or low-level theft (Austin and Irwin 2001).

During the 1980s, the public concern over drug use eventually focused on crack cocaine. This was driven to a large degree by the media hype surrounding the death of college basketball star Len Bias, purportedly from smoking cocaine. Although there is no consensus about the means by which he ingested cocaine, a comment made by a member of the medical examiner's office attributed the death to freebasing. In fact, there is evidence that he snorted rather than smoked the cocaine that caused his death. But the media had picked up the story, and the damage was done. Crack became the new drug scourge (Shelden 2001). This demonization of crack cocaine ultimately culminated in the infamous Anti-Drug Abuse Act of 1986, with its draconian punishments for crack. This law provided penalties for possession of crack cocaine that were equivalent to the penalties for one hundred times as much cocaine hydrochloride, commonly referred to as powder cocaine (U.S. Sentencing Commission 1995; Shelden 2001). This law had the effect of punishing street-level crack cocaine dealers more harshly than the higher-level suppliers of the powder cocaine used to make the crack. As a result, poor low-level drug sellers in the central city, many of them women, were incarcerated for a minimum of five years.

Additionally, legislation during this period abolished parole in the federal system. That was not the only drug legislation that targeted the poor during the late 1980s and early 1990s (Austin and Irwin 2001; Sentencing Project 2010). The Anti-Drug Abuse Act of 1988 instituted a mandatory minimum sentence for possession of more than five grams of cocaine base, the only drug with a mandatory minimum for a first possession offense (Shelden 2001). Additionally, several states rapidly began adopting similar strategies, with fourteen states having a disparity in sentences for crack cocaine and powder cocaine (Sentencing Project n.d.). The War on Drugs, although purportedly focused on drug kingpins, shifted by the end of the 1980s to a focus on arresting and prosecuting low-level drug offenders, the "low hanging fruit," those most visible to law enforcement. This had a disproportionate effect on minorities, especially minority women (Bush-Baskette 1998; Alexander 2010).

The effects on the criminal justice system have been predictable, but also rather astounding. Drug crimes resulted in longer sentences as well as a higher likelihood of incarceration instead of probation. This "tough on crime" approach was primarily linked to drug crimes. At the federal level, sentences for murder actually decreased over 28 percent between 1982 and 1994. At the same time, sentences for drug offenses increased about 45 percent (Shelden 2001). At the state level, there has been a similar trend, causing noted criminologist Randall Shelden (2001, 143) to conclude, "It has become progressively more serious to have been caught with drugs than to kill someone."

The proliferation of crack cocaine is tied to another reason for the rapid expansion of America's correctional system. During the same time period as the escalation in the War on Drugs, the economic plight of those living in central cities, especially black people, became increasingly worse (Wilson 1987; Wilson 1996). Unemployment rose, as did the number living in poverty. In fact, there was a 27 percent increase between 1980 and 1996 in the total number of Americans below the poverty line (Austin and Irwin 2001). Likewise, the income of black families compared to white families reached a low in the mid-1980s that had not been seen since the 1960s (Austin and Irwin 2001).

Not only were minorities impacted by the shifting economy, but women in particular experienced negative changes. Illegitimate births almost doubled, and female-headed households experienced rapid growth (Austin and Irwin 2001; Shelden 2001; Jacobson 2005). These women remained segregated in lower-paying occupations despite their need to support their families. At the same time, there was a concerted effort to end or at least drastically reduce the number of women on welfare. Crime began rising, especially property crime and crime related to drug sales, quickly followed by a huge increase in the number of women entering prison. The intersection of race, class, and gender has been an important aspect of the rise in female incarceration. Indeed, the group that experienced the highest growth in incarceration was poor black women, causing some feminist researchers to claim that the War on Drugs was in fact a war against women of color (Bush-Baskette 1998).

PRIVATE PRISONS AND THE RISING INCARCERATION RATE

As America's prison population began growing rapidly, entrepreneurs saw new opportunities. The private, for-profit prison industry experienced rapid growth. Companies such as Wackenhut, a security provider, and Correctional Corporation of America began contracting with various governmental agencies to provide needed bed space (Greene 2007).

Because the growth in the incarcerated population was so rapid, governmental bodies could not keep up with the demand. Private corporations did not have many of the constraints that departments of corrections had, such as obtaining consent of neighboring communities, and this allowed them to build facilities more rapidly (Austin and Irwin 2001; Shelden 2010). By cutting costs in ways less accessible to state-run facilities, private prison corporations purported to save state governments money (Greene 2007). However, at least one study has found that prisoners who spent more of their incarceration time in a private facility were more likely to recidivate than those who had spent proportionally more time in state facilities (Spivak and Sharp 2008). This has implications for the growth of the prison populations, since a higher recidivism rate can lead to a higher overall prison population. It is noteworthy that during the period in which I was conducting the research for this book, Oklahoma had a higher proportion of its prisoners in private facilities than most states (Harrison and Beck 2005; Greene 2007).

Collectively, during the 1980s and 1990s the United States rushed to incarcerate those who offended its collective conscience. Harsher laws were passed, sentencing reforms were enacted. The end result was that we were putting more people in prison, and for longer stretches. Crime rates peaked and then began dropping, but the incarceration rate did not drop off. Today, the United States has the dubious distinction of having the highest per capita rate of its citizens imprisoned of any country in the world (Sentencing Project 2005).

Again, this had a disproportionate effect on women, especially women who used drugs. Owen (1998, 15) refers to these women who violate both the laws and gender expectations as "double deviants," noting that not only do women commit less serious crimes but they tend to persist in their behaviors despite legal repercussions. This persistence suggests that there may be something qualitatively different about women who offend that is not being deterred by harsh punishment. Addiction and the need to support children are both likely contributors to the persistence of female crime. The U.S. criminal justice system has continued the harsh responses, nonetheless.

In recent years, the trend has been to develop intermediate sanctions that fall somewhere between minimally supervised probation and imprisonment. These include a variety of sentencing innovations such as day-reporting, which allows individuals to spend their evenings at home, as well as nighttime incarceration, which allows individuals to work during the day and to continue to support their families. Day-reporting centers, modeled on programs in Great Britain, are often used as an early release mechanism that allows individuals to step down to a lower level of supervision. However, utilizing these programs as a step toward release is often less effective with women than men, due to the short sentences served by female offenders (McDevitt and Miliano 1992).

Intensive supervision probation, with or without electronic monitoring, is another popular alternative (Lurigio and Petersilia 1992; Palumbo, Clifford, and Snyder-Joy 1992; Petersilia, Turner, and Deschenes 1992). However, these methods often result in high levels of revocation due to their emphasis on technical violations such as being away from the home after curfew or urinalyses that are positive for drugs (Palumbo, Clifford, and Snyder-Joy 1992; Petersilia, Turner, and Deschenes 1992). The majority of women in prison have substance abuse problems that are often not addressed in prison. It is foolish and dangerous to assume that incarceration will solve these problems. Indeed, unless underlying issues such as abuse are treated, it makes more sense to assume that they will continue to use drugs and therefore be at risk of reincarceration.

The belief that we are incarcerating far too many people is not a new one. Many alternatives to incarceration were originally developed more than three decades ago for this very reason. However, as prison costs began skyrocketing during the 1980s, these alternatives were revamped to include those who had been on regular probation. In effect, the focus of alternatives to incarceration had switched from keeping low-level offenders out of prison to providing more control over the probation population (Palumbo, Clifford, and Snyder-Joy 1992). Furthermore, incarceration was the consequence for failure to walk a very narrow line dictated by some of these programs. The result was that policies and programs that might have reduced the high rate of incarceration ultimately increased it. This had a particularly strong impact on women offenders, as a high percentage were in the system for problems with drugs, and those drug problems, often untreated, have resulted in continued drug use and thus revocation.

Drug Courts and Other Specialty Courts

Drug courts, mental health courts, and other specialty courts have been important innovations in the quest for alternatives to incarceration. These courts are more costly than regular probation but less costly than incarceration. While the research is mixed regarding the efficacy of drug courts, a number of best practices have emerged. These include ensuring offenders receive effective screening, providing drug treatment quickly, and utilizing sanctions appropriately. Regular face-to-face interaction between high-risk offenders and the court, graduating a fair number of participants, and treating the offenders with dignity and respect are also important aspects of effective drug courts (Fox 2005).

Oklahoma's use of drug courts is somewhat different from that in most of the United States. First, rather than serving as an intervention early in an offender's history, the majority of participants are those who would otherwise be headed to prison. In fact, counties that refer too many first-time offenders to drug court are penalized through a reduction in their drug court funding. An additional problem is that those who fail drug courts receive heftier sentences than in most states, and their sentences tend to be greater than similar defendants who do not attempt drug court rehabilitation (MGT 2007).[1]

There is also some inconsistency with the sanctions handed down in drug courts. Notably, one county (Rogers County) sends those who are having difficulty in drug court to the Department of Corrections (DOC) for stays of four to twelve months, then brings them back into the drug court for further review (MGT 2007). Not surprisingly, Rogers County ranked as one of the top ten counties for sending new female receptions to the DOC in FY 2010 (Oklahoma Department of Corrections/Division of Female Offender Operations 2010). This policy obviously contributes to the high female incarceration rate in Oklahoma and seems counterproductive to the stated drug court goal of reducing incarceration.

The average sentence for drug court failures in Oklahoma is 74 months (MGT 2007). In other words, those who attempt drug court are harshly penalized for failing to complete the program successfully. This harsh response to failure often deters offenders who might be helped through drug court participation. Furthermore, most of the failures are for either failed drug tests or being late to appointments rather than new crimes. Indeed, one in four of the drug court failures were terminated for positive drug tests, and almost one in three were terminated for being late to either a drug test or an appointment. This is counterproductive, since these failures tend to receive much longer sentences than similar non-drug court offenders. One recommendation is to reduce the sentences for failures to be similar to offenders who did not go through drug court (MGT 2007). Another suggestion is to respond to problems in meeting the expectations of drug courts with intermediate sanctions rather than sending the struggling offenders to prison.

Selection of participants is yet another issue with Oklahoma drug courts. In particular, the primary drug charges involved are methamphetamine, alcohol, and marijuana offenses (MGT 2007). This means that heroin, cocaine, and prescription drug offenses are less likely to receive admission to drug courts. The failure to admit those using heroin and cocaine disproportionately precludes participation by blacks. Another difficulty with Oklahoma drug courts is that policies vary widely around the state. In some counties, the probation officers participate in the drug court team, but in others they do not. Perhaps even more germane to the issue of high female incarceration, a few counties use the drug courts as an intermediate sanction for probation violations such as testing positive for drugs. This is a policy that, if extended throughout the state, could have significant impact on the incarceration rate. In contrast, some counties (most notably, Comanche) send only first-time offenders to drug court (MGT 2007). However, Comanche also has the third highest rate in the state of sending women to prison (Oklahoma Department of Corrections/Division of Female Offender Operations 2010). It would seem that this county could reduce the female incarceration rate by utilizing drug court as an intermediate sanction to divert repeat offenders from prison, but it is failing to do so.

In Oklahoma, females are disproportionately represented in drug courts, accounting for about 43 percent of the admissions. While at first glance this might seem to be a good thing, the failure rate (42 percent) means that a large number of drug court participants in Oklahoma go on to prison for longer terms than they would have otherwise served. Because of this, there is no net decrease in incarceration from drug court, and the director of the DOC has commented that it should not really be considered a diversionary program.[2] In fact, both admissions to prison and the total number of drug offenders in Oklahoma prisons have grown since the inception of drug courts in the state. A relatively high percentage of those in drug court have no prior offenses (37 percent) and probably would not have been sent to prison, but they end up in the DOC because of the high drug court failure rate (MGT 2007).

Another problem with drug courts is that they are used with a small proportion of the offender population, often fewer than five percent of offenders in a state (MGT 2007). Yet another problem is that some drug courts do not allow offenders with drug trafficking offenses or any history of violent offenses to participate, although many crimes in these categories may have been committed as a consequence of addiction. In Oklahoma, anyone with a violent felony charge or conviction is ineligible for drug court. Consider the following example: Darlene (a pseudonym) has been convicted of two violent offenses, both of which resulted in lengthy incarcerations. In the first offense, she was the driver of a car used as the get-away vehicle in a robbery, was charged with robbery, and served six years. In the second offense, she grabbed a purse lying on the side of the road after an automobile accident. This offense was also classified as a robbery since the owner of the purse was present. Altogether, Darlene served nineteen years for the two offenses. She has a long history of addiction, first to heroin and later to crack cocaine. She has always been ineligible for drug court participation, although it is likely that she would benefit because she is a high-risk, drug-addicted offender with a strong need for the kind of behavior modification that occurs in drug courts.

OKLAHOMA'S WOMEN PRISONERS

Oklahoma has long been the state with the highest female incarceration rate. In 2011, the imprisonment rate for women was 129 per 100,000 residents, almost double the national average for females of 66 per 100,000 residents (Carson and Sabol 2011). At the same time, Oklahoma has a crime rate only slightly higher than the national average. Furthermore, the state's incarceration of females has been rapidly growing over the last two decades. On July 30, 2010, there were 2,762 women imprisoned in the Oklahoma DOC (Oklahoma

Department of Corrections 2010), compared to 1,689 women incarcerated in 1995 (U.S. Department of Justice 1995), 1,582 in 1993 (Harrison 2000) and 751 in 1988 (Harrison 2000). From 1995 to 2001, the state experienced an increase of more than twenty percent in female incarceration (Damphousse 2003). It is readily apparent that there has been an increase in the incarceration of women over time, but what is not as readily apparent is the reason for this.

First, the state is punitive towards all offenders. While Oklahoma has ranked first in the nation in female incarceration for almost two decades, the overall incarceration rate for Oklahoma has also been high. In 1994, Oklahoma ranked second in overall incarceration rates, surpassed only by Texas (U.S. Department of Justice 1994). By 2008, Oklahoma had dropped to fourth overall, with an overall incarceration rate of 661 per 100,000 residents that was approximately 31 percent higher than the national average of 504 per 100,000 residents. Oklahoma also ranked fourth in the incarceration of men, at 1,203 per 100,000, approximately 26 percent higher than the national average. However, Oklahoma's 2008 female incarceration rate of 135 per 100,000 was double the national average of 67 per 100,000 for female incarceration (Sabol, West and Cooper 2009). Clearly, something is going on in Oklahoma that disproportionately affects women. To fall in line with the national averages, Oklahoma would have to release around 9,000 prisoners, and about 1,300 women, nearly half of the women who are incarcerated (Delcour 2009; Oklahoma Academy 2009). Given that Oklahoma ranks 17th in violent crime (U.S. Census 2006; Delcour 2009), it is clear that the high rate of incarceration is not solely due to criminal activity in the state. Furthermore, Oklahoma's crime trend has been about the same as that of the nation since the mid-1980s, so prior high crime rates are not an explanation for the high female incarceration rate (Sandhu, Al-Mosleh and Chown 1994).

The increase in incarceration in Oklahoma, especially of women, has had some devastating effects on the state's economy. During the economic recession, funding for all state agencies, including Corrections, was slashed. By the end of 2009, the DOC had funding for only 75 percent of the correctional officers needed. Halfway house contracts had dropped almost 20 percent over a two-year period. Shifting of the state budget towards Corrections and away from other agencies had already impacted social services and transportation in the past, and by early 2010, state-supported residential drug treatment was virtually nonexistent (Davis 2010). The lack of drug treatment facilities has only made the situation worse.

An analysis of the absolute number of women prisoners, as well as their percentage of the incarcerated population over time is informative. On January 1, 1982, there were 294 women in Oklahoma prisons, accounting for 5.8 percent of the total prison population. By January 1, 1986, the female prison population had risen to 396, an increase of almost 35 percent in just four years. However, women still constituted about the same proportion of the total incarcerated population, or 5.9 percent. In 1987, the women's share of the incarcerated population rose to 7.3 percent (555 women), and by 1991 there were 914 women in Oklahoma prisons, accounting for 8.7 percent of the incarcerated population. By 2008, over 2,500 women were incarcerated in Oklahoma prisons, and their share of the total population had increased to more than 10 percent.[3] The annual total female prisoner population and the percentage of the total incarcerated population that was female are reported in Table 2.1. Figure 2.1 graphically represents the growth in absolute numbers of female prisoners from 1982 through 2008. It is clear that there was a rapid increase in the number of women in prison in Oklahoma in the early 1990s through 2000. There has been some leveling off in the overall population of women in Oklahoma's prisons since 2000. In Figure 3.2, the percentage of the total prison population that was female is presented in graph form. The female share of the total prison population began increasing slightly earlier than the increase in the female population itself, with a large increase in 1987 and another large increase in 1993.

TABLE 2.1

Oklahoma's Women Prisoner Population

	No. of Women Prisoners at Year End	Percentage of Total Prison Population
1982	294	5.8
1983	320	5.3
1984	410	6.2
1985	396	6.0
1986	396	5.9
1987	555	7.3
1988	632	7.5
1989	620	7.0
1990	825	8.4
1991	914	8.7
1992	1,075	8.5
1993	1,582	9.6
1994	1,607	9.7
1995	1,815	10.0
1996	1,940	9.9
1997	2,053	10.0
1998	2,091	10.0
1999	2,316	10.3
2000	2,394	10.3
2001	2,290	10.1
2002	2,336	10.0
2003	2,320	10.3
2004	2,361	10.3
2005	2,455	10.5
2006	2,394	10.3
2007	2,607	11.2
2008	2,524	10.4
2009	2,649	10.5
2010	2,760	10.6

Source: The data for 1982 through 1991 came for the archives of the Oklahoma Department of Corrections. The remaining years were obtained from the *Prisoner Series* of the Bureau of Justice Statistics.

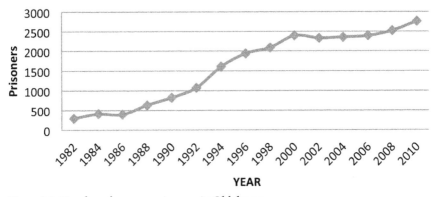

Figure 2.1 Number of women prisoners in Oklahoma
Source: Oklahoma Department of Corrections archival data, 1982 through 1991. The remaining years were obtained from the *Prisoner Series* of the Bureau of Justice Statistics.

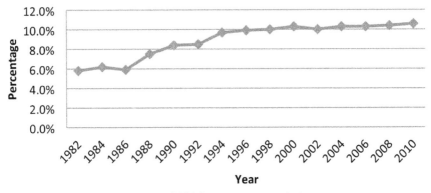

Figure 2.2 Women as percentage of Oklahoma prison population
Source: Oklahoma Department of Corrections, 1982 through 1991. The remaining years were obtained from the *Prisoner Series* of the Bureau of Justice Statistics.

Thus, there appear to be two different trends. First, the overall prison population began rapidly increasing in the early 1990s. Second, the female proportion of that overall prison population began increasing slightly earlier. To understand these trends requires close examination of policy and law changes in the state that affected the incarceration rates. However, Oklahoma is not unique. It is also important to contextualize these changes within the framework of changes across the United States.

It is noteworthy that the increase in incarceration in Oklahoma began in the late 1980s, at the same time the crime rate was beginning to fall. One possibility for this is that the higher crime rates in the early 1980s led to the creation of new prisons. After crime rates had peaked and begun their dramatic decrease, these prisons and their beds became available. The private prison industry took note of the need for more prison beds in the state. This meant that, as violent crime decreased during the latter part of the 1980s, the incarceration rate of nonviolent offenders increased dramatically. A recent study demonstrated that the number of drug offenders sent to Oklahoma prisons increased sevenfold between 1983 and 2001 (Damphousse 2003). This disproportionately affected women, who were more likely to be arrested for drug offenses than any other crime.

In 2010, possession of or obtaining a controlled dangerous substance (CDS) was the number one controlling offense category for new receptions of female offenders in the Oklahoma DOC, accounting for almost 24 percent of new admissions to the system. This was trailed by distributing a CDS at 19.1 percent, forgery at 8.5 percent, larceny at 7.1 percent, and assault at 7 percent. It is quite clear that drug crimes are driving the high female incarceration rate (Oklahoma Department of Corrections/Female Offender Operations 2010). However, it is also important to note that arrests for drug crimes have decreased since 2002, while new prison receptions have increased (MGT 2007). Thus, the punitive response to drug use is driving the incarceration rate.

Ten of Oklahoma's 77 counties were responsible for nearly two-thirds of the women sent to prison in fiscal year (FY) 2010. While two of these were the counties with the two largest cities in the state (Tulsa County and Oklahoma County), others were smaller. Table 2.2 reflects the top ten counties, showing the number of women per county received by Oklahoma DOC in FY 2010. The final two columns show the percentage of women from these counties who were imprisoned for possession of a controlled substance or for distribution or manufacture of drugs. It is evident that drug charges account for a significant number of women sent to prison. Of course, these numbers mask the fact that most of the other women admitted to Oklahoma's prisons were sentenced for drug-related crimes. The majority of those not sentenced specifically for drug offenses were sentenced for property crimes committed to support a drug habit.

POLICIES AND LAWS CONTRIBUTING TO THE HIGH RATE OF IMPRISONMENT

There are many reasons for Oklahoma's extraordinarily high rate of imprisonment, primarily laws and policies in the state. Oklahoma is not the most dangerous or criminal state, according to the statistics. In 2008, the overall crime rate (property and violent crimes) for Oklahoma was 3,969.1 per 100,000 residents, only slightly higher than the 3,667 rate for the United States as a whole (Federal Bureau of Investigation 2009). Nor has crime increased dramatically in the state. For example, in 1980, the murder/manslaughter rate for the state was 10 per 100,000 residents, and the property crime rate was

TABLE 2.2

Top Ten Oklahoma Counties for Receptions of Women Prisoners, FY 2010

	Population	No. of Women Sent to Prison	Percentage Sent on Possession Charge	Percentage Sent on Distribution/ Manufacturing Charge
State	3,687,050	1,393		
County				
Oklahoma	716,704	324	26.9	13.0
Tulsa	601,961	315	20.0	17.4
Comanche	113,228	47	29.8	4.3
Creek	70,244	46	19.6	15.2
Pottawatomie	70,274	32	12.5	12.5
Garfield	58,928	31	12.9	16.1
Grady	51,649	31	22.6	9.7
Carter	48,326	27	14.8	14.8
Kay	46,110	27	22.2	18.5
Rogers	85,654	26	26.9	23.1

Source: Oklahoma Department of Corrections Division of Female Offender Operations 2010.

4,633.4 per 100,000 residents. By 2008, those rates had dropped to 5.8 per 100,000 and 3,456.6 per 100,000, respectively (West and Sabol 2010). Thus, despite incarcerating at a far higher rate in 2008, the state was actually safer. In addition, the number of violent offenders incarcerated per year was lower in 2001 than in 1983, but the number of non-violent offenders received by the Oklahoma DOC had doubled (Oklahoma Alliance for Public Policy 2003). Despite falling crime rates, Oklahoma has continued to have high incarceration rates and in fact has increased its rate of incarceration.

There are several apparent causes. First, Oklahoma is less likely to use probation as a sanction and more likely to incarcerate than most states. The 2001 probation rate in the state was under 1,200 per 100,000, while the national average was 1,834 per 100,000 (Glaze 2002). In support of this, a 2007 audit found that 84 percent of the female offender population had no Class B offenses or reports, concluding that Oklahoma's female prisoners posed little risk (MGT 2007). Another way one might look at this is that the vast majority of the women in Oklahoma prisons probably do not need to be incarcerated.

Furthermore, a fairly high percentage of new receptions to the Oklahoma DOC are for violation of probation. In 2010, 410 of the 1,393 women received by the DOC were probation violators. Of these, 167 had new cases and 243 were violated for technical violations, including positive drug urinalyses or failure to report. In other words, 29.4 percent of the women sent to prison during that fiscal year were probation failures. Another 17.4 percent of those sent to prison were sent due to a technical violation rather than an additional offense. This is an increase in the use of prison as a response to probation violation: In 2008 25.4 percent of the new female receptions were probation violations, and 15.5 percent were for technical violations only (Oklahoma Department of Corrections/Division of Female Offender Operations 2010).

Longer sentences are another cause for the state's higher incarceration rate. One study suggested that sentences in Oklahoma are approximately two or three times longer than those for similar crimes in other states (Damphousse 2003). Of particular relevance to female offenders, the mean sentence in Oklahoma for drug possession was 6 years, compared to the overall U.S. mean sentence of 4.2 years. In even sharper contrast, the mean sentence for drug trafficking in Oklahoma was 16 years compared to an overall U.S. mean of 5.5 years (Damphousse 2003).

Finally, the actual sentence length and percentage of time served affect the incarceration rate. Again we see that Oklahoma appears more punitive than other states. The mean sentence length increased 6.3 percent between 1993 and 1999, while the mean time served increased a startling 38.2 percent. By 1999, prisoners in Oklahoma were serving over 40 percent of their sentences on average (Damphousse 2003). Parole was used less often, as was probation. Many community corrections programs were eliminated, further driving up the incarceration rate.

According to an external audit, the parole rate in 1991 was 40.8 percent. By 2006, it had dropped to 18.9 percent, a more than 50 percent reduction since 1991 and a startling 39 percent decline between 2003 and 2006. Currently, although investigators recommend parole in close to half of the cases, the parole board only recommends parole in less than one-third of the cases. Three-fourths of the cases heard are low to moderate risk, making the low level of parole recommendations even more disturbing (MGT 2007). The same report goes on to note that the expansion of the "85 percent rule" means that the number of prisoners serving 85 percent of their sentences will almost double between 2007 and 2017 (MGT 2007).

The use of incarceration as the preferred punishment for felony convictions by certain counties in the state has also contributed to the high incarceration rate. For example, Grant County sent 70 percent of those convicted of any felony to prison. However, in 2001, this translated to only 10 felony convictions and seven prisoners. In contrast, Tulsa County sent over

50 percent of those convicted of a felony to prison, or 1,508 prisoners; Stephens County sent 48 percent to prison (122 prisoners), and Comanche County sent 41.6 percent of those convicted of a felony to prison (200 prisoners). These percentages compare to the overall state incarceration rate of 26.8 percent of felony convictions (Damphousse 2003).

Additionally, wording in the Oklahoma Statutes allows prosecutors to sentence offenders with extremely short sentences directly to prison rather than to county jail. In most states, sentences of one or two years are normally served in the county jail rather than in the state department of corrections. Oklahoma law allows those convicted of a felony to be sentenced directly to the DOC for any length of time, sometimes weeks or even days. More than one in four of the Oklahoma women received by the DOC during FY 2010 served less than one year in prison. In fact several were released immediately upon admission (Oklahoma Department of Correction/Division of Female Offender Operations 2010). This policy allows district attorneys to save their own jurisdictions money, placing the financial burden back on the state. The Oklahoma DOC has expressed concern about this policy, pointing out that a sizable proportion of the 1,393 women received into their custody in 2010 served very short terms.

> As of November 1, 2010, of the women received in FY 2010, 377 had completed their sentences and were released. Three hundred and fifty-seven (95 percent) of these women served less than one year in prison. Five were released on the same day as admission.
>
> While the majority of the 377 women discharged (238 or 63 percent) were required to undergo a period of community supervision, many (139 or 37 percent) were not. (Oklahoma Department of Correction/Division of Female Offender Operations 2010, 12)

As noted above, another problem is what is commonly referred to as the 85 percent rule. In the late 1990s, the state attempted to pass a truth-in-sentencing act. The idea was to incarcerate violent offenders for 85 percent of their sentences but also to have non-violent felons serve 75 percent of their sentences. The advisory committee also recommended that the state divert non-violent offenders to community corrections. The act was passed, but eventually repealed. In its place, Oklahoma created a list of offenses for which it would be mandatory to serve 85 percent of the original sentence prior to eligibility for parole or even eligibility to earn credit that would reduce time served to less than 85 percent of the sentence. The crimes included in the original bill were Murder I, Rape I, Burglary 1, Child Abuse, Child Pornography, Lewd Molestation of a Child, Robbery with a Dangerous Weapon, Arson 1, Bombing, Forcible Sodomy, and Child Prostitution. However, legislators have jockeyed to demonstrate their "tough on crime" stance by modifying the original list of crimes. One of the more recent additions to this list of "deadly sins" has severely impacted women prisoners: trafficking in illegal drugs.

In Oklahoma, trafficking does not necessarily mean the woman has sold or transferred drugs to another person. Instead, trafficking is defined by the amount possessed. The Trafficking in Illegal Drugs Act sets out the list of drugs and amounts that qualify for 85 percent sentencing. This list includes 20 grams of methamphetamine, the drug most commonly abused in the state at this time, and 5 grams of cocaine base, the drug most commonly abused by blacks in Oklahoma (O.S. 63-2-415). These relatively small amounts of the two drugs have resulted in both long sentences and the requirement to serve 85 percent of those long sentences for many of the women now in prison in Oklahoma.

Furthermore, a conviction for trafficking may over-represent the criminal behavior of the women. Women are often only tangentially involved in drug manufacturing and distribution. For example, allowing a spouse or boyfriend to manufacture relatively small amounts of methamphetamine (20 grams) in the home or to use the woman's telephone to make a drug deal has resulted in drug trafficking convictions with long sentences, as well as the requirement to serve 85 percent of that sentence prior to becoming eligible for parole. This is further compounded by the fact that the excessive penalties allowed by the laws result in plea bargains for long sentences (Oklahoma Alliance for Public Policy Research 2003). In 2010, 9.5 percent of the 1,393 new female receptions were classified as 85 percent offenses, suggesting that this will continue to be a problem for some time (Oklahoma Department of Corrections/Division of Female Offender Operations 2010)

In a few cases, women have been sentenced to Life without the Possibility of Parole (LWOPP) for drug convictions. Perhaps the best-known case is that of Sheila Devereux. A typical housewife, Sheila's descent into crime began with her divorce. She began using alcohol and drugs to self-medicate, finally overdosing on cocaine in 1998. The overdose resulted in a conviction for possession of a controlled dangerous substance. Then in 2001, she was convicted of possession of marijuana when one joint was found in her stalled vehicle. She had two drug convictions prior to the case that resulted in her LWOPP sentence, and the final conviction was the result of a drug raid at a house where she was visiting. The man who lived there had six grams of crack cocaine hidden in the house, and the law allowed prosecutors to charge everyone present with trafficking since the amount was greater than the statutorily defined five grams. Sheila, who claimed no knowledge of the drugs, chose to go to trial rather than accept a plea agreement for seven years. Under the Oklahoma law, her two prior convictions allowed the prosecution to enhance the penalty to LWOPP (Tulsa World 2010; Families against Mandatory Minimums, n.d.).

There is no logical reason for giving a life without parole sentence to a low-level drug offender who is battling addiction, but between a state law that allows this type of sentencing and a prosecutor who was probably irritated that the defendant did not accept a plea bargain for a seven-year sentence, the outcome was far in excess of the level of offending. While Devereux's case received national attention because of the ludicrousness of the sentence based on the amounts of drugs involved in her three offenses, she is not the only woman serving a life without parole sentence in Oklahoma for a drug offense. Two other women are serving LWOPP for similar offenses. In one case, the woman's past association with a high-ranking member of an outlaw motorcycle club earned her the prosecution's wrath. Her own participation in the crimes was minimal. Her biggest crime was being married to someone whom law enforcement detested.

Another problem stems from a cumbersome parole process in Oklahoma. The parole process in Oklahoma is two-tiered. Once eligible for parole, the inmate must go before a parole board. If that board recommends early release, this recommendation is then sent to the Governor; he or she, in accordance with the Oklahoma State Constitution, must then also approve the parole. Because the governor is elected, decisions about parole are tied to political ambition, thus reducing the number of early releases. A 2010 attempt to remove the governor from the parole process failed, in large part due to get-tough-on-crime rhetoric and the argument that having the governor in the process provides yet another level of protection for the public. Apparently we need to be protected from women with sad lives and drug problems.[4]

Nor is the parole process the only area in which public officials use rhetoric that results in a high incarceration rate. The get-tough-on-crime rhetoric, often following a particularly egregious offense, is frequently used by politicians from local to national levels as a campaign platform, fueling public fears. At times, the media, and politicians may focus on one terrible incident, or "atrocity tale," to increase negative sentiment (McCorkle and Miethe 2002). This may in turn create a moral panic, wherein the public, the media (Altheide 2002), and politicians (Kappeler, Blumberg, and Potter 2000) join in voicing concerns and rush to formulate new laws in reaction to a newly discovered social problem.

According to experts, a moral panic occurs when there is an increased level of concern about how some group in society is behaving. In addition, there must be some reason to believe that this behavior will have negative consequences for society as a whole. Furthermore, the members of this group engender hostility in the rest of society, who somehow see them as a threat to the norms of the mainstream. There must also be a reasonable level of consensus about the threat's seriousness and, this fear or concern must be out of proportion to the actual threat. Finally, a moral panic arises quickly and just as quickly disappears in most cases (Goode and Ben-Yehudah 1994). Moral panics are volatile. They erupt fairly quickly and nearly as suddenly vanish. While some panics do become institutionalized, most simply disappear. However, laws placed on the books during a moral panic do not so easily fade away, nor do prosecution policies.

In the United States, the formulation of the so-called crack baby epidemic as a social problem contributed to overly harsh sentencing of women who used drugs during pregnancy. More recently, and especially in Oklahoma, attention has been turned to mothers who use methamphetamine.

The crack baby scare began with an article in the *New England Journal of Medicine* by Dr. Ira Chasnoff, who was concerned about 23 babies exposed to cocaine *in utero* (Chasnoff et al. 1985). Interestingly, these mothers had been injecting or snorting cocaine rather than smoking crack, but when the media picked up the story, the focus was on crack cocaine. Although the study was preliminary and Dr. Chasnoff later expressed grave concern about the widespread panic, his findings were nonetheless used to fuel the War on Drugs, especially against women who used crack cocaine. By 1989, laws were in place allowing the state to prosecute mothers who passed drugs to their unborn children through the placenta. Ultimately, in 1999 a woman in South Carolina with a low IQ was convicted of murdering her unborn child (Gomez 1997). However, research has indicated that while cocaine is certainly not good for the fetus, environmental factors such as poor or nonexistent prenatal care and poverty are even more harmful (Chavkin 2001). In other words, research does not clearly indicate that any drugs other than alcohol and tobacco cause birth defects or fetal death.

Regardless of the reality, the consequences of the moral panic over crack babies have been quite real. The panic has served to demonize women who use drugs in general, and it has led to zero-tolerance approaches to their drug use (Humphries 1999; Chavkin 2001). Women who use drugs have been held accountable for many of the country's social problems. In part, this helped divert attention away from the consequences of policies enacted during the administrations of Ronald Reagan and George H. W. Bush that diminished access to social programs. The moral panic was also part of the backlash against women who failed to adhere to social norms about "proper" womanhood (Rosenbaum 1997). Nor did things improve in the Clinton administration. Although initial rhetoric indicated that the focus of the War on Drugs would shift from interdiction to prevention, intervention, and treatment, almost two-thirds of the budget for the war continued to go to law enforcement during Clinton's terms (Rosenbaum 1997).

The crack baby panic has also had harmful effects on pregnant addicts and their unborn children, due to the harsh consequences that could occur if they sought prenatal care. A woman who tested positive for drugs at delivery could lose custody of her child or even find herself charged with delivering drugs to a child. If the child was stillborn, she might face manslaughter or even murder charges (Gomez 1997; Rosenbaum 1997; Humphries 1999). Some women, therefore, will not seek medical care during pregnancy due to fears of incarceration and loss of their children.

Oklahoma is one of the most conservative states in the Union, and the panic about drug-using mothers and their ability to destroy the fabric of society has found fertile ground in the state. Oklahoma's brand of conservatism has been characterized as values-conservatism, placing particular emphasis on what its proponents characterize as traditional family values such as a "pro-life" agenda (Engle 2008). It does not take much imagination to see how women who use drugs would run afoul of traditional Oklahoma conservatism. Use of drugs is seen both as a threat to unborn children and as a failure to adhere to religiously ordained ideas that attempt to define the role of women. It comes as no surprise that women drug users have been prosecuted zealously in the state.

In April of 2004, Theresa Hernandez had a stillborn child during her thirty-second week of pregnancy. Ms. Hernandez was charged with first-degree murder because she tested positive for methamphetamine at the time of the stillbirth (Amicus Brief 2007). Prosecutors argued that the death of the fetus was attributable to the use of methamphetamine. Women's advocates struggled to support her and get the charges dismissed, but after three years in the county jail awaiting trial and with no contact visits with her other children, Theresa Hernandez pled guilty to the reduced charge of second-degree murder and was sentenced to fifteen years in prison, with the contingency that after one year in prison her sentence could be revisited. In the fall of 2008, her case was heard again and the remainder of her sentence was suspended, with the requirement that she undergo drug treatment (Real Cost of Prisons blog 2008). Altogether, Theresa spent four and half years incarcerated for use of drugs during pregnancy. After her release, Ms. Hernandez was able to go to a drug treatment program due to the generosity of an unnamed donor. But the impact on her family of her four years in custody has been great. She is now living in the Midwest, and her other children are being raised by their paternal grandmother.

Theresa Hernandez's story is not atypical. She was molested by a stepfather, became pregnant in middle school, and was summarily married off to one of her stepfather's friends. She had five children prior to the stillbirth. Her husband became abusive during the marriage, and she turned to her mother-in-law for help with her children. Given her traumatic history, it is not surprising that Theresa began abusing drugs. When her child was stillborn in 2004, however, her history was not considered. The district attorney at the time saw the opportunity to take a strong stance against drug use during pregnancy, leading him to charge her with first-degree murder.

In Oklahoma, as in many conservative states, the rights of the fetus often surpass those of the mother. The fetus is insured protection against the actions of the mother. In contrast, the mother often cannot access needed social services and health care. While many in the state clamor for protection of the unborn, there is a failure to realize that protection for both the unborn child and the mother includes far more than simply disallowing abortion or punishing drug use.

> . . . the United States stands alone among developed countries in failing to guarantee access to health care to women and children throughout their lives and in failing to provide other economic, legal, and social supports (including treatment for drug and alcohol addiction) in order to increase the chances that women can nurture and provide for their children, as well as reduce the incidence of women's addiction. (Fentiman 2008, 4)

While it is certainly true that the use of any substance during pregnancy should be avoided, it is also true that addiction is powerful: many women do not want to use drugs during their pregnancies but are powerless to quit (Rosenbaum 1979; Sharp 1998; Rosenbaum 1997; Humphries 1999). Furthermore, medical experts tend to agree that taking a punitive approach to drug use during pregnancy can have far worse consequences than most drug use, with women being afraid to seek medical care or drug treatment (Lester 2007). The case of Theresa Hernandez, however, demonstrates the judgmental and punitive attitude in Oklahoma towards women who use drugs, helping to explain the high female incarceration rate.

JUSTICE REINVESTMENT

Justice reinvestment is a new concept designed to reduce prison populations and increase public safety. Under Oklahoma HB 3052 (2012), this has involved two important aspects that may have long-term consequences for women offenders. First, the new law requires a minimum of nine months of supervision for all offenders upon release from prison. Second, it establishes intermediate revocation facilities under the DOC. These intermediate revocation facilities will house offenders for six months and tentatively provide substance abuse counseling, mental health counseling, and domestic violence counseling. The success of this will be largely dependent on the quality of treatment the DOC can afford to offer.

Both of these requirements could increase, rather than reduce, incarceration and the costs of the system. According to Oklahoma DOC Director Justin Jones, HB 3052 will require the hiring of new probation/parole officers, more office space, and more equipment. This has not been as well-funded as necessary, either:

> We received one million dollars for mandatory supervision start up and should receive another two million this next legislative session based upon projections from the Justice Reinvestment researchers. Eventually we will need six million and will have 4,500 additional offenders under supervision.
>
> We will not have the luxury of designating one facility as an Intermediate Revocation Facility so we are working on a business plan to designate beds at all security levels for these technical probation violators who must serve six months with no earned credits. This section of the bill received no funding so the mandatory intensive drug treatment, etc., for these revoked offenders will not be available until at some point funding is secured. (Jones 2012: 3)

In other words, policies put into place to reduce the prison population could ultimately increase it. Oklahoma's version of justice reinvestment focuses on the more punitive aspects, such as revocation of probation for any violation with no good time credit, but it fails to incorporate the most crucial aspect—increasing available drug treatment for those who need it. Plus, an important aspect of the original bill had to be deleted in order to get the bill passed. The bill's author, Kris Steele, then Speaker of the House, wanted to incorporate a policy that would allow those serving sentences under the 85 percent rule to accrue good-time credits that would be applied once the offender reached the 85 percent threshold. Under Oklahoma law, those serving under the 85 percent rule are not allowed to begin receiving good-time credits until 85 percent of the sentence has been served. Thus, they often end up serving over 90 percent of the sentence before becoming eligible for parole. This effort to allow this class of offender to earn good-time credits was stricken from the final bill.

HB 3052 requires anyone convicted of a felony to undergo risk, mental health, and substance abuse assessments prior to sentencing, to aid the courts in appropriate sentencing. The DOC has been tasked with developing a matrix of sanctions for technical violations. The offender then has the option of complying with the proposed sanctions or facing revocation.

> The hearing officer shall determine based on a preponderance of the evidence whether a technical violation occurred. Upon a finding that a technical violation occurred, the hearing officer may order the offender

to participate in the recommended sanction plan or may modify the plan. Offenders who accept the sanction plan shall sign a violation response sanction form, and the hearing officer shall then impose the sanction. Failure of the offender to comply with the imposed sanction plan shall constitute a violation of the rules and conditions of supervision that may result in a revocation proceeding. If an offender does not voluntarily accept the recommended sanction plan, the Department shall either impose the sanction and allow the offender to appeal to the district court, or request a revocation proceeding as provided by law. Every administrative hearing and sanction imposed by the Department shall be appealable to the district court (HB 3052, Section 5).

SUMMARY

Oklahoma is not unique in its astronomical increase in the number of incarcerated women over the past two or three decades. Many of the same factors have created this situation in the United States as a whole. Oklahoma, however, has some particularly punitive policies and laws that have exacerbated and hastened the state's burgeoning population of women in prison. Long sentences, significantly minimal use of probation, the 85 percent rule, and a complex parole process have all contributed. Furthermore, some counties tend to send almost all offenders to prison, and in many cases a drug court sanction may include time in prison. All of these factors have driven up the rate of female incarceration in Oklahoma.

While the state is definitely punitive and harsh in its approach to women who offend, it is also important to note that many women are sent to prison for very short sentences. Wording in the state statutes allows county and district officials to save their jurisdictions money by sending women with short sentences directly to prison rather than keeping them in county jails. Oklahoma's high female incarceration rate may thus be deceptive if one takes into account the rates of county jail incarceration in other states.

Oklahoma's version of justice reinvestment, while well-meaning, is rife with potential for negative consequences. The new law is based on Beccaria's argument that to act as a deterrent, punishment must be swift, certain, and severe. HB 3052 has incorporated swift and certain responses, and Oklahoma's punishments are inarguably severe. However, by failing to provide adequate funding for treatment of substance abuse and mental health issues, the law may simply increase the problem in the state. Sorely needed is action by future legislatures to more adequately fund all aspects of the bill.

There have been positive changes occurring in the state. The MGT 2007 audit of the correctional system recommended elimination of maximum security classification for females, and this has been almost completely accomplished. Additionally, in 2008, the Division for Female Offender Operations (recently renamed Division I) was formed, and Dr. Laura Pitman was appointed as the Deputy Director for Female Offender Operations in January of 2009. This has led to considerable innovation and change in the system. Many of the programs available to offenders are now gender-sensitive and gender-appropriate. While incarceration rates remain high due to "mean" laws and policies, positive changes are starting to occur within the penal system itself. In chapter 8, I will discuss in greater detail the positive changes that are occurring in the state. In chapter 3, I will present a brief description of the methods used to produce this book, followed by profiles of the prisoners themselves and descriptions of the prison experience in Oklahoma.

CHAPTER 3

Mean Women or Mean Lives?

ADVERSE CHILDHOOD EXPERIENCES AND ADULT ABUSE OF WOMEN PRISONERS

WHEN I first moved to the state in 1996, the largest women's correctional facility, the Mabel Bassett Correctional Center was located in Oklahoma City and housed approximately 350 women. In 1998, the Central Oklahoma Correctional Center, a private women's prison in McLoud, Oklahoma, was opened. The prison housed Oklahoma women as well as women from other states such as Hawaii and Wyoming. In 2001, reports of sexual abuse by guards and rampant drug use began to emerge, and so the state purchased the facility in 2003 for $40 million and moved Mabel Bassett to this location. The facility has a capacity of over 1,100 women, and the Department of Corrections (DOC) moved all female assessments and receptions for the state there in 2009. The facility also houses the mental health unit, the segregated housing unit, and is the primary facility for pregnant prisoners and women with severe physical health problems.

The second largest facility in the state is Dr. Eddie Warrior Correctional Center in Taft, Oklahoma. Eddie Warrior is a minimum-security facility with a capacity of about 800 women. In addition to these two largest faciliteis, there were two community corrections centers for women in the state, Hillside Community Correctional Center and Kate Bernard Community Correctional Center, which recently was closed. Kate Bernard housed women who worked at jobs in the Oklahoma City community during the day. Hillside housed both women who work in the state government offices and at other jobs as well as women in a residential treatment program. There are a few other programs and institutions scattered around the state, including the Turley Halfway House in Tulsa, which houses around 160 women, most on work release, and the Center Point residential therapeutic community, which houses around 40 women.

My immersion in the complicated story of Oklahoma's women prisoners began when Susan Marcus-Mendoza and I submitted a proposal to the Oklahoma DOC for a research project entitled, "A Preliminary Analysis of Gender

Differences in the Impact of Imprisonment on Children and Spouses of Drug Offenders" in early 1997. The Oklahoma Criminal Justice Resource Center and the Oklahoma Consortium on Criminal Justice had become very interested in the effects of Oklahoma's drug policies on the families of offenders, following the publication of the proceedings of a Vera Institute (1996) conference on the collateral effects of incarceration. These papers were republished as a special issue of the *Journal of the Oklahoma Criminal Research Consortium* (1996), which stimulated considerable interest among state correctional professionals.

Our initial study focused on both male and female offenders and their families. A random sample was drawn of prisoners convicted of drug offenses who were incarcerated by the Oklahoma DOC during 1997 (with females oversampled). A questionnaire was administered on site at two women's facilities (Eddie Warrior and Kate Bernard) and three men's facilities (Jackie Brannon Correctional Center, Oklahoma City Community Correctional Center, and Clara Waters Community Correctional Center). This initial study was based on a sample of 144 females and 124 males.

I quickly learned that collecting data in prisons was fraught with complications. The majority of our female sample was to come from Eddie Warrior. The DOC had drawn up a list of every female prisoner housed there, chronologically ordered according to the offender's initial reception into the DOC system. We had a sample drawn of every third woman at Eddie Warrior and every other woman at Kate Bernard). However, the night before our visit to Eddie Warrior, eighty-five prisoners were suddenly moved to a Texas prison with virtually no notice. We therefore ended up administering the questionnaire to every drug offender housed at Eddie Warrior who was willing to participate. The women were upset because of the sudden move of a large group of women, and were worried about the possibility of being moved away from the state themselves. We ended up spending time talking about the move with the women and the DOC staff person assigned to assist us.

I began to get a clearer understanding of the degree to which prisoners are at the mercy of the state. They may be moved, sometimes to facilities without the programs in which they are enrolled, or far from their children. This is often to satisfy a need to ensure the system is in compliance with requirements related to overcrowding. This can be particularly difficult for women with children, as movement to another facility may create difficulty in maintaining already fragile connections with families.

When we visited Kate Bernard, we discovered another problem. DOC personnel, not understanding the requirement of voluntary participation, had told all prisoners drawn in the sample that they had to complete the survey. Thus, when the research team arrived, we were met by a very hostile group of prisoners who felt they were being coerced into participating in the research. Dr. Marcus-Mendoza and I spent considerable time explaining to the women (and staff) that their participation was voluntary. We explained the purpose of the research and how we hope the findings could be used to impact public policies. Eventually, some of the women elected to remain and to participate in the survey. This was to be the first of several problems that arose over the years while conducting research.

From this project, we were able to begin untangling the differences between men and women prisoners' families in the state. Some interesting differences emerged that informed later projects. For example, we discovered that while high school education was the modal category of completed education for all prisoners, males were more likely to report education beyond the high school level. Males were also more likely to report prior felony convictions and prior incarcerations.

Women were also more likely to report having other family members who had been incarcerated, a spouse or partner who had been incarcerated, or a spouse or partner as a co-offender. The women were far more likely than the men to report histories of childhood physical and sexual abuse and domestic violence victimization. In other words, the women were more likely than the men to report growing up in dysfunctional families and to have histories of trauma (Sharp and Marcus-Mendoza 1997). This was followed by another study and a 98-page report to the State of Oklahoma, a report to the Oklahoma Sentencing Commission, and several book chapters and journal publications (Sharp and Marcus-Mendoza 1997; Marcus-Mendoza and Sharp 1998; Sharp et al. 1998; Sharp and Marcus-Mendoza 2001).

I became increasingly interested in the topic of incarcerated women based on what we had learned, and I edited a collection of articles on incarcerated women that was published in 2003. I also began teaching a course that focused on race, gender, and the criminal justice system, furthering my interest in this topic.

The bulk of the research reported in this book occurred from 2004 to 2009. In 2004, Oklahoma State Senator Barbara Staggs and Oklahoma State Representative Debbe Leftwich passed a joint resolution, SJR 48, which mandated that the Oklahoma Commission on Children and Youth (OCCY) conduct an annual study on Oklahoma's women prisoners and their children. I was contacted by the director of OCCY, and I agreed to do the research. Other organizations became involved in planning the research, including the Department of Human Services, the DOC and the Department of Mental Health and Substance Abuse Services. Together we crafted a plan that would allow an in-depth examination of both the backgrounds and issues of women prisoners and the impact on the lives of their children. A more detailed

Age and Education

The mean age of each sample remained consistently in the mid-thirties, consistent with the mean age of the female offender population in the Oklahoma DOC. There was a decline over time in the level of education reported, but this is partially an artifact of the questions asked. From 1997 through 2007, we asked participants the highest level of education they had completed. In 2008 and 2009, that question was divided into two questions, one measuring education prior to incarceration and the other measuring education completed after incarceration. According to the Oklahoma DOC, 71 percent of the women prisoners who entered prison during FY 2010 and 70 percent of all women incarcerated at fiscal year's end were assessed as needing basic education. Perhaps more disturbingly, 29 percent of the female prisoners who were assessed as needing basic education were discharged without completing any educational program (Oklahoma Department of Corrections/Division of Female Offender Operations 2010).

There are at least two reasons for this. The first is that funding for programming within the prison is limited. Second, because some women have very short sentences, they receive priority of placement into programs. This creates two issues. First, these women are often discharged without completing the program. Second, women with longer sentences have difficulty accessing the programs. During FY 2010, there were 1,500 completions of educational programs, including 51 women age 21 or younger who came under Title 1. Of these, 247 completions were in literacy coursework, 311 in adult basic education, 452 in college courses, and 252 completed the General Equivalency Diploma program. An additional 238 prisoners completed Curriculum and Instructional Materials Center (CIMC) Life Skills coursework. It should be noted that some offenders completed multiple courses and therefore are counted two or more times in the 1,500 completions (Oklahoma Department of Corrections/Division of Female Offender Operations 2010).

Vocational Training

The Oklahoma DOC has also partnered with *CareerTech* to provide skills training. There were 222 completions during FY 2010, and only 22 women were counted as non-completers. In all, 329 women were enrolled in these courses, and 82 continued their training into the new fiscal year. Two vocational programs in particular are starting to result in paying jobs for women after their release from prison. Both of these programs are through Prison Industry Enhancement. The Jacobs Trading Company repackaging program at Dr. Eddie Warrior Correctional Center prepares prisoners for warehousing work outside of prison, training them in pallet shipping and invoicing.

The second program is the the Back Office Support Systems (BOSS) tele-marketing program at Mabel Bassett Correctional Center. BOSS employs women in the program while they are still incarcerated, and upon release, the job continues, providing them with steady employment at the time of release. There has been considerable improvement in the kinds of vocational training offered to prisoners over the past twelve years. Not only are women being trained for non-traditional work, but some are being employed by companies that will hire them on release while they are still in prison. Furthermore, these jobs, while paying the women very low wages while in prison, may pay an adequate wage to sustain them on release.

ABUSE HISTORIES

Research has documented the importance of negative childhood experiences in explaining women's crime. In particular, the link between sexual abuse and later offending has been well-documented (Chesney-Lind and Rodriguez 1983; Widom 1989; Rivera and Widom 1990; Widom 1995; Kaufmann and Widom 1999; Widom and Maxfield 2001; Chesney-Lind and Shelden 2004; Kempf-Leonard and Johansson 2007). But there are other experiences that should be considered. Most work has been limited to the effects of physical and sexual abuse experienced by young girls, but abuse does not generally exist in a vacuum. Homes that are abusive physically or sexually generally are also characterized by other forms of dysfunction. This clustering of negative experiences during childhood is the focus of the Adverse Childhood Experiences (ACE) study (Felitti et al. 1998; Anda n.d.; Anda et al. 2002; Dube et al. 2002; *ACE Reporter* 2003b; Dube et al. 2003; Felitti 2003; Dong et al. 2004; Felitti and Anda 2010).

Beginning in 2004, we asked questions drawn from the ACE study. We found that an extremely high number of the women came from chaotic and abusive homes. More than half came from homes where one or both parents had been violent towards other family members, with approximately one in four reporting only a father had been violent and one in eight reporting only a mother had been violent. An additional one in eight reported both parents had been violent. More than two-thirds had experienced either physical or sexual abuse, or both, during childhood. These experiences continued into their adult lives. Four out of five had experienced intimate partner violence or rape as adults. Thus, in subsequent studies we expanded our consideration of adverse childhood experiences.

The ACE study helps shed light on the pathways of women into crime and drug use. Dr. Vincent Felitti, principal investigator of the ACE study, has stressed the importance of the research in understanding how addictions arise. He notes that many individuals are disturbed by the implications because the findings clearly demonstrate that the source of addiction is not found in either the substances used or in weaknesses of the individual. Instead, chaotic and damaging childhoods are clearly a significant factor:

> (W)e found that the compulsive use of nicotine, alcohol, and injected street drugs increases proportionally in a strong, graded, dose-response manner that closely parallels the intensity of adverse life experiences during childhood. This of course supports old psychoanalytic views and is at odds with current concepts, including those of biological psychiatry, drug-treatment programs, and drug-eradication programs. Our findings . . . suggest that billions of dollars have been spent everywhere except where the answer is to be found. (Felitti 2003, 3)

The ACE study focuses on types of abuse and neglect that may occur during childhood, including physical abuse, sexual abuse, emotional abuse, emotional neglect, and physical neglect. General household dysfunction is also considered to be a contributing factor to negative outcomes. Household dysfunction includes growing up with someone with a mental illness, growing up with someone with a substance abuse problem, seeing one's mother being abused, an absent parent or parental divorce, or having a family member in prison (Felitti 2003). Furthermore, these problems do not tend to occur in isolation from each other. Most individuals who experienced one adverse childhood experience have experienced several. This increases the likelihood of negative outcomes. Simply put, the more adverse experiences one has during childhood, the more likely it is that, as an adult, one will develop physical health problems, mental health problems, and substance abuse problems.

The link between adverse childhood experiences and both substance abuse and mental health problems has great relevance when looking at incarcerated women. The relationship between these negative experiences and addiction is even stronger for women than for men. In fact, Felitti reports that a startling 78 percent of injecting drug use by females is attributable to adverse childhood experiences (Felitti 2003, 7). He goes on to discuss a factor that has relevance to any discussion of drug use and addiction. Referring to the use of heroin by U. S. soldiers in Vietnam, he points out that not everyone who uses a drug, even frequently, becomes an addict. Instead, he views addiction as a result of short-term coping through drugs. This is reminiscent of Agnew's argument that crime and other deviant behaviors are coping strategies (Agnew 1992, 2006).

> [T]he major factor underlying addiction is adverse childhood experiences that have not healed with time and that are overwhelmingly concealed from awareness by shame, secrecy, and social taboo. The compulsive user

appears to be one who, not having other resolutions available, unconsciously seeks relief by using materials with known psychoactive benefit, accepting the known long-term risk of injecting illicit, impure chemicals. The ACE study provides population-based clinical evidence that unrecognized adverse childhood experiences are a major, if not the major, determinant of who turns to psychoactive materials and becomes "addicted." (Felitti 2003, 8)

When drug use is viewed as a strategy to reduce the inner turmoil that is the result of cumulative abuse, we then have a clearer understanding of how painful and dysfunctional childhoods may lead to drug abuse in women, ultimately leading them into prison. The hidden and unacknowledged nature of adverse experiences in childhood results in a failure to intervene with appropriate services. The emotional pain, however, remains. When the woman (or girl) experiments with alcohol and drugs, she may find short-term emotional relief. The ACE researchers even suggest that these traumas can cause chemical imbalances in the victim (Felitti 2003). What they stress, however, is that it is not just an isolated abusive event that is the culprit. Instead, it is the systemic nature of family dysfunction that predicts risky behaviors that are in turn used to diminish the emotional pain that has resulted from adverse experiences. Furthermore, attempts to address the problem of addiction through interdiction and punishment will be unsuccessful. The addict will continue to use drugs to reduce the pain of past traumas. Instead, the researchers recommend prevention and early intervention.

In 1997, we had no awareness of the emerging medical literature on the cumulative effect of negative childhood experiences. Most of the existing literature on women offenders focused on physical abuse and sexual abuse, and their relationship to drug use. My first research project on women prisoners in Oklahoma examined only those two types of abuse. Sexual abuse was reported by 37.5 percent of the subjects, physical abuse was reported by 42.7 percent, with both types of abuse experienced by 26 percent (Sharp and Marcus-Mendoza 2001). It was clear that these women had a high likelihood of experiencing abuse, with more than one in four experiencing both physical and sexual abuse, and more than half reporting at least one form of abuse during childhood.

In 2004, questions were added about violence in the home. I found that 14.8 percent of the women had experienced only physical abuse, 18.5 percent had experienced only sexual abuse, and 44.5 percent had experienced both types of abuse. Some 55.6 percent reported that one or both of their parents had been violent around the family. Not surprisingly given what we know about intimate partner violence, 46.3 percent reported that their fathers had been violent (Sharp 2005a; Sharp 2005b).

In 2004, I also asked about mental health treatment. Little intervention had occurred with the women prior to their imprisonment, despite the high rate of reported abuse. Only slightly more than one in three had received counseling specifically to address abuse. However, almost one in five had been hospitalized in the past for mental health problems. Furthermore, about three-fourths reported using drugs more than once a week in the month before incarceration, but more than half had not received substance abuse treatment before coming to prison, even though some had tried to get into a treatment program. This included almost half of those who reported heavy drug use (Sharp 2005a; Sharp 2005b). The 2004 study preceded the creation of the Division of Female Offender Management, and trauma-focused gender-specific programming was just being initiated in the prison system. There have been significant improvements in the quality of services offered since that time, although the number of prisoners receiving both mental health treatment and substance abuse treatment is still limited due to budgetary constraints.

By 2007, seven of the adverse childhood experiences were incorporated into the survey. Only the questions that measured physical neglect, emotional neglect, and emotional abuse were absent. As you can see in Table 3.2, the women in the study grew up in highly disorganized households and experienced high rates of abuse.

The childhoods of these women were disorganized and chaotic, with family violence and abuse, drug or alcohol abuse in the households, and other types of dysfunction common. Table 3.3 presents the distribution of the seven adverse childhood experiences in the sample of women prisoners from 2007.

This table demonstrates that adverse childhood experiences clearly cluster together in this group of incarcerated women. A significant number of the women experienced four or more types of adverse experiences (46.6 percent).

TABLE 3.2
Percentage of Adverse Childhood Experiences of Women Prisoners, 2007

Physical abuse	44.8
Sexual abuse	53.7
Mother battered	36.2
Lived with substance abuse	73.3
Lived with mental illness	35.3
Parents separated/divorced	63.8
Someone in household went to prison	22.4

Source: Oklahoma Study of Incarcerated Women and Their Children: Phase I data (Sharp 2007).

About one out of eight reported six or seven adverse childhood experiences. This is startlingly different from the insured population in the Kaiser Permanente/CDC study. Although direct comparisons cannot be made to the Kaiser Permanente study due to the different numbers of adverse childhood experiences, the early ACE study publications only counted eight adverse childhood experiences as opposed to the ten found in later publications and reports (Table 4.4). Furthermore, a 1998 publication examined only seven, although one was different from those included in study of women prisoners. The 2007 prisoner data did not include psychological abuse, and the original ACE study article did not include parental separation or divorce (Felitti et al. 1998). It is also noteworthy that in the Kaiser Permanente study, women were far more likely than men to report four or more adverse childhood experiences (8.5 percent compared to 3.9 percent). While almost half of the women prisoners had experienced four or more adverse childhood experiences, the Kaiser Permanente subjects had a far lower prevalence.

What is perhaps even more important is the relationship between these adverse experiences and risk behaviors. In the Kaiser Permanente sample, subjects reporting four or more adverse childhood experiences were 10.3 times as likely to report injecting drug use as those who reported none, and those reporting three or more adverse childhood experiences were 7.1 times as likely as those reporting no adverse childhood experiences to inject drugs (Felitti et al. 1998). Clearly, there is a strong link between abusive and dysfunctional childhoods and drug use. Those reporting four or more adverse childhood experiences in the Kaiser Permanente sample were also 4.7 times

TABLE 3.3
Distribution of Adverse Childhood Experiences among Women Prisoners, 2007

No. of Adverse Childhood Experiences	Percentage of Women Experiencing	Cumulative Percentage
0	5.6	5.6
1	14.7	20.3
2	15.9	36.2
3	15.5	51.7
4	15.1	66.8
5	19.0	85.8
6	9.5	95.3
7	3.0	98.3

Source: Oklahoma Study of Incarcerated Women and Their Children: Phase I data (Sharp 2007).

Note: Total is less than 100% due to missing data on some women.

TABLE 3.4
1998 ACE Study Subjects and Prevalence of Adverse Childhood Experiences

Adverse Childhood Experiences	Percentage of Kaiser Permanente Enrollees
Physical abuse	10.8
Sexual abuse	22.2
Mother battered	12.5
Lived with substance abuse	25.6
Lived with mental illness	18.8
Parents separated/divorced	
Someone in household went to prison	3.4
Psychological abuse	11.1

Source: Felitti et al. 1998.

as likely to report any illicit drug use and 7.4 times as likely to consider themselves alcoholic (Felitti et al. 1998). This may explain why 61.6 percent of the women in the 2007 prisoners' sample reported using drugs (other than alcohol and marijuana) more than once a week, 24.1 percent reported daily marijuana use, and 14.7 reported daily alcohol use.[1] Taking a feminist pathways approach informed by specific strains from the ACE study, I found that the majority of the women fit the childhood strain model.

In the last two years of the study, the data included measures of all ten adverse childhood experiences from the ACE study. When those two samples were combined, there were 598 subjects. I compared the two years and found no major differences, so I will present the data for the two years combined in Table 3.5. As noted in chapter 1, these women experienced far higher incidents of adversity than subjects in the Kaiser Permanente Study. Each adverse childhood experience occurred at a higher rate than in the Kaiser Permanente sample, and about two-thirds of the women reported four or more adverse childhood experiences, with 17.9 percent reporting eight or more (See Table 3.6).

The feminist pathways approaches clearly suggest that childhood sexual abuse is an important precursor of drug use and criminal behavior (Acoca 1998; Katz 2000; Holsinger & Holsinger 2005; Belknap & Holsinger 2006). Not surprisingly, the women in my research reported extensive histories of childhood sexual abuse. Furthermore, about half of the women in the 2004 and 2005 studies reported that their abusers were family members, with 1 in 5 reporting a father or stepfather as the perpetrator. In subsequent years, the numbers were even higher.

Childhood sexual abuse, in and of itself, is traumatic. However, when the perpetrator is someone the child should be able to count on for care and

TABLE 3.5

Adverse Childhood Experiences of Women Prisoners, 2008 and 2009

Adverse Childhood Experiences	Percentage Experiencing ACE
Childhood Abuse	
Emotional	62.9
Physical	49.3
Sexual	55.7
Childhood Neglect	
Emotional	69.9
Physical	46.8
Dysfunctional Household	
Battered mother	34.4
Substance abuse in home	70.4
Mental illness in home	46.0
Parental divorce	64.5
Family member went to prison	26.9
$N = 598$	

Source: Oklahoma Study of Incarcerated Women and Their Children: Phase I data (Sharp 2008, 2009).

protection, not exploitation, the trauma is even greater. Furthermore, it often sets the victim up for a lifetime of revictimization (Heney and Kristiansen 1998; Girshick 1999). Sexual abuse during childhood leads to sexualization of the child, feelings of powerlessness, stigma, and feelings of betrayal (Finkelhor and Brown 1985). The victim often grows up feeling ashamed and vulnerable. She may place herself in situations where she is at high risk of being victimized yet again. This is the story of Oklahoma's women prisoners. Many reported abuse by multiple perpetrators before the age of 18. Being raped as an adult, often multiple times, further compounded the victim's vulnerability.

Many of the women have stories similar to Darlene's (chapter 2). Because she grew up victimized by a number of male relatives, she learned to view herself as a commodity. She engaged in prostitution off and on as an adult and frequently hooked up with abusive men who coerced her to prostitute herself in order to support both of them. When she was released from prison in her early fifties, she quickly hooked up with a former pimp and began turning tricks at truck stops. This led to drug use and eventual reincarceration.

However, she was more fortunate than many of the women. She was lucky enough to land a coveted spot in the "Helping Women Recover" program at

TABLE 3.6

Distribution of Adverse Childhood Experiences among Women Prisoners, 2008 and 2009

No. of Adverse Childhood Experiences	Percentage of Women Experiencing	Cumulative Percentage
0	4.0	4.0
1	7.2	11.2
2	9.2	20.4
3	10.2	30.6
4	9.5	40.1
5	13.4	53.5
6	13.5	69.0
7	7.7	76.7
8	8.2	84.9
9	6.0	90.9
10	3.7	94.6

Source: Oklahoma Study of Incarcerated Women and Their Children: Phase I data (Sharp 2008, 2009).

Note: Total is less than 100% due to missing data on some women.

Mabel Bassett. The program is gender-responsive and trauma informed, based on the work of Stephanie Covington (Covington 2002a, 2002b). Darlene wrote me that she started to understand how her early experiences shaped her life for nearly forty years. She hoped to parole to a women's halfway house soon, and appeared motivated to continue dealing with her history of trauma and her drug and alcohol abuse. As Covington notes, women who are addicted often suffer from a weakened self-concept, and neglect their own needs (Covington 2002b). This is perhaps the most apt description I have seen of Darlene and of many women prisoners I have come to know. They do not see themselves as worthy or deserving of a normal life or good treatment. As a result they tend to partner with abusive men and men engaged in crime.

Not surprisingly, when examining drug and alcohol abuse, I found that the women in Oklahoma prisons reported high levels of drugs and alcohol use in the month prior to being incarcerated. These high rates of substance abuse were linked to three things. First, the ACE study clearly predicts that women with such high levels of adversity in childhood would be far more likely than the general population to use drugs. Second, the women in Oklahoma prisons have a very high rate of drug problems. Indeed, most of them are in prison because of drug problems. Third, the mediating link between adverse childhood experiences and drug use is the reaction to the strain, especially depression and anxiety, caused by the adverse experiences during childhood. For many of these women, drugs were a solution for psychological problems and mental illness that resulted from this strain. Thus, it is also important to examine mental health problems in this population.

Agnew (1992, 2006) stresses that not all individuals who experience strain will respond with deviant coping strategies. Higher levels of self-esteem and mastery may act as protective factors. However, woman prisoners tend to have low self-esteem and low levels of mastery or self-efficacy. The women in the 2007–2009 samples were asked a series of questions related to this. Overall, the levels of both self-esteem and mastery were relatively low, although there is no control group for comparison. When an individual lacks protective factors, she is then more likely to respond to strains such as abuse with drug use and other non-legitimate behaviors.

Oklahoma prison officials have become increasingly aware of the mental health problems faced by the women in their custody. With the appointment of Dr. Laura Pitman as the first deputy director over all aspects of female offenders, emphasis increased on trying to meet the mental health needs of these women. In two annual reports published by the Oklahoma Department of Correction, it was reported that from 62 to 69 percent of the women in Oklahoma's prisons had major psychiatric problems, including major mood disorders, psychotic disorders and post-traumatic stress disorder (PTSD) (Oklahoma Department Corrections/Division of Female Offender Operations 2009, 2010). Of these women, almost one in three were receiving psychotropic medications (Oklahoma Department of Corrections/Division of Female Offender Operations 2010). The prisons then have to find adequate funds to provide not only medications but also crisis intervention, suicide prevention, and individual and group therapy. Those with the most severe problems are housed at Mabel Bassett, which has 45 beds for seriously mentally ill offenders.

One of the greatest strengths of Division I (Female Offender Management) is a clear understanding of the intricate link between trauma, mental health problems, and substance abuse. Many of the women receiving psychiatric and psychological services were also involved in substance abuse treatment programs. These include the aforementioned Helping Women Recover program and the Beyond Trauma Treatment Program (also developed by Covington), offered at both Mabel Bassett and Dr. Eddie Warrior Correctional Centers. These programs are both gender-sensitive and holistic: they are based on an understanding of the interlocking nature of trauma, mental health, and drug use.

The women in Oklahoma's prisons also talked about how they supported themselves prior to incarceration. For most years, over half the women supported themselves and their children through their own work; only one in seven reported receiving Temporary Aid to Needy Families (TANF). About one-third received child support, and almost one-fourth reported that their spouse or partner helped support the family. This belies the mental picture many people have of women prisoners. As I often tell my students, they are more normal than abnormal. Most are doing the best they can with limited financial and emotional resources to provide a loving home for their children. The difficulty is that those resources are usually quite limited.

These women also are frequently not the first in their families to be incarcerated. In 2009, almost 10 percent reported their mothers had been to prison, and nearly one in five reported their fathers had been incarcerated. In some case, both parents had gone to prison. And almost one in three had a sibling who had been to prison. This underscores the instability of their childhood homes, where parental alcohol and drug abuse was common, as was mental illness. Not surprisingly, given the chaotic family lives and abuse, more than half had run away before age 18.

While the stories of the women vary considerably, there are common themes throughout many of their lives. One woman, Melissa, shared how her co-dependent relationship with a drug-using male and her own inability to cope with life led to her incarceration. Like many of the women, once she found herself having difficulty meeting the demands of her probation, she quit reporting. With a history of physical and emotional abuse from a past marriage, she suffered from severe depression. Ultimately, she ended up in prison, and her parental rights were terminated.

In Melissa's case, it seemed like all efforts she made backfired. Melissa was arrested in 2007 for selling a prescription drug. Her boyfriend kept a couple of guns in her closet, which the police found, leading to additional charges. She received a deferred sentence and her children were placed into state custody. Her options were limited, so she went to stay with her boyfriend's family after she got out of jail. When he was released from jail, he also returned to that household. Hoping to stay out of more trouble, Melissa found a duplex that she could almost afford, and moved out.

Melissa was required to work and undergo counseling, as well as to attend parenting classes. With no transportation and little education, she looked for work close to where she lived. Her work schedule frequently conflicted with her counseling schedule, especially her parenting classes. Since she had to pay her bills, she opted to place a priority on work. She was in the process of trying to regain custody, so her failure to regularly attend the parenting classes received a negative appraisal. She also continued to see her boyfriend. One day, the

Department of Human Services paid a surprise visit to her duplex. Melissa was at work, but her boyfriend and some of his friends were at her duplex drinking. The caseworker then reduced Melissa's visitation with her children to a one hour supervised visit per week, and Melissa began using drugs heavily. She managed to find a sober-living house, then she made contact with her probation officer, who had her arrested on the spot. The judge released her with the requirement that she remain at the sober-living facility. The new living arrangements added three more groups per week to her requirement and placed her on a curfew. Melissa was still working to pay for her rent there, and she was kicked out for curfew violation due to her work hours. She relapsed again. At this point, fear set in. Melissa did not let the court or her probation officer know she had been kicked out. She still tried to work and to attend the required counseling and classes, but she found this very difficult and had not completed her mandatory parenting classes. Eventually, she missed a court date, and the court filed to revoke her probation. Melissa wanted to see her children again, and knowing she would be arrested, she still made an appointment with the caseworker to see them. When she arrived, she was arrested and sentenced to two years in the DOC.

The state filed to terminate her parental rights in 2009. Her attorney advised her to sign the papers or she would never see her children again. So, Melissa signed away her rights. She was told that she would be able to maintain some contact with the children, but her letters to her children were returned, and she was threatened with legal action if she made any further attempts to contact them. Her children were adopted, and she has no idea where they are.

At first blush, it might appear that Melissa had been given many opportunities and that she had failed to take advantage of any of them. However, Melissa did not receive drug treatment, the one type of assistance she most needed, until she went to prison. Like many caught up in the criminal justice system, she faced competing demands that could not all be satisfied. It is very easy to order someone to undergo counseling or to attend classes. It is often something quite different for that woman to be able to juggle multiple appointments, responsibilities at home, and a work schedule. Melissa is not a well-educated woman with career options. She worked fast food and waitress jobs where, if she could not be on time and stay her shift, she could be easily replaced.

Abuse during Adulthood

While childhood abuse contributes to drug use and crime, for most of these women, abuse did not end when they left their childhood homes. From 2007–2009, almost 80 percent of the women reported being the victims of domestic violence, and nearly 40 percent reported they had been raped.

Childhood abuse was a strong predictor of experiencing abuse in adulthood. Nearly half the women who reported sexual abuse as a child were later raped. Likewise, around half of those whose fathers were abusive towards their mothers reported being raped in adulthood, and about half of those who were physically abused as a child were adult rape victims. Nearly 90 percent of those who said their fathers were violent towards their mothers themselves became victims of domestic violence as adults. Similarly, about 80 percent of those who were physically and/or sexually abused as children later became victims of domestic violence.

We do not do a good job protecting or intervening with this population during childhood. They are frequently victimized, and they are not given tools to deal with that victimization. They grow up to form relationships that repeat the violence and abuse of their childhoods, further traumatizing them. Then, because they use drugs to cope with the emotional pain of their extensive histories of abuse, we label them criminal and lock them up, often for many years. If they are among the most fortunate ones, they may then receive help.

Their relationships with criminal men are linked to their abuse histories, especially in adulthood. Over 80 percent of those whose husband was also involved in the crime for which they are imprisoned and about three-fourths of those whose boyfriend was involved reported being victims of domestic violence.

Most corrections officials acknowledge that many of the women were convicted of crimes in which their partner was far more culpable. If you then consider that they are domestic violence victims, it is not hard to make the leap to the argument that they may have been coerced into crime. One woman summed up the relationship between the men in their lives and the women's convictions:

> And the ones in for life—drug crimes. They're basically in prison because the boyfriend did something. Some of them knew the boyfriend was doing something, I'm not gonna sugarcoat it. Some of them knew the boyfriend was—some of them didn't. And there's no way to decipher between who's telling the truth and who's not. There's a lot of women in prison who are scorned—I know one in there, she basically walked in on a man molesting her son and she killed him and she got life. And that's her protecting her own child.

Clearly, most of these women do not know how to have healthy relationships with men. They become involved with drug-using and abusive men because that is what they know and these are often the only men who will have anything to do with them. Unfortunately, those relationships eventually help destroy the fabric of their own lives. If they do not receive appropriate counseling while incarcerated, they may very well become involved again with the same type of man, once they are released.

SUMMARY

It is readily apparent that Oklahoma's women prisoners have had mean lives. The vast majority have experienced physical or sexual abuse growing up. This abuse has continued in their adult lives, with an overwhelming number of these women the victims of intimate partner violence and rape. In contrast, a fairly low number have been able to access trauma therapy or substance abuse. Oklahoma is a state that focuses on individual accountability, and when the traumatic lives of women prisoners are pointed out, citizens are usually quick to point out that they personally know someone who has overcome such adversity. However, if we inform the pathways approach with Agnew's theory, we can better understand why only some abused women become offenders. These are women who lack the internal and external resources to deal with their experiences, and the state shows little interest in providing treatment for either trauma or substance abuse to those lacking health insurance. Instead, the first treatment many of these women received occurred after they entered the Oklahoma DOC. Chapter 4 focuses on the prison experience of Oklahoma's women prisoners. It is sad to note that despite the trauma of incarceration, for many women it is also their first opportunity to receive much-needed help. It is perhaps even sadder to realize how many of those who need help may not even receive it in prison, due to dwindling state budgets. Chapter 4 focuses on the daily experiences of the women in prison and the programs available to them.

CHAPTER 4

The Prison Experience

UNTIL THE realignment of Oklahoma Department of Corrections (DOC) and creation of the Division for Female Offender Operations in 2008, female offenders entered the system through the Lexington Assessment Center, the same place where men entered. Since 2008, women have been assessed at Mabel Bassett Correctional Center where the administration uses gender-sensitive assessment tools. The entire system has been revamped, in recognition that women prisoners are qualitatively different from men. In the words of a recent warden, "It's icing on the cake, in terms of meeting them at the door" (Riggs 2008).

The process involves medical, educational, and mental health assessments that focus on the specific needs of women prisoners. Up to 93 women can be housed in the assessment center at one time.

Having the assessment done at a women's facility can reduce the stress for the new prisoner, especially if she remains at Mabel Bassett, as about one in five new receptions do. In the past, women were housed at a men's facility for reception, which created a cumbersome process and added to the trauma of entering prison.

ENTERING PRISON

Arrival at the facility can be highly stressful for the new woman prisoner. Mabel Bassett Correctional Center, unlike Dr. Eddie Warrior Correctional Center, looks like a typical institution. Surrounded by razor wire fencing, the prison is a gray concrete structure. It sits on a lonely two-lane road in central Oklahoma, and the approach to the facility can itself instill a sense of foreboding.

In contrast, arrival at Eddie Warrior inspires less fear. This all-woman facility looks much more like a boarding school than a prison, with dormitories and buildings spread out over the grounds. In fact, the facility has at various times housed the Indian Mission Haloche Industrial Institute; the Deaf, Blind, and Orphan Institute for Children; and various children's homes. Most recently, it was the state Department of Corrections Training Facility. In 1988, it became Dr. Eddie Warrior Correctional Center, a minimum security facility for Oklahoma's women prisoners. The prisoners maintain a vegetable garden, although according to some, they rarely get the fresh vegetables they have grown, a fact I was unable to confirm.

There were two community correctional facilities in the state until 2013, both located in Oklahoma City. One has recently been closed due to the need for more repairs than are feasible. The beds are being relocated as much as possible to the other facility, the name of which has been changed . Many women are released to that facility as they near the end of their sentences. Finally, the DOC contracts with private businesses to operate three halfway houses, two in Tulsa and one in Enid. There are approximately 300 halfway house beds available for women coming out of prison. The state releases nearly 1,200 per year, so a significant majority of the women do not go to halfway houses.

PRISON PROGRAMMING

Life for women in prison is not easy. Most of them struggle with being in close confinement with so many other women and with being away from their families and loved ones. Additionally, they are faced with long hours to fill. The overwhelming characteristic of prison life is boredom, and the women look for ways to fill their time. However, while the Oklahoma DOC has instituted innovative programming for the women, a dwindling budget makes it difficult to provide the programs to all who have a demonstrated need.

Substance Abuse Treatment

Substance abuse beds are severely limited. This is very problematic because drug problems are the number one reason women go to prison, and many women have a documented need for substance abuse treatment but do not receive it while incarcerated. "During Fiscal Year (FY) 2010, 885 female offenders who discharged or completed their sentences had a need for substance abuse treatment. Of these, 252 (28 percent) completed treatment prior to release, and 633 (72 percent) did not" (Oklahoma Department of Corrections/ Division of Female Offender Operations 2010). Those who are fortunate are able to get into programs such as Helping Women Recover and Regimented Treatment Program. Helping Women Recover has been particularly helpful to women with long-term substance abuse issues. However, not all those who receive treatment are successful. One woman—who had been incarcerated nearly 20 years then paroled—is typical. While she had completed a faith-based program and received substance abuse education prior to parole, she had done little to deal with her underlying problems. Once released, she quickly returned to what she knew—prostitution, drug use, and drug-using men. Not surprisingly, her parole was quickly revoked. However, through the intervention of individuals outside of the prison system, she was able to obtain one of the coveted slots in Helping Women Recover. In her words:

> I wasn't at all familiar with my triggers nor did I have any coping skills to maintain sobriety. This is a deadly combination that caused my selfishness and my survivor skills to resurface, causing me to become once again a failure in the eyes of everyone counting on me to include myself . . . This program is thorough and very intense and it offers four months of digging up roots that cause demise. I am excited to learn and experience the ways that could change my future forever, by transforming into the person I was always destined to be, without the additives. Today I am a prisoner of hope . . .

This prisoner was one of the fortunate ones, garnering one of the coveted spots in Helping Women Recover during her most recent incarceration. However, the number of beds available is far fewer than the number needed. Indeed, as of the end of 2011, only 127 women had completed the program (Oklahoma Department of Corrections/Division I 2012). This shortage of beds is true for all substance abuse treatment in the system.

Education

Nor is substance abuse treatment the only area that is inadequately funded. Consider the experience of one woman, who was serving a 65-year sentence and was eligible for parole consideration after 13 years. One of the stipulations of her parole was that she had to obtain education. In the prison, the education department was unclear whether the stipulation meant she had to complete General Educational Development (GED) testing, Adult Basic Education, or Literacy. She had completed some school work while in a private facility, but when the facility was taken over by the state, her records somehow did not transfer. To make matters worse, one of the ways the DOC manages inadequate resources is to reserve education slots for those with a short time remaining on their sentences. This approach is logical, but for this woman, and probably others, it had negative implications. Not only did she have to wait to get into educational programs, but she found that the long gaps between classes often led to her forgetting what she had learned before. She often found herself having to start over almost completely once she was able to get into a class, so her progress was limited.

Prisoners who already have a high school diploma or GED can take college courses, although they must find their own funding. In FY 2010, 452 college courses were taken by women prisoners in Oklahoma. The prisoners are generally limited to correspondence courses, and many seek financial support for their education from church groups and other organizations. Some with long sentences have been able to complete associate's degrees while incarcerated.

Very young offenders can also take courses that are paid for by grants under the Youthful Offender Act. One woman talked about the problem with that funding source. Based on her own experiences in the system, she feels that opportunity is available for women who are too young to truly appreciate it. She has been incarcerated more than once, and during her last incarceration, she completed several college courses.

> Well, when I first, when I went there the second time, to prison, I had a friend, she was doing life, and she said, "You need to go to school." So I started taking my basics in school, so the whole time I've been gone, I've just been taking the classes they give us. I got all my basics done. School was free. 25 and under you can go, you can get a grant, and then they raised it up. I wasn't gonna be able to go this time around 'cause I was too old, But they made it 35 and under and so many years from parole. You can go to school, you get like a Federal grant thing, it's like a Youthful Offender Grant is what it's called. And then you make certain—you make all good grades you get a higher grant. So I made As and Bs, I got the extended amount where I could take more classes. And I took every class that they had that I needed.

This woman went on to note that the younger women in prison are less motivated to change, and she expressed the opinion that the grant was somewhat wasted on them. The Oklahoma DOC also provides many of the college classes as telecourses. At Eddie Warrior, which is a minimum security facility, some courses have been offered on site. Those not qualifying for a Youthful Offender Grant can also enroll in classrooms on a space-available basis. There are some other funding sources available to women who want to take college courses. In some cases, their families pay for the tuition. Private foundations also offer scholarships, including Friends of Eddie Warrior and Little Light Ministries, which offers a Loving Touch Scholarship to a few women prisoners.

Numerous volunteer groups have been bringing programs into the women's prisons for the past few years, as well. In 2011, two individuals brought their life-coaching class, Life On Purpose, into Mabel Bassett on a strictly volunteer basis. The focus is on teaching the women prisoners to think in depth about their own values and relationships, to develop listening skills, and to expand their communication skills. Many of the women who have completed this training have now become life coaches to administer it to other women.

Health

Health issues in prison are often problematic as well. Shrinking budgets have led to various strategies to reduce the cost of medical care, including contract physicians and telemedicine (Anderson 2003). Oklahoma, like many states, has consolidated the more extensive medical treatment into one facility, Mabel Bassett. Any woman who is pregnant or needs substantial medical care must be housed at that facility. This means that women are often placed in a more restrictive and austere setting than necessary, just so they can receive medical treatment.

More than 16,000 requests for medical services were submitted at three facilities during FY 2010, resulting in more than 10,000 scheduled appointments, 134 emergency room visits, and 87 hospital admissions. Women prisoners have often neglected their health care for years before they are incarcerated, and one nurse commented that for many of the women, prison is where they receive their first annual checkups and PAP smears, as seen in the video *Women Behind Bars* (Benalioulhaj 2010). Because of their lifestyles prior to incarceration, women in prison often have chronic illnesses as well (Anderson 2003).

One woman related a story of her difficulty getting needed services. She suffered from congestive heart disease and an enlarged heart. In the spring of 2009, she had accumulated so much fluid that she was having difficulty breathing. She was sent back to her cell once after seeking assistance, but the nursing staff followed up and sent her to the hospital in critical condition. While in the hospital, she was told that her condition had been diagnosed four years earlier, but she had not received treatment for it. Not surprisingly, this prisoner developed a very negative attitude towards the prison staff. Lacking the ability to communicate her concerns effectively, she began bombarding staff with requests. In her words, "I just feel so abandon in here. I cry so much . . . I am so overwhelm with pain." However, she eventually received a pacemaker and defibrillator. She said that she was grateful she had not paroled when she first was eligible, as she might not have received the life-extending procedure. Ultimately, her incarceration meant that her medical condition was treated. It is highly unlikely that she would have received the needed treatment if she had been living on the outside and lacking health insurance.

Another woman has had multiple bladder surgeries, all but one of them to repair damage done during the first surgery. She expressed anger and frustration with the system, but she was relieved to have at last had a successful corrective surgery. This woman, who I will call Donna, is serving a very long sentence. She works hard to maintain a positive attitude and to gain education and treatment while in prison. For a while, she had one of the coveted paying jobs with outside industries, but she is currently working within the prison system. According to her, maintaining her health and staying positive and busy help pass the time.

Work

Work is important to the women, but opportunities are limited. Those employed to work in the prisons receive up to $20 per month. There are also a few contracts with external employers. For example, at Eddie Warrior, up to 15 women at any given time work at repackaging damaged goods, for minimum wage. But given the almost 800 women at the facility, this makes little impact.

At Mabel Bassett, the Back Office Support Systems program (BOSS) is a telemarketing endeavor that employs up to 90 offenders at a time, for less than $2 per hour. However, there are over 1,100 women at Mabel Bassett, so competition is stiff for the positions.

Both jobs serve several purposes for the women. First they help fill the hours with constructive activity, thus lessening the boredom. Second, they provide the women with some money that they can use to buy items in the commissary or even pay for college courses at times. Finally, sometimes the women who have worked at these jobs while imprisoned can go to work for the companies after their release. The less positive and even dark side of these industries, however, is that the women are essentially being exploited by private industry because they work at far below the minimum wage of the country as a whole.

Filling the Hours

The dearth of jobs and limited education slots mean that many of the women have little to fill the long hours of their days. Those who are in for short sentences may get into programs but often are unable to complete them before discharge, so they often do not take them seriously. Those with longer sentences who are not eligible for programs tend to find ways to occupy their time. Some spend considerable time reading and educating themselves.

At Eddie Warrior, there is more freedom of movement and nicer grounds, so when the weather is nice, many women spend time outside. However, movement is strictly limited at Mabel Bassett, even though one-fourth of the population is minimum security and more than half is medium security. The facility looks and operates more like a maximum security facility, with limited movement and few places to sit outside.

Many of the women take up hobbies to pass the time. Sometimes, these hobbies can be used to make small amounts of money. One of the most creative projects has been undertaken by a woman who is serving life without parole on a drug charge. She uses cardboard boxes and candies to make all types of gifts, including fire trucks, tractors, and houses. She told me that she can basically make just about anything if people tell her what they want. One day I came home from work to find a package from Mabel Bassett Correctional Center on my front porch. This woman had made my granddaughters a house out of candy, with popcorn packages for windows and Hershey bars for doors; the remainder of the "house" was covered in hard candies. The roof of the house could be lifted off to place small gifts inside. She saves her money, buying small amounts of candy each month until she has enough on hand to make a few of her creations. The families of other prisoners often buy them from her, as do many of the staff and volunteers. The money is placed in her canteen account, allowing her to buy what she needs, including more supplies. Her creativity speaks to the efforts that many women in Oklahoma's prisons put forth to reduce the boredom and pain of their incarceration.

Visitation

Visitation days are highly anticipated. However, most of the women do not receive visitors. Prison staff members frequently comment that it is heartbreaking how few have families that come to see them regularly. In contrast, according to people who have worked at multiple facilities in the Oklahoma DOC, visitation days at the men's prisons are quite busy. In recent months, due to the budget constraints, visitation has become more problematic for all prisoners. The DOC has been operating at about 75 percent of full staffing, resulting in too few correctional officers available to allow visitation on some weekends. Visitation is regularly canceled for no other reason than the inability to effectively monitor the prisoners and their visitors.

Friendships and relationships with other prisoners are also important. While some do form sexual relationships and others form families, other research has documented this well. I will instead focus on the importance of friendships and being of service to other prisoners.

One woman has availed herself of every opportunity she can find to train as a mentor for other women. She is serving a life without parole sentence for a drug crime, so she has found a way to have a life inside. She has taken every program that she is allowed to take,[1] and wherever possible, she has trained to help provide the programs to others. Other women who have some formal education or are more literate often try to help other prisoners with their legal paperwork. One woman, no longer in prison, said she had found her calling while doing this. She has recently taken the Law School Admissions Test (LSAT) and hopes to enroll in law school next year. While she was in prison, she filled her hours with providing legal assistance to the other women. She hopes to eventually turn that into a career and not only plans to attend law school but also has started an advocacy business.

While some friendships formed in prison serve simply to stave off loneliness, others become lifelong bonds. One woman talked about a friend who had recently died. "She always did think she was my mother." She went on to say that the other woman had broken through her own resistance and "led me back to God." These two women remained very close both inside and outside of prison. When the older woman died, the younger one was devastated.

SUMMARY

In the present political and economic climate, prison is a harsh experience for Oklahoma's women. Limited programming and limited job opportunities mean that days are long and empty. The women try to find ways to fill their time, through self-improvement projects, hobbies, and friendships. While the younger women may get into fights, the older ones tend to seek ways to stay out of trouble and make the time pass. Visitation is often limited, so the relationships they form inside the prison are very important to them. Most will eventually return to society and hopefully to their families, but while inside, it may simply be too painful to think about their loved ones, especially their children.

Unfortunately, the dearth of available programs means that not all of those released into society will be well prepared for success. In chapters 5 and 6, we turn to the experiences of women who have been released. Those in chapter 5 have been returned to prison, while those in chapter 6 have been able to stay out. The role of social support in the ability to stay out of prison leads to a clear understanding of the kinds of issues faced by women upon returning to their communities, and the interventions that help them succeed.

CHAPTER 5

Going Back Again

Juanita Ortiz

CHALLENGES TO REENTRY

VERY LITTLE research has been conducted on female offenders and their experiences with reentry. Even less research exists on female recidivism and the factors that influence women's return to crime. To prevent their recidivism, it is important to understand the challenges individuals face upon leaving prison. While many reentry needs of female offenders are similar to those of male offenders, some of those needs are unique. Many female offenders live below the poverty line, both at the time of incarceration and following release (Jacobs 2000; Olson, Lurigio, and Seng 2000; Severance 2004; Holtfreter, Reisig, and Morash 2004). Women also have higher rates of substance abuse and mental illness than male offenders. These distinctions are important in determining successful reentry for women, since having experienced adverse events is correlated to engaging in crime, as well as an increased likelihood of experiencing further mental and physical health problems (Holsinger and Holsinger 2005; Messina and Grella 2006).

Released individuals face difficulties in key areas of their lives, in part because they lack assistance in addressing the issues that brought them into prison in the first place. Released prisoners consequently enter society having to deal not only with the stigma associated with their criminal convictions, but also having to deal with problems present in their lives before and during their incarceration. The most documented areas of life in which reentering prisoners will experience difficulty on the "outside" include employment, housing, health, substance abuse, and families (Petersilia 2003; Travis 2005; Travis and Visher 2005). These difficulties, on their own or combined, can help to explain the high rate of recidivism among former offenders.

The risk of recidivism has been found to be highest during the first year of release (Petersilia 2003). In the most comprehensive study of recidivism in the United States, 67.5 percent of 272,111 prisoners released in 1994 were rearrested for a new crime within three years of release (Langan and Levin 2002). However, Allen Beck (2001) argues that recidivism figures are problematic because there are varying definitions about what is counted as recidivism and the time frame used to measure it. Having qualified recidivism statistics, Beck and Shipley (1989) found a reincarceration rate of 42 percent for men and 33 percent for women within three years of release, while Patrick Langan and David Levin found higher rates of recidivism for both males and females, 53 percent and 40 percent respectively (2002).

Not much research exists on female recidivism specifically. A recent study on female recidivism followed 506 women released from prison in one state, finding that 47 percent of these women were reconvicted or reincarcerated, with most women reconvicted or reincarcerated within the first two years following their release (Huebner, Cobbina, and DeJong 2010). Other research has found that almost 60 percent of the females in the Langan and Levin (2002) recidivism dataset were rearrested within three years of release, linking higher numbers of prior arrests with higher rates of recidivism. It also determined that women incarcerated for drug possession and property offenses had the highest recidivism rates (Deschenes, Owen, and Crow 2006). In Oklahoma, the state reports a 14.7 percent recidivism rate over three years for Oklahoma female offenders, from 2006 to 2009 (Oklahoma Department of Corrections Female Offender Operations 2009).

Unfortunately, the challenges that released individuals encounter in reentry make sense. In terms of employment, ex-offenders must struggle not only with lack of education and job skills in their search for work, but they must also struggle with the stigma resulting from their criminal background (Mukamal 2001; Seiter and Kadela 2003; Henry and Jacobs 2007). Many states, including Oklahoma, restrict ex-offenders by limiting the occupations in which they can work (Hahn 1991; Dietrich 2003; Harris and Keller 2005). These challenges in securing employment are correlated with higher recidivism rates (Harer 1994; Piehl 2003). If employment is found, it is typically in low-paying, secondary-labor-market positions (Western 2002). Negative experiences in locating employment can lead to disillusionment and apathy about working in the legal job market, especially in the face of greater profits in the illegal job sector (Rose et al. 2008).

Additionally, former prisoners typically lack financial resources to obtain housing after their release (O'Brien 2001). They are often ineligible for any type of housing assistance or, when eligible, they may be placed on extremely long waiting lists for assistance (Travis, Solomon, and Waul 2001). While some women are lucky enough to secure transitional residential housing (e.g., halfway houses), most female offenders return to the neighborhoods from which they were arrested and convicted: typically impoverished, run-down communities with few resources to offer toward employment and overall reintegration needs (Leverentz 2006b).

Released offenders may not be able to return to living with their families, either because their staying there would make their families ineligible for housing assistance, or because the offenders might have ruined their family relationships through their criminal activities and incarceration. These challenges mean that many returning prisoners will face homelessness immediately upon their reentry into society, despite the finding that stable housing is conducive to preventing recidivism (Travis, Solomon, and Waul 2001). Challenges in securing employment and housing augment family problems for reentering female offenders, as oftentimes these women cannot regain custody of their children without meeting rigid state social service requirements (Dodge and Pogrebin 2001).

Substance abuse and mental health issues are also problematic for newly released women. Tammy Anderson states, "Women in prison have higher rates of substance abuse, antisocial personality disorder, borderline personality disorder, post-traumatic stress disorder, and histories of sexual and physical abuse than their male counterparts. Women frequently engage in self-mutilating behaviors, are verbally abusive, and report numerous suicide attempts" (2003, 51). Anderson reports that, overall, female prisoners are more likely than male prisoners to have recurring and more severe mental health issues, based on their lifelong experiences of victimization. This higher likelihood of mental illness among female prisoners is important because women respond to mental illness in more self-harming or even suicidal ways (Covington 2002a). Due to the paucity of treatment while incarcerated, many women leave prison with severe mental health issues. Outside the prison, the problem may be even worse, as community mental health services for low-income individuals may not even be available, especially in non-urban communities.

Additional research points to factors that intersect with sex to explain higher rates of mental illness, HIV/AIDS, STDs, and chronic illness among certain populations of criminal women over others (Anderson, Rosay, and Saum 2002). Incarcerated women with histories of abuse are more likely to engage in problematic risky sexual behavior such as sex without protection, sex with multiple partners, and sex while under the influence of drugs and alcohol (Fogel and Belyea 1999). Failure to diagnose and treat these issues in prison and after release likely contributes to unsuccessful reentry efforts (Petersilia 2003; Travis 2005; Baer et al. 2006).

Reentering female offenders face other specific health care needs during their incarceration and release. Biologically, women need gynecological services as well as services related to pregnancy, breast health, and menopause. Serious illness may go undiagnosed prior to discharge from prison due to funding problems, and when they do receive health services in prison, women may have difficulty finding follow-up care in their communities. One important issue is the lack of preparation that incarcerated new mothers receive to deal with their separation from their baby, along with how to deal with that child upon release (Anderson 2003).

Research suggests that maintaining connections with family, specifically children, during incarceration is important to preventing recidivism. Presence or absence of an intimate partner during incarceration and upon release from prison is important, as a partner can often provide social and financial support. While male prisoners may often return to their pre-incarceration intimate partner upon release, however, this is often not an option for women prisoners (Leverentz 2006a; Arditti and Few 2006).

Limited visitation schedules and policies, the prisons' distance from family members, lack of public transportation to prisons, and lack of affordable telephone communication are also not conducive to supporting family unity (Mumola 2000; Austin, Irwin, and Hardyman 2002; Christian 2005). These challenges make it difficult for family members to sustain contact with an incarcerated individual, which strains reunification attempts upon release from prison.

Incarcerated mothers face additional issues with the placement of their children. While the incarceration of a parent is traumatizing for a child, the presence of the other parent can help to alleviate some of the trauma by providing some parental stability. However, children of women offenders are more likely to have children who had no parent in the home. This presents tremendous challenges to women seeking to reunite with their children, especially in light of the fact that female prisoners are less likely than male prisoners to see their children while incarcerated (Bloom 1995). Mothers who do not have the option of family members with whom to leave their children during their incarceration report significant distress over not knowing who was caring of their children or even where their children might be residing (Forsyth 2003). In Oklahoma, the female prisoner's parent was the most common placement until recently (Sharp and Marcus-Mendoza 2001; Sharp et al. 2008). These issues can lead to increased likelihood of problematic and even questionable reunification with their children upon release.

Female prisoners are further disheartened in their efforts to succeed economically and to support their families in the face of all of the fines that they encounter upon their release from prison (e.g., restitution, court costs, parole supervision fees, etc.). Female offenders find it incredibly challenging to meet the economic requirements necessary to reunite with their children.

Yet these critical needs for successful reentry of female offenders are often not addressed. Furthermore, even if some of these issues are dealt with while these women are incarcerated, no transitional services are normally offered to them upon their release. Because incarcerated women typically lack healthy social support networks in the community, they are returning to prison at high rates (Reisig, Holtfreter, and Morash 2002). Successful addressing of these issues for female offenders is arguably directly correlated with prevention of recidivism (Visher and Travis 2003).

Recidivism and Oklahoma's Women Prisoners

Twenty-one women who were incarcerated for a second or subsequent time were interviewed for this chapter. A description of the women and the research can be found in Appendix A. Pseudonyms are used throughout the chapter to protect their anonymity.

Reentry: Housing, Jobs, and Transportation

Reentry challenges begin immediately after women are released from prison. Yet most of these women reported being previously released into society with no money, secure housing, or plan for success. The most immediate needs following discharge from prison are food, clothing, shelter, and personal hygiene products. However, except for two of the women in this study, the released women had no one to turn to for help in securing these necessities. It was consequently a huge decision for many of these women about how to spend the $50 with which they were released from prison.

Many women reported having to decide whether to rent a cheap motel room and have enough for a fast-food meal, which would only cover one day of living expenses. In the face of not knowing when their next meal might be, some women chose to sleep outside on park benches, under bridges, in ditches, or in garage stairwells to save their $50 for food for as long as possible.

Another immediate challenge these women reported was clothing, as they reported that they had been released from prison with clothing that was ill-fitting or not suitable for the weather at the time of their release. For example, Cody shared that she had gone into prison a younger woman, so the clothes which fit her upon her entry into prison not only did not fit her anymore, but she found the clothing to be unsuitable for her as a middle-aged lady upon her release. Vivian summarized the concerns of these women about being released without weather-appropriate attire and without the resources to address this situation.

So, if you get out December 31 and it's cold outside and you don't even have a coat, you're standing out there freezing at the bus stop. And you're hungry, and you don't even have money for something to eat. It just goes on and on and on. They give you $50 when you leave . . . So we get released with $50 and the clothes I'm wearing. Yeah, what I got on right now. With the "inmate" stamp back there.

Housing was another serious challenge facing these women upon their release. They understood the importance of housing as a pillar of stability in their quest to succeed outside of prison. Housing provided necessary shelter for the women and their children, and stable housing offered the first point of a transitioning relationship between the newly released woman and her children. Stable housing was also important to note on employment and social service applications. Housing provided a sanctuary from the judgment they experienced from others, as well as the motivation to keep working and stay out of trouble. This sentiment was best expressed by Beverly.

Housing is important, you know what I'm saying? If you out there, you homeless, what can you do when you homeless? What? You know what I'm saying? If you got a roof over your head, you got responsibilities. You know you gotta pay your rent, you know you gotta pay your gas, you know you gotta pay your lights, that's motivation, you know what I'm saying, to go get you a good job, to keep your stuff up. That's motivation to keep a roof over your kid's head, you know what I'm saying, so housing is important.

Despite the acknowledgement of housing as a critical need, the little amount of money with which the women were released from prison did not leave much room for negotiating safe housing options. They were thus very likely to return to housing within communities that held connections to their prior offending friends, family members, or partners, thereby returning them to crime-promoting elements. Or, they were left to risk housing situations with unknown people and environments. The women's housing situations were likely to be unsafe and often criminal. For example, Sweet had to lease an apartment with her sister, as she was not able to qualify for her own lease, based on her felony conviction. Yet living with her sister brought her back to drugs, because her sister was a drug addict.

As another example, Vivian also had no place to go after her release from prison, so she resorted to living with people she did not know well. It turned out that she was living in a known meth house. When she figured out that they were making and using drugs, she left that residence, fearing the trouble she would get into if she were discovered to be living among criminals. She also feared resuming her prior substance abuse issues. However, her desperation to find a place to stay after that put her back into trouble, as she moved in with an older man and some of his friends, and he eventually started pressuring her for sex in exchange for housing.

Some might propose homeless shelters as a temporary solution for women leaving prison. However, many of these women expressed difficulties in finding shelters, even for temporary housing. Many of the women were released after years of incarceration, with little knowledge about the areas into which they were being released. No reentry transitional assistance had been given them, so they were not aware of shelters they could turn to for housing. Even when they did locate a homeless shelter, there were challenges of finding one that was not full, that accepted women, or that was safe.

Another dimension to consider in the women's decisions of whether or not to pursue housing in a homeless shelter was introduced by Bad Girl. Bad Girl gave a poignant description of the challenges incarcerated women encounter at these types of facilities, based on their institutionalization due to years of incarceration. She stated that the shelter reminded her too much of prison, in terms of not being able to control when you arrive, when you have to leave, and standing in line to eat. She thus made it a priority to get out of the shelter by selling drugs and prostituting herself enough to save money to get into a hotel room.

Several of the women in this study thus shared stories of extremely difficult transitory housing experiences. Bree's experience is typical of the housing experiences these women faced immediately upon getting out of prison.

BREE: I walked. To my dad's house. And it was, "Oh. It's good to see you, but you can't stay here."

INTERVIEWER: So what was the housing situation then?

BREE: Staying from pillar to post. From here, maybe one night I could stay over at this person's house, and the next night I could probably stay at this person's house. "Oh, well, I'll let you stay a couple of days." . . . About seven months that I moved from friend to friend.

INTERVIEWER: Were you ever homeless during that time?

BREE: Yes. I remember sleeping in a parking garage. As a matter of fact, downtown, right by the Union Bus station. There's nobody there, so you, um, sleep in the stairwell. 'Cause you know the stairwell doors close, 'cause you can open the stairwell doors to go from the next level. Well, I slept in the stairwells, with no blanket or anything. I just had what I had on my back . . . housing has been very unstable.

In terms of the housing situation for released prisoners, Lone Wolf provided an interesting new facet that should be considered. Lone Wolf was Native American, and she stated that, normally, had she been impoverished and homeless, she would have had access to tribal assistance with housing, food, clothing, utilities, and education. However, her felony conviction made her ineligible for assistance from her tribe. She stated that ineligibility for services varied from tribe to tribe, so it was her bad luck that her tribe had such a rule. Left without assistance options, she went from friends to family to homelessness until her return to prison.

Another significant reentry challenge reported by the women involved securing employment. A few of the women mentioned that the employment situation had worsened over just the past few years, as background checks had become a standard practice after the September 11, 2001 attacks. This made employment difficult to obtain in even the areas of employment not typically desired by most of society, like retail and fast food.

Fifteen of the twenty-one women discussed how difficult it was for them to get a job after their release from prison. (Of the six remaining women, one didn't have to work; one couldn't work due to medical issues, two had job offers waiting for them from family or a friend, and two chose to go straight back to crime instead of looking for a job.) All fifteen of the women who had problems finding a job after their release specifically stated that they believed it was directly related to their felon status. Most of the women reported having been trained, through prison programs, to tell the truth about their criminal backgrounds on employment applications, as employers would be willing to work with them based on their honesty. However, they soon discovered that advice was not accurate, as reported by Vanda here.

> But as soon as they see that prison or ex-felon, you're out. They're not even gonna look at your application. So you don't stand a chance, actually. Especially if you're a woman. I think it's worse against women, because we're women. And, quote, unquote, in society, women are supposed to be home, taking care of the kids, the husband, and the house. So it's just harder on women, all around. Over half of the jobs that I applied to wouldn't even look at it.

The women reported incident after incident of going somewhere to apply, only to see an immediate shift in the potential employer's demeanor once he/she found out that the woman had a criminal background. Their inability to get a job was not based on lack of effort, as evidenced by the fact that then would spend all day, every day, trying to find employment. It took a long time for Beth to find work:

> And it was six months, of Monday through Friday, focusing, like that was my job, finding a job. And so from 8 in the morning until about 6 in the evening, I was actually beating the pavement. I know a lot of people don't, but I mean, I did the newspaper thing, I got out and walked, I did

applications, I went places. And I was beating down doors. And it was rejection straight for six months.

These women were trying to succeed and to stay out of prison. Bree even reported that her parole officer did not believe how hard she was working to get a job, as she told him that she had pursued 39 jobs in 45 days. The parole officer made her go back to each of the 39 places to have them document why they would not hire her, and the vast majority of the employers wrote that it was because she was a felon. Missy looked for a job for two years and was never able to get one, because she refused to lie about her criminal history, sure that she would be fired if they found out she lied. Even those with education and skills could not find work, as Pooty described:

> I don't know. I'm thinking, honestly, because of my criminal history, a lot of times, I don't get jobs. Because I don't go looking like me, I go looking like a whole different person. And I have the credentials for it. I have suits, I have education, I have the skills. What else could it be? I'm there. I'll be the first to open and the last to leave, if you want me to. I'm not too proud to do anything. I just want a job. I'm willing to work. And I just couldn't ever get hired.

Their felony records also made their training irrelevant in many cases. For example, Laci had a chemistry degree but could not obtain professional employment, so she used her chemistry skills to start producing drugs, arranging to supply people in exchange for money, food, and housing. Sweet had worked in the nursing field prior to her incarceration, but her felony conviction made her ineligible for employment in that profession. Anne had been working on a child psychology degree before her incarceration, but she realized that her felony conviction would make her ineligible for the licensing necessary to pursue that occupation. Also, Missy had a business management educational background, along with computer skills, but she could not gain employment professionally after her release from prison.

When the women in this study were able to obtain employment, it was typically in low-paying positions in food service or through temporary employment agencies. As the women learned that being honest about their criminal background would almost always translate into immediate refusal of employment, many of them began to lie on that part of the application. However, a few of them experienced great disappointment when a background check was eventually conducted and they lost their employment. Pooty had accepted a job offer as a clerical worker with an educational institution, which would have paid for her to attend school as an employee. However, her job offer was conditional on her passing a drug test and a criminal background check. She thus offered the details of her incarceration and, despite the employer's assurance that she would be fine in the process, she got home to find an email from the employer that she no longer had the job. Pooty reported, "That crushed my spirit, seriously. That hurt. It knocked my self-esteem down, when it came to that, because I was excited, seriously." Overall, six women were fired after it was discovered that they had a felony conviction. They reported having had a great work ethic and reputation at their place of work, but the revelation of their felony conviction through background checks was enough to suspend their accomplishments at that position. If these women were not fired immediately, their employers found trivial or false reasons to fire them soon enough.

Transportation was another obstacle upon release from prison. Most of the women reported that they were released with no information whatsoever about the transportation options available to them in their communities. When they walked out of prison they had no idea about how to reach desired locations or where to find information about public transportation options. Relying on word-of-mouth to gain directions, the women reported riding around aimlessly for hours, then trying just to return back home rather than to the places they needed to be.

The women reported multiple responsibilities—meeting with parole officers, finding and maintaining employment, and consulting with social service providers for assistance with basic needs and even child custody issues—that they had to meet on a regular basis in order to stay out of prison. Many of these responsibilities involved traveling significant distances and so required access to transportation, but the women reported that transportation issues were not considered a reasonable excuse for missing any of them. They thus expressed fear of failing to meet their obligations and returning to prison. Bree and Vivian reported being paralyzed with fear of missing the bus to their appointments or jobs. Another interesting point they both brought up was that issues with transportation led them to bus stops and situations in troubled communities that exposed them to illegitimate behaviors and opportunities.

Transportation options also limited many of these women's employment opportunities. Several women stated that the cities they returned to lacked a dependable, far-reaching transportation system. This meant that they were limited in where they could seek employment. Women reported finding work, only to be unable to get there or to keep the job because buses did not travel there or else the buses did not offer regular access to that area of the city, especially at the hours when they might need to be at work. Consequently, even if they were able to get to work on the bus, they might not be able to get home that way.

Another issue related to the women's use of the public transportation system was having the money to use it. Putting all available money into simply trying to keep afloat with fines and survival needs, the ability to pay for transportation was essentially nonexistent for many. A couple of women had parole officers who would give them enough bus passes to get them to work and back, as well as to required appointments, until their next parole visit. Most of the women, however, were on their own to fund their public transportation needs. Whether the women were using bus passes or depending on others for transportation, some would enter a cycle of debt, based on borrowing money for their transportation, only to pay it back with their next paycheck and then have to borrow again.

Not only were their jobs and parole obligations at stake based on transportation challenges, but the women themselves were often in perilous situations as a result. For example, Cody started work at 11 P.M. five or six days a week, but the bus to her employment location would quit running at 6 P.M. each evening. Serious about keeping her job, Cody would ride the bus and sit at work for five hours between the last bus and her shift start time. She would then leave work exhausted and either walk, hitchhike, or beg her coworkers for a ride. Cody grew so physically tired after working this schedule that she almost burned her grandmother's house down one day as she fell asleep cooking.

Another dangerous situation arising from transportation issues involved Tamara. Tamara got pregnant soon after her release from prison, so she needed money to pay for bills, food, and other necessities. The only job she was able to find was at a fast-food place that was over five miles away from her home. Lacking both access to public transportation and the money to pay for it, she walked to her place of employment every day. She passed out twice from exhaustion and heat, as it was during her later stages of pregnancy and she was walking in intense August heat in Oklahoma. She was also walking anywhere she needed to go, like to doctor's appointments and the grocery store. Her doctor regularly informed her that she was jeopardizing herself and the baby, but she felt she had no choice if she wanted to stay out of prison.

While Cody and Tamara definitely faced frightening situations, perhaps the most chilling accounts of dangers encountered due to transportation shortcomings came from Lone Wolf. Lone Wolf stated that she had no car and no money to pay for anyone to drive her around. She lived in an isolated, rural area, so there were no public transportation options. Not only did Lone Wolf face transportation issues, she also had significant substance abuse addiction problems. Based on her inability to stay sober, she eventually quit her job. At that point, she fully succumbed to the substance abuse issues and placed herself in extremely dangerous situations, hitchhiking for alcohol, drugs, and food.

Lone Wolf: When I quit my job, I just walked to the next place where I'm going to go get drunk and probably lay my head down. Trying to find a place to stay and drink. If I couldn't find me a place to stay, I just had me a little blanket in my bag and stuff. I'd just go underneath the bridge and just pass out and just go to sleep.

INTERVIEWER: Did anyone ever try to hurt you while you were out there hitchhiking or sleeping?

LONE WOLF: There's a few times that I got by them. I was riding in this car with these two guys, and I never knew these people. I'd just get in the car. I'm drunk and I'm a brave person when I'm drunk. So I get in the car with these two guys and we go riding around. And we start getting real messed up and drunk. And pretty soon, I noticed they start whispering to each other when I wasn't looking, and my senses told me, "Next stop. Run. Get out of the car." And so we stopped at the store, to get some more beer. Okay. They get out to go get the beer. They get back and they set the 12-pack down. And the woman, she let them use the phone. So what I did is that they had I don't know how much money they had in their seat, in the console, so I grabbed all the beer and stuck it in my bag and all the money and took off. But I felt that they was wanting to go away, out in the field somewhere and party and do whatever they wanted with me, and I was just supposed to get some beer and stuff, but I just took off on them before anything happened.

This other time, I got a ride from this guy, and he said, "I've got to use the restroom." And I'm already drunk, like a said, I always have a bottle with me, drinking. And he went down into this field, way down in there, and I was like, "Man, we're going too far out here. I want out." And I was going to jump out, and he grabbed me by my hair. And I had my bottle in my bag, and I turned around and I hit him in the face with it. He let go, I jump out, and I start running. And it was dark. That's probably why I got away, because it was dark. I could hear him looking for me in the woods, and I lay underneath in the bush, still. And I could hear him walking around and stuff, looking for me. And I've almost gotten run over, walking in the night, drunk. It's like one night, I was walking through, and a little voice tells me, "Be on the other side now." So I just stagger myself on over to the other side. About that time, a car comes by without no headlights on. Just, voom, right where we were standing. And I've been through some crazy stuff. It's a wonder I survived. Yep.

Finally, even when a few of the women were able to secure their own transportation, they still faced issues of driving without a license, or else driving vehicles that were not dependable or that were attached to problematic situations. As an example, Missy was able to save enough money to purchase a car, but it broke down two weeks after she bought it. She then used a friend's car to get to work and to pick up her children from school, on the condition that she would pick up her friend's children from school as well and have the car back to her friend in time for her to get to work as well. This schedule soon grew too complicated, and Missy lost her friend, her job, and access to any transportation, as her small town did not have a public transportation system. Transportation issues thus presented serious obstacles to women's success outside of prison, impeding them in meeting both their basic needs and their requirements to stay out of prison.

Other Issues: Training and Participation in Programs While in Prison

The women also described severe deficiencies in education and skills, which were not alleviated during their former or current incarcerations through relevant, effective programming. While the women wanted more education, skill development, and program opportunities, they were discouraged about the likelihood of receiving such programming. One of the main reasons that they were not able to take all of the classes that they deemed necessary for themselves was the existence of significant waiting lists. Many women were not in prison long enough to outlast the lists, so they were released from prison before their name came up for a class or program. Other women were in prison for so long that they were not considered a priority for taking classes or programs. Even if they had been on a waiting list for years, they were prioritized behind women who were leaving sooner. These women reported that it was essentially a matter of luck   whether they were able to take a class or program while incarcerated. This held for programs as basic and essential as GED and Adult Basic Education training. Consequently, women reported days full of boredom and lack of productivity.

> So there's nothing for me to do except lay in my cell and watch TV. That's what I do every day. Some days you don't even want to get up and make your bed, because you know you're just going to get right back in it. Just stay on your bunk all day long and just watch TV. This is the most exercise I've had today, walking up here. Because I just live in that little corner room right there. (laughs) (Shoshone)
>
> So there's a lot of depressed people here, with no jobs or programs, just sitting on their bed or sitting around with nothing to do. (Young)

Women described programs they had participated in as being irrelevant and ineffective. They reported that the programs were run by untrained volunteers or current female prisoners who lacked any formal educational or professional experience. Because these programs were run by volunteers, the courses met irregularly, often going months without meeting or even terminating before the completion of all of the goals set forth for the participants, who said they were not kept informed as to when the program would resume or why it was terminated. Volunteer program staff also experienced significant turnover rates, further adding to the delays in program delivery. Beth's sentiments here were consistently expressed by the other women in this study.

> In my opinion, the parenting classes were completely terrible. Actually, to be honest, I think all the programs I've taken are really not very good. I hope this doesn't sound very critical. I'm not trying to sound ungrateful. But this is why I think women come back . . . Um, so I think that these programs are so schoolbook thought out and really have no basis in anything that they'll do for us. They haven't for me, and I was looking for things to use . . . They are just not relevant. It's so inappropriate. I know these girls are going, "Whatever!" And I've seen, I don't know how many of them, that I went through the class with, saying, in front of the person who taught it, "Yeah. I've learned a lot. I've really changed." And then they'll go out and get thrown in lock. Just like that. They didn't learn anything because it was so irrelevant.

Beth went on to describe how the programs typically consisted of role-playing with what she perceived as unrealistic, irrelevant scenarios. These scenarios taught women what to do to keep their husbands happy, like agreeing with the men to avoid arguments. Beth made the point that the women taking the classes were not married, so the lessons were less applicable to them.

Vanda similarly expressed that she had received over 500 hours of substance abuse rehabilitation programming during her last incarceration period. She called it "a joke." She said it did not help anyone overcome substance abuse addictions, as the program consisted of outdated workbooks, a journal, an occasional video, and untrained prisoners and volunteers running the program. Vanda stated that the female prisoners in this program routinely faced meetings where they were unsupervised and left to figure things out for themselves. Finally, Bree admitted that her program participation during her previous incarceration had not rehabilitated her. In fact, it had only served to make her a better criminal, as she had moved on from stealing to writing checks.

Another issue that deserves serious consideration is the over-representation of faith-based organizations among programming efforts in prisons. Of course, with low funding arising from our current economic crisis, it is understandable that volunteer groups would be utilized and welcomed into the correctional environment. Also, the women who described these groups' programs did not disparage the volunteers or say that they were unkind or disrespectful. They tended to see these groups as benevolent and earnest in their attempts to help incarcerated women. However, the women saw these individuals as lacking in experience and knowledge about what is needed to succeed outside of prison. They described these groups' focus on the use of prayer and paternal morality as a path to success in life. The morality lessons to submit to your husband and the father of your children are not very applicable or well-received among this group of women. Nevertheless, these were the types of programs that were consistently available without a waiting list. Some of the programs these groups offered asked participants to consider God's views and the consequences of their actions prior to doing or saying anything. Other programs provided by these groups included substance-abuse education, Bible studies, parenting classes, marriage classes, and religious worship services.

Beth brought up some interesting information about the complex set of issues introduced by granting religious-based groups a presence in the prison. She mentioned that prison administrators forced prisoners' participation at religious speakers' presentations. She said that the prison officials would encourage high attendance at these events, so they would be able to attract speakers regularly to the institution. This forced attendance of prisoners was especially high during a few of the presentations that were being videotaped for distribution nationally. Beth believed that religious groups enjoyed advantages entering the prison compared to other groups. In fact, she expressed surprise that the researcher was allowed entry for this project. One of the biggest points of contention she had with these groups being in the prison was the fact that they did not attempt to separate their faith's lessons from the lessons they were supposed to be objectively providing to the prisoners. She argued that there were some women in prison who could not find a program to participate in, as they were not Christian and refused to be subjected to a continuous stream of Christian ideas. Beth believed that incarcerated women should be able to access programs similar to the ones taught by the Christian groups, but independent of the religious curriculum.

Finally, incarcerated women did not view as beneficial the various vocational training programs made available to them after a long wait. Pooty stated that the prison administrators were quick to put people to work in the kitchen or cleaning around the facility. However, she argued that such experience would not help the women to obtain employment in the future. In line with these views, the women asked for more opportunities with diversified vocational education, as they knew they had a small chance of being able to participate in the vocational education system that currently existed. They wanted programs involving computer training, and access to college courses as well.

Some of the good job training programs included the truck driving program, the telemarketing program, and the garment industry. These programs were seen as lucrative in pay compared to the other prison positions. They were also seen as providing skills that would be beneficial in the workforce upon reentry. However, gaining a position in one of these programs was reserved for the long-term prisoners, and the waiting list was years long.

Health and Mental Health Issues

Another major obstacle that the women reported involved issues with their health and medical needs. Some of the women reported less than satisfactory medical attention upon their arrival in the prison system. Cody was actually injured in her efforts to evade the arrest that brought her back to prison. Trying to escape from the police, she wrecked her car, her ear was severed, and she had her entire scalp sewn back together and reattached to her skull. She also had a broken back, a dangling left arm, and severe physical trauma to her chest and breasts. She was in a coma for two weeks after the wreck. She awoke from her coma to find that she had been transferred after two days in the hospital to the prison infirmary. According to Cody, she was transferred into the general population at the prison once fully conscious, remaining in a full body cast for the next four months. Cody had to regain her mobility and to navigate prison life while severely disabled, without much-needed therapy. She stated, "I had to teach myself to use the bathroom again, I had to do a lot of things, if it wasn't for someone else being in the room with me, it wouldn't have happened." Cody's negative experience suggests the level of medical attention offered to prisoners, and other women offered similarly grim accounts.

Unfortunately, most of their struggles for medical attention were also difficult once released into society. Laci was diagnosed with cancer during her prior incarceration. She said the treatment she received for her cancer was so delayed that she almost died. Based on the poor treatment she received, she was in a coma for almost a year, and suffered numerous health complications. After about two years of dealing with her cancer, the Department of Corrections released her on medical parole. Despite the fact that they knew the severity of her cancer, and even though Laci was so frail that she was released in a wheelchair, the Department of Corrections did not help her to secure any housing or medical attention upon her release from prison. She went to her father's home, but he only let her stay one night. She was thus homeless and severely ill for weeks.

At this point, Laci was still able to get limited medical assistance from the doctors in Oklahoma City that had overseen her cancer treatment during her incarceration. However, she eventually lost even that assistance, as she was surviving homeless in Norman and was too sick to travel to Oklahoma City. In a desperate situation, Laci had an epiphany to lie to a battered women's shelter, telling the administrators there that she had been hit and kicked out of her home by an abusive male partner. She was thus allowed to stay there, and it was only through the shelter's services that she was able to locate medical attention and assistance for her cancer. The shelter administrators put Laci in touch with a local nonprofit healthcare agency. During the three months that she stayed at the shelter, she was able to receive chemotherapy, radiation, physical therapy, and other much-needed medical services. She shared that she could otherwise not get medical attention because she was uninsured, and she was ineligible for Medicaid because she was not a mother of dependent children. Despite the nonprofit agency's assistance, Laci accumulated approximately $100,000 in medical bills in the span of two years. Even with that debt, she shared that she was often not able to get her much-needed prescriptions filled because she did not have the money for them, and she had exceeded her prescription refill privileges at local nonprofit health agencies.

Laci was reincarcerated this time because she failed to check in with her parole officer, who ordered her to take a drug test in which she tested positive for drugs. She stated she had started doing drugs after she had exceeded the maximum stay time at the shelter and was forced to move out. While the shelter's administrators had helped her find housing, she said she started using drugs to help her deal with being lonely, depressed, angry, anxious, and in pain. Laci was in such poor health that she was transported immediately and directly from the jail's infirmary to the prison infirmary upon her reception into the prison system.

Dirty Lucy endured years of stomach pain and never-ending diarrhea during her incarceration, yet she claimed that she had never received professional medical attention. Upon her release, she was diagnosed with a life-threatening bacterial condition in her stomach that she contracted while incarcerated. She had no medical insurance, and she claimed that her medicine cost approximately $4,000 a day, so she was unable to get rid of or even maintain a tolerable level of comfort. She thus resorted to selling drugs to try to earn enough money to pay for her medicine, also using the drugs to self-medicate.

> So I had major medical issues . . . And I was so sick, so I was like, "Well, I'll do a little bit of morphine here, and it'll make me feel better." And one thing led to another and I was right back in the place I was before. So while I was sick, I was selling drugs, to help pay for my medicine and stuff and to continue my drug habit. They made me feel better when I was sick.

Another area of concern for a few of these women was their mental health and the accompanying need for services and medication not only while incarcerated, but also when they left prison. Most of the women in this study discussed experiences with physical, sexual, and emotional abuse while growing up and as adults. Yet most of them did not specifically discuss having mental health issues. It is not clear if the absence of any mention of mental illness among the women interviewed is because this sample was somehow not representative of the typical female offender. My own suspicion is that part of the reason is due to their failure to identify their emotional struggles as mental illness. Of course, not all emotional difficulties cause mental illness, but the way these women spoke nonchalantly about experiences that most people would see as extremely traumatic and violent led me to suspect that these women had either repressed their emotional struggles or else they simply denied the intense mental distress that they had suffered from such events.

Bree, Young, and Bad Girl were the only women who talked about mental health issues. Bree discussed the root of her mental illnesses coming from her experiences as a child. She was abandoned by her mother, and she and her brother were discovered by the police and fire department. Bree and her brother were separated and grew up apart from each other. Yet she still remembered her experiences with her mother.

> My brother mentally blocked everything out. I remember every single thing. I remember every punch, every scream, every holler. I remember. And it trips me out, because things happened like when I was little, little, and I thought I dreamt it, and my aunt was like, "No. That really happened." You know. So that's where a lot of mental issues come in. Like abuse. Mental abuse. Physical abuse. Sexual abuse.

Young reported an extremely negative response to her encounter with mental health services in prison. Essentially, it involved the mental health expert dismissing the severity of her experiences and issues. The mental health professional told her that she was simply engaging in self-pity. This resulted not only in her needs continuing to go unmet, but also in further traumatizing an already fragile individual.

Bad Girl was released from prison previously without any medical transitional assistance for the psychotropic drugs she needed to maintain her emotional stability. In desperation, she turned to the local health department, who then diagnosed her with tuberculosis. The health department then set her up with medication and treatment for her tuberculosis and her mental illness. She considered herself lucky, as she had no other resources to secure medication and treatment.

The final health-related issue the women in this study faced involved their substance abuse, addiction, and lack of access to adequate and effective treatment. Many of these women came into prison with substance abuse issues. Some of them had lifetimes of abusing drugs and alcohol. Vanda started drinking when she was nine or ten years old, and said she had steadily consumed alcohol from that age. She also started using methamphetamines in her late teens. Laci stated that she "first shot dope" when she was eight years old, "for my birthday. I've been shooting dope ever since. I did speed, but I never did heroin. I was scared of it. Speed, cocaine, marijuana." Dirty Lucy started doing and selling drugs when she was fourteen years old, in order to deal with her parents' divorce and the subsequent move from her home state, and to help her mother pay the bills because her mother was now on her own. Angel started smoking marijuana when she was eleven years old. She then began using powder cocaine when she was twelve years old and crack cocaine when she was seventeen. Tamara started doing methamphetamines when she was sixteen, and eventually started using marijuana as well.

However, the woman who appeared to have the most serious substance abuse issues—specifically involving alcohol abuse—was Lone Wolf. As described previously, Lone Wolf was so dependent on alcohol that she would resort to hitchhiking, prostitution, and stealing to get it. Her alcohol dependency put her in extremely dangerous situations.

LONE WOLF: So I just hopped around everywhere. I even slept under bridges and things like that. Walked miles in the dark, drunk, with a bottle in my hand, because I didn't care. I hid the feelings, and nothing mattered.

INTERVIEWER: What would you do after you woke up under a bridge? How did you decide what to do after that?

LONE WOLF: First thing I'd be thinking is that I've got to get me another bottle. Because I always made sure, if I'm going to pass out, I've got to have me a bottle when I wake up, because I'd be sick. I'd be real sick. And I always had another extra bottle in my backpack. And I would sit there and drink that and then catch a bus . . . I might go to the creek and wash off, wash my hair, change my clothes, and take off walking down the road. And usually when I'd take off walking down the road, somebody would pick me up and usually, 45 percent of the time, it's a single man, and they're just looking to have a good time and drink and stuff. And they'd buy me beer or whiskey, whatever . . . And some would just buy it for me and just send me on my way. Some just wanted something else. And if I wanted to eat, if I wanted to drink, then I had to do what I had to do.

These women thus had serious, established histories with drugs and alcohol. But the initial problem in dealing with these issues arose from the way that the prison handled substance abuse treatment. The women thus reported enduring programs that seemed to be experimental, with no known effectiveness. And whatever substance abuse treatment was available involved the dreaded waiting lists, with the recognition that it could be years before a woman potentially got into a treatment program.

INTERVIEWER: So what does it take to get into those programs?

SWEET: A drug addiction. Substance abuse . . .

INTERVIEWER: You have one, right? You said . . .

SWEET: Oh, yeah, I do! But so do 6,000 other women. I mean, you know, it's just waiting until you can get into it and they prioritize those people that are in delayed sentencing, uh, there's kind of like a probationary period, that, you know, they let some people come in and do six months and then go before the judge again, for those ladies they prioritize. So, I mean, for anybody that's just waiting on the yard, you just be waitin' up to a year, two years to get out to those programs.

INTERVIEWER: So have you ever done any substance abuse programs?

SWEET: Um, not during an incarceration. I haven't.

The women expressed that they left prison the last time with strong intentions to never touch drugs or alcohol again. Even if they had not had access to substance abuse treatment, they considered themselves strong enough to withstand the pressures and addiction pulling them back toward drug and alcohol abuse. However, it did not take long for some of them to fall back into their old patterns with drugs and alcohol. Tamara used the same day she was released, as a result of pressure from the boyfriend who picked her up from prison. Bree also resumed her drug and alcohol use immediately after her release from prison, for a similar reason—it was right in front of her, and she had not had enough counseling and support inside of prison to help her learn to resist. Young also turned back to drugs soon after her release. She shared that she resorted to drugs to help her cope with the rejection of her family and the denial of employment. She also declared that she felt pressured to use drugs, as they were rampant in her community: "To me, I mean, that's all I knew, and that's what I turned back to. I guess like a therapy. I just did it to numb the pain and to make me forget what was going on around me. 'Cause it was just hurtful."

The Role of Attitude

Many of the women reported overwhelming feelings of institutionalization, frustration, and discouragement upon their release from prison. These women had grown so used to the prison environment and the emotional isolation they cited as necessary to survive in prison, that even things nonprisoners would consider basic overwhelmed them. Socializing, eating in restaurants, or even keeping food in the home presented challenges. Others found themselves overwhelmed by silence or by social situations. In fact, even leaving their room or their home paralyzed many of them. Essentially, their time in prison had institutionalized them.

It is logical that these women would report such shocks and difficulties during their transitioning back into society. They moved from an institution where every action and interaction was heavily monitored, to an environment where they were able to exercise most of the freedoms that they were denied while incarcerated. The transition from total structure to no structure was difficult for several, such as Pooty.

That was scary because, as bad as I wanted out of here, they provided everything for me. And when I got out, I provided them for myself. That was the plan. It was the unsureness of what was going to happen to me. Where was I gonna go? What was I gonna do? After seven years, it wasn't familiarity. I didn't have that. I was scared I wasn't gonna make it. I was scared to . . . I don't know.

It is understandable that the women found these sudden freedoms to be intimidating, and that their reactions to that apprehension included isolation and overall emotional volatility. In fact, women in this study reported that a large part of surviving the incarceration experience involved their becoming hardened and stoic in their overall interactions, as any evidence of weakness or vulnerability made them easy prey for other offenders and even prison staff. Unfortunately, daily adherence to such a demeanor and conduct made it difficult to shed these characteristics once they reentered society. And so they took that protective shell back into their interactions with others in the "real world" upon their release.

Many of the women in this study thus expressed intense fear of returning to society after their current incarceration, based on their recollection of what their experiences had been with their prior releases from prison. It was interesting to observe that most of them did not seem excited to leave prison, as they shared the realization that they were likely to be released back into society with no transitional assistance, resources, or support. They were also often being released back into the very conditions that had led them to commit crime in the first place.

It was scary going back, because I know that I have a problem, and I know that there's plenty of drugs out there. And they're just waiting for me, calling my name . . . Just being afraid of what I'm going to do when I get there. I'm more afraid of myself than I am of what's out there. I'm not afraid in here. (Dirty Lucy)

And now, right now, I'm supposed to be gettin' back out and I'm not even looking forward to it. Because I know I'm fixin' to go out there and I have to start all the way over . . . (B-Dog)

Financial Obligations

Many of the women reported having to pay debts that they had incurred either prior to their incarceration or related to the crime for which they had been sentenced. These fines and fees could be for traffic tickets, medical bills, or debts accrued trying to survive. The women also amassed debts based on fines and fees for prior offenses. While challenges centering on finances came as no surprise, the specific issue of problems arising from debts was new and surprising, as the existing literature on women and reentry has little to say about how previous debt awaits reentering women and can affect their likelihood of recidivism. And yet encountering debts upon their release from prison is daunting, and can lead otherwise rational individuals to risk their freedom to alleviate financial obligations.

The biggest debt challenges facing women upon reentry were fines and fees imposed by the criminal justice system. Failure to deal with these could affect parole requirements, staying out of prison, and trying to satisfy requirements for essentials like getting some form of identification or a driver's license. While the women realized the importance of meeting these obligations, they were understandably overwhelmed. Young described the tremendous financial pressures she was under the last time she was released from prison. Based on her multiple felony convictions and traffic tickets, she had lost her driver's license and was required to go to supervision meetings with her parole office, as well as counseling and drug classes that she had to pay for and complete before she could regain her driver's license. She was paying her counselor $75 each time she met with her, and she had to pay her parole officer's supervision fees. She also had to pay $600 to have her license reinstated, and she was paying about $125 in required minimum payments for $8,000 in fines she had accrued. In addition to these fines and fees, Young stated that she also had to pay for a babysitter while she was attending her counseling and parole visits. All of these expenditures were in addition to her trying to meet her and her family's basic needs.

To a lesser extent, some women faced debts from things like accessing health services without insurance during their prior release from prison. Cody serves as an example of the decisions that must be made by an offender laden with serious debt as she returns to the outside world. Prior to her current incarceration, she had to go to the emergency room for a cut on her foot, because she had no insurance. While she was paying that debt incurred before incarceration, she knows that it is continuing to grow while she is currently in prison. Her plan was to go straight to jail after prison, as each day served in jail would earn her money towards her debts. She estimated that she would be in jail for about a year after her release from prison this time in order to pay back her debts to the state. Many women are thus leaving prison not only with the debts they left behind from their prior sentence, or even medical bills, but they are also going to incur responsibility for new costs that will arise based on their current incarceration and release.

Family and Relationships

The major area of concern expressed among female offenders was the possibility of reunification with their family and loved ones, especially their children. Vanda summarized these sentiments perfectly, with her statement: "Anytime you do time, your family does time right along with you." Many of the women reported difficulties with family reunification after prison because of their physical and emotional absence. As Beverly stated, "You have to re-bond with them, you have to, you know, reestablish your bond with your family." This is in the best-case scenario, when family reunification might still be a possibility, as other women, like Laci, reported that prison had cost them their relationships with family and children.

> I lost my kids when I came to prison . . . I'm their mother, because I gave birth to them, and they love me and I love them. And I tried to have a relationship with them, but they've grown now. The relationships are gone. I was married, whenever I came to prison, I lost my husband. After a couple of years, we grew apart . . . But prison affected everything. It [prison] destroys relationships. It destroys your family. It destroys everything.

One of the most frequently reported challenges by mothers in this study was interacting with their children after absence from them. These women reported returning to children who did not know them, as they had left them at a very young age, only to return to them in early adolescence. Mothers also described children who had grown timid and cautious around them, as they expected to be abandoned again and wanted to avoid reattachment to their mothers. Some reported that children were angry and hostile toward them for leaving them during their incarceration. Young talked about her experiences with her children as she moved in and out of prison and their lives.

> My daughter was two years old when I started going to prison. And I've been in and out of her life every since. She's sixteen now. And my son, I had to leave him when he was three, and he just turned eight, so I don't know how to be a mom, and it scares me. They don't know how to be around me. . . . I don't know them. I don't know what they like, what they dislike. I just know that they're mad, they're angry and confused. My daughter was playing with my son whenever I got out, and he ended up getting hurt. And I got onto her and said, "What are you doing to him? Why are you treating him like that?" She was like, "Well, what do you care? You ain't ever been in our lives. You haven't ever been here for me or my brother." That was the reality of it.

Mothers in this study received confirmation from their families and children of the massive effects that incarceration was having on their children. Children experienced tremendous separation anxiety when their mothers returned from prison and then left for any reason whatsoever. In fact, Beth's son was so terrified of her leaving or being taken away from him again, that he refused to sleep anywhere but on the floor next to her bed every night after she returned from prison. He felt that sleeping there, he would wake up if she tried to leave or was taken away.

Nor were the children's fears limited to loss of their mothers. Children also felt abandonment and loss, to the point that they feared that current family members would leave them, just as their mothers had. Such feelings manifested themselves among these children as anger, with children lashing out at peers, teachers, and anybody around them. Mothers also reported their children growing depressed and isolating themselves, losing attachment from anyone and anything around them. In even more extreme situations, Young reported her daughter becoming bulimic, while Amanda's daughter ran away and could only be found occasionally. The women thus reported difficulties in interacting with their children upon their prior releases from prison, as well as during their current incarceration, which affected their ability to parent and discipline in any setting.

The women in this study also reported experiencing significant anger and resentment from the family members they left behind. Mothers, fathers, sisters, brothers, children, and romantic partners consistently reminded them of the harm they had done to the family through their incarceration. Family members vented about having had to assume these women's responsibilities for their children while they were in prison. Women also heard about the shame they had placed on the family through their involvement in crime and their imprisonment. While some women were lucky enough to have continued support from their family and children during their incarceration, most of the women in this study experienced temporary or permanent estrangement as a result of their repeated incarceration.

> And my family had to take on all my responsibilities, and it affected hard my family. It wasn't a good effect, because they don't believe in me no more. It's like nothing that I do or did is enough for them anymore. I wasn't the smart granddaughter, the intelligent niece anymore. I was just the bad person, the one that didn't have any sense no more. And nobody trusted me, and nobody would help me. That's just how it is. (Missy)

Despite realizing the effect that separation from their children has on families, women in this study experienced significant challenges in maintaining contact with family and children. A few of the women had family who refused to visit or contact them in prison, which meant that their children could not visit or contact them either. Several women reported that if family were willing to visit, it was nearly impossible because of the distance they would have to travel and the cost of such travel. Phone calls were reported to be very costly, and women in this study mentioned that it was pretty difficult to squeeze in conversations with everyone in the family because there was a fifteen-minute limit on calls.

In addition to the challenges associated with maintaining family relationships, mothers in this study also reported concern about the placement of their children during their incarceration. While a few of these women did not have custody of their children prior to incarceration—based on their unstable lifestyles and substance abuse—most of the women did have custody. Most of the children were placed with grandparents or the incarcerated women's siblings. Yet several women had lost custody of their children while incarcerated, through questionable means that they were helpless to resolve. Laci had no knowledge of what had happened to her youngest son, as she was not kept informed of his placements and received no responses to her repeated inquiries for information about him from the state's social service system. Anne's brother had assumed custody of her son when she was incarcerated, but he had grown tired of dealing with the child's acting out (due to being separated from his mother and having experienced sexual abuse as a child). The brother had consequently given her son over to a social service shelter without notifying her, and she had not been able to get information on her son's placement since then. The father of Beverly's daughter essentially kidnapped the child and successfully filed for sole custody while Beverly was in prison. Tamara's children were placed into her mother's custody upon her incarceration, despite the fact that Tamara and her mother did not have a good relationship. Consequently, upon her release from prison the last time, Tamara had to fight through the social service system for 18 months before she was able to visit her children.

These women also were concerned about the experiences with abuse that their children had suffered. The women felt angry and helpless about these situations, as they were frequently unable to get any information or updates from state child protective service agencies or from family members or friends about the initiation or progress of any investigations around the children's claims. The majority of the abuse experienced by the children involved sexual abuse. Beverly's daughter had been molested by her new stepmother's older teenage sons. However, despite Beverly having reported this situation while she was out of prison, her daughter was placed back into the care of her father and stepmother when Beverly returned to prison. Her daughter was thus living again with her sexual abusers. Anne and Laci's children were also sexually molested during their mothers' prior incarcerations, and Vivian's children were exploited physically and sexually while she was incarcerated. Finally, one woman disclosed that she had heard that her son, who was living separately from his sibling, was not being fed regularly by his guardians, and was too young to seek out food for himself. Based on these experiences, women in this study reported great anxiety about their children's well-being and placement during their incarceration.

The importance of their children to these women was obvious during the interviews, through the voicing and tears of anguish and regret that these women shared. Yet a couple of women in this study specifically mentioned having committed their crimes to meet the needs of their children. Missy stated, crying, that her main motivation for her crimes was to secure basic necessities for her children.

> Things that I did do, I did it for my kids. Because I can't let them go without. And if it's all because I made a mistake, because I messed up, I messed up for them. If I can't get it right, if I can't get it the way that it's supposed to be, at the time, I would do whatever it is that needed to be done to get them what they needed, what they had to have. I mean, there was no issues that I had, like drugs. No habits or nothing like that for me. If my kids needed clothes, I'm gonna get them clothes. Even if I ain't got no money, I'm gonna get them some clothes. Stealing or whatever I had to do. If they needed shoes, whatever I had to do. If they needed food, whatever I had to do. Which, they never needed food, I always had that for them. But whatever it was that they needed, I was going to get it.

Missy later elaborated on the specific crimes she had committed in order to provide for her children, including the crime for which she was currently incarcerated.

> Well, when I was talking about having to do everything necessary to take care of my kids, I've had to steal. In fact, I'm in here right now on a robbery case, and it got that bad. I had no money, and I had no means of transportation. I had nothing. And I went to get us money. It was almost winter time. I didn't have no electric in my house, and there was no food or nothing. The kids needed to eat. And I went to go get money. From a check cashing. I want to say that there is not one day that I do not regret doing what I did . . . And I regret that every day. Every day. (starts crying) I was stealing, I tried to rob. I sold drugs. Stuff I had to do. So we need help once we get out there, so things don't have to go to that level ever for anyone to provide for their kids.

Lone Wolf also stated that she committed crimes not primarily to support her drug and alcohol addictions, but to help her parents provide for her children, as well as to grant her children any nonessential items that they desired.

> They [her children] basically know me when I'm buzzed or drunk. But they know I'm mama, and their mama will do whatever it takes to get there to see them and help them, if my mom and dad didn't have money. If it took

me tricking with a guy to get money, then I'd tell my mom and dad I borrowed the money, instead of telling them the truth. If they wanted them $100 shoes, then mama's going to go and get the money to get you shoes. My drinking was bad, but if I had like my last $60 and my kids wanted something, then I'm going to do for them and I'm going to have to go without or I'm going to have to go find something else for me.

Finally, in terms of family relationships, incarcerated women's experiences with abuse were substantiated through the women in this study. Numerous women reported intimate partner violence nonchalantly, as if it was something to be expected and tolerated. For example, Tamara willingly returned to an abusive ex-boyfriend after her prior release from prison because she had no one else to turn to. Shoshone reported enduring domestic violence for so long that she eventually killed the man abusing her. Several women also shared how they had experienced sexual abuse from men all their lives, with Laci even reporting that her mother had traded her to men sexually for drugs. Young, another victim, was sexually abused by her male cousin when she was 10.

Relationships with children, parents, siblings, and romantic partners have all had a strong impact on the incarcerated women in this study and their criminal offending. The incarcerated mothers in this research expressed anxiety about the possibility of reuniting with their loved ones, especially their children, after their extended absences brought about by their incarceration. They also shared the difficulties they faced in being able to parent or discipline their children after an absence from their lives, due to their children's resentment and anger toward them. These mothers' interactions with their children were oftentimes not made easier by family members or romantic partners, based on their own feelings of resentment toward these women, their prior abusive relationships with them, or else their abandonment of the women.

In terms of relationships, the women who were mothers emphasized their children as their main priority and concern during their incarceration and after release. They were often justified in their concerns for their children's well-being, as some of their children had experienced horrific abuse, primarily sexual in nature, during their mothers' prior and/or current incarcerations. Yet the women were often unable to secure any information about their children's safety or placement, either from loved ones or the state child protective services system. Further affecting the women's relationships with loved ones were their prior experiences with intimate partner violence and abusive experiences from childhood to adulthood.

Summary

The women in this study encountered serious concerns and challenges when they were previously released from prison, in line with the limited research that exists in these areas. Their experiences often proved to be over-whelming enough to lead them back into crime and, eventually, back to prison. In fact, some women like Amos and Missy expressed relief at having been reincarcerated.

> I don't even know if you'll understand this, I was relieved . . . Cause I was tired of wondering, I was tired . . . tired of struggling. I was just tired, and once I got right with everything and I was provided everything when I got put in jail, I do my time better now. (Amos)
>
> I was really upset that I was back here, but at the same time, I was kind of, not happy, but relieved, because I was going through a lot out there. Not having a job, not going to school, barely making it with my children. (Missy)

Aside from meeting their basic immediate needs, the major issues that these women faced upon their reentry were related to needs in housing, employment, paying debts, transportation, educational opportunities, and medical attention. Based on the intersecting of these challenges and the mag-nitude of the obstacles that these women faced upon their reentry, it is not hard to understand why they recidivated.

> Oklahoma just pushes you out there. "Oh well if you don't have nowhere to go. Sorry about your luck." A lot of people go out sick and stuff like that. Pretty soon, if you're hungry, angry, cold, and tired, you're going to do something to survive. A lot of people turn to drugs or to criminal things, because they don't know anything else. (Tari)

It was obvious that these women realized that they were being released back into environments and situations that would promote their failure, and they openly expressed their worry at being placed back into the very com-munities that contained the exact people and problems that had led to their criminal involvement. These women were pouring out the factors that had led them back to crime and back to prison to a researcher that had known them for only a few minutes. It was therefore hard to imagine that they had not expressed these concerns to any of the professionals who worked with them regularly in the system.

The criminal justice system appears to have no qualms about releasing these female offenders without ensuring that they have somewhere to go and that they have a safe way to get there. The Oklahoma system does not seem to focus on how they will meet their immediate needs upon release from prison. According to the women, there is little indication of any effort by the system to verify that these women will have access to any form of an ongoing support system. Lacking such basic emotional and physical necessities immediately after leaving prison, the women are left with few options conducive to their success outside of the system. They are left to cover all of the requirements for daily living—as well as any requirements imposed by the criminal justice system for parole, with the meager funds with which they tend to be released from prison. The impossibility of such expectations causes them to struggle with how they can attempt to meet those obligations. This can understandably lead them to feel frustrated, angry, and disheartened, —promoting their return to problematic methods of coping and survival with crime and substance abuse. Chapter 6 discusses women who have been more successful in staying out.

CHAPTER 6

Coming Home and Staying Out

CHAPTER 6 explored the experiences of women who had returned to prison. In this chapter, we turn to the experiences of a group of women who have successfully stayed out of prison. Both groups of women face the same issues upon release, including employment, housing, transportation, economic, and family issues. However, those who have stayed out successfully have learned to negotiate reentry in a more positive manner. By examining the experiences of those who have stayed out one or more years, we can uncover some of the attributes that have led to success. In turn, that could lead to the development of reintegration policies that work.

To understand what works, a quick review of the profile of returning women prisoners and the issues they face can be informative. According to a recent report, women prisoners tend to have certain characteristics that place them at severe disadvantage (Greene and Pranis 2012). These characteristics include:

- They are disproportionately women of color.
- On average, they are in their early to mid-thirties.
- Drug-related offenses are the most likely reason they are in prison.
- They come from fragmented families that include other family members who also have been involved with the criminal justice system.
- The majority are survivors of physical and/or sexual abuse both as children and adults.
- They are individuals with significant substance abuse problems.
- They also have multiple physical and mental health problems.
- The majority are unmarried mothers of minor children.
- On average, they have high school or general equivalency diploma (GED) but limited vocational training and sporadic work histories.

In the 2008 Oklahoma Study of Incarcerated Women, I asked women who were imprisoned for a second or subsequent offense about problems that they experienced after their prior release from prison. There were 103 women who provided responses. Those responses may be seen in Table 6.1. Among

TABLE 6.1

Problems Experienced between Incarcerations

Problem	No.	Percentage
Finding a job	58	56.3
Finding an affordable and safe place to live	51	49.5
Paying court costs, restitution and fees	64	62.1
Staying drug free	77	74.8
Staying away from friends/ family who engaged in crime or drug use	70	67.9

Source: Oklahoma Study of Incarcerated Women and Their Children: Phase I data (Sharp 2009).

Note: N = 103 women who were serving a second or subsequent incarceration.

those women, the biggest problem reported was staying drug-free, with almost three-fourths of the women reporting that as a problem they experienced. More than two-thirds also reported difficulties saying away from friends or family who engaged in drug use or crime. They were almost equally likely to report that they had problems with court costs, fees, and restitution. More than half the women also reported they had experienced trouble finding a job, and nearly half said they had problems locating safe housing.

SUCCESSFUL REENTRY AND OKLAHOMA'S WOMEN PRISONERS

Successful reentry requires that the women find ways to overcome the deficits described above. It is apparent that certain shared traits are more likely to lead to failure: single parenthood, fractured families, little education, few job skills, and drug problems. However, some women are able to overcome these shortcomings.

Twelve women who have successfully stayed out of prison for one or more years were interviewed. In some cases they have successfully reintegrated into society despite the obstacles they faced. In other cases, they are still struggling but able to stay out of further legal trouble. A description of the women and the research can be found in Appendix A. Pseudonyms are used throughout the chapter to protect their anonymity.

Reentry: Housing, Jobs, and Transportation

Stable housing is usually the most pressing need for women returning to the community. In the 2009 survey of Oklahoma's women prisoners, 49.5 percent said that finding an affordable place to live was a major difficulty. Options are limited for the woman who is a former prisoner. She may be able to stay with family temporarily, but that is often not conducive to staying out of trouble. These women tend to come from families rife with drug problems and criminal behavior. Returning to that environment can be a recipe for disaster. However, the newly released woman usually lacks the financial ability to find and rent an apartment or house on her own. Deposits and rent can easily add up to a thousand dollars or more, and she may have no resources whatsoever.

Even if she has the money to get into an apartment, she often faces housing discrimination. Many landlords are simply unwilling to rent to someone with a criminal history. Twice in the past three years, I assigned the students in my Women, Girls, and Crime course a project that required them to interview people in our community about their willingness to hire or rent to women returning from prison. The students began the project convinced that I was exaggerating the difficulties the women faced. However, when they presented their projects to the class, the majority were dismayed at the level of prejudice faced by women coming out of prison. Some landlords said they threw applications from convicted felons into the trash immediately. Others said it was company policy to not rent to anyone with any criminal background. Only one student in each class found a landlord who said he would rent to them. This is even more disturbing since we live in a university town where the general populace tends to be more progressive than people in the rest of the state. Thus the students' experiences did not bode well for women returning to other communities.

For many of these women, the solution has often been to try to find a man to help take care of them and their children (Schram 2003). However, women with felony convictions, unlike men, can rarely find a partner who is noncriminal. They are considered doubly deviant. First, they are deviant because they have been convicted of a crime, a handicap also faced by males returning from prison. However, they also face a more insidious type of judgment: they are seen as deviant because they have not lived up to the expectations of society of what it means to be a "good" woman (Schur 1984). Their choices of partners are therefore often limited to criminally involved men. If a returning woman is unable to establish housing on her own, she may return to a previous boyfriend, often one who led to her incarceration. Or she may find a new male to hopefully provide for her and her children. Unfortunately, these men usually end up getting the woman into more legal trouble. Gina saw this as a roadblock for many women upon release:

> I mean, that's what a lot of women do, they return—because either they're married or they have some kind of emotional commitment with somebody, and they want to, you know, they—our, our core need when we get out of prison is we want somebody to love us.

So when that becomes a priority, and, you know, it becomes a real issue, because you got women like now their judgment is skewed toward that.

Arlena also talked about how difficult it had been for her after release because it had been so long since she had been in a relationship with a man. When she was first released, she immediately got involved with a man who sold drugs. This led to a relapse. Eventually, she found him with another woman and was able to end their relationship and get off drugs again. But, she believed that women leaving prison needed to be prepared for the loneliness they would feel and warned about the dangers of getting involved with a man too quickly: "The women need to know that the dumbest thing they can do is to go back to one of their old men or find a new one. And, they need to have some way to deal with the loneliness. I wasn't prepared for that, and I ended up messing up." Virtually all of the women that I interviewed who had stayed out successfully came out to family support, with the exception of Arlena. In fact, that seems to be one of the predictors of success. Sometimes they were able to live with family who were maintaining stable environments. In other cases, family helped them become reestablished. For example, a relative helped Gina get on her feet.

> I was very well resourced. Um, my aunt lived in Washington, DC and was very, um, very, very, very supportive. I mean, I could not have asked—I don't think a person would actually have that kind of support. You know, I mean, she—when I got out, I mean, literally from the time I stepped out of the gate, everything she orchestrated. She put together, like, my plan of living, um, she financed that, she bought me a vehicle. Um, she worked for the U.S. Department of Education, so she made sure that all my paperwork got done for me to get into college. So I got out in November and I was in (a university) as a full-time student in January.
>
> She provided me with the one thing that I was always missing and that was the financial wherewithal to do what I needed to do, I mean, she was in DC, so she really didn't run my life—but she did provide me with—she provided me a) with money, and, b) because I knew she was there, I had a lot less fear about the whole thing. And I had a lot more responsibility to her, uh, you know, just the idea that she believed in me enough made me, you know, the times that I wanted to do something—you know, like maybe I want to have a beer or whatever—I didn't. Because of her. Because, I mean, you know, she believed in me enough, um, and I'd never had that before. Never had anyone that believed in me enough to, to always be there. Like, I could always count on her, you know, whatever, she was always there. And so, that was, that was the success factor. That was the success factor. That's what got me from, from literally the first—well over five years.

Of course, most women prisoners do not have family willing or even financially able to set them up in a new life. However, those who had stable family to whom they could parole felt like that gave them the opportunity and breathing room to figure out how to negotiate a crime and drug-free life on the outside. For example, Misha has lived with her grandparents for more than a year. They live in a middle-class neighborhood where she is not constantly exposed to drugs and crime. She is acutely aware that having a safe place to live as long as she needs is not only helpful but essential to success. Without, the immediate future of the newly released woman prisoner is, in her opinion, very bleak.

> As a felon, I'm gonna have to find somebody to go help me get an apartment. I can't go to an apartment complex and get an apartment with seven felonies. They'll do a background check and nine times out of ten they'll deny me an apartment. So I'm stuck with having to try to find me a house. Which I can't really afford because I'm not making too much money. I can't get a good job right now because I don't have a degree. And I'm a felon. So, it's the bind for us—jobs and housing.
>
> And it might even be housing, like the Exodus house—just a place, like an apartment complex where we can get apartments. And maybe with rules or maybe without rules, but to be able to have our own place. Those are two things the state could help with so far as providing. They need to change the laws on housing. You can't even get a Housing Authority house. Or housing through Section 8 'cause you're a felon.

Although she does have safe housing with her grandparents, she would like to have her own place someday. However, on her income, her opportunities are limited. She expressed hope to rent an apartment with her sister in the coming months. She believes that it will have to be in her sister's name because of her own record.

Misha mentioned that having halfway houses can be helpful, and that was Tara's experience, as well. She was initially released to a halfway house. She wanted to be released to one in another state, since she had both state and federal charges, but she ended up being released to her own community. She felt that being released to an environment with some structure was very helpful to her in the first few months. She then went to live with her grandparents and got her children back. However, that environment was less healthy, so she began looking for an apartment. She was able to get her own apartment because her background check did not turn up her felonies for some reason. A year later, when she tried to renew her lease, the apartment manager discovered her record.

When I went to, when I went and did my, uh, my background check, for my apartment. Well, they did it. And nothing came up on OSBI.[1] Yeah. But, a year into it, on the recert, it came back. I guess the OSBI didn't have it but the Oklahoma County pulled up all those, you know, the cases that I had. So they were saying that, you know, you have a felony. And I was like, yeah, but I had the felonies when I came into the apartments. You know. And they looked back on the application and I had put that I had a felony. I never lied about it or anything. And she just showed me how, we got past that but that's why I think they didn't kick me out.

I was worried to death about them kicking me out. Because it was a low income . . . you know . . . it was . . . it was my first home on my own that I didn't have to have a man to help me pay for it. (Laughs). So I was really happy.

Twyla was perhaps the most fortunate of the women I interviewed. When she was released, she returned to the upper middle-class neighborhood where she and her husband owned a house. However, few women prisoners have a non-criminal husband waiting for them upon release, and even fewer own a home to which they can return.

For those women without supportive family, release and safe housing are more difficult but not unobtainable. Arlena had developed a relationship with a woman who brought a Bible ministry into the prison. When she was released, she paroled to that woman's home. Because she was disabled, the prison staff had set her up to begin receiving Supplemental Security Income (SSI) upon her release, so she quickly had enough money with which she could rent her own apartment. However, because of her criminal record, the only place she found that would rent to her was in a neighborhood riddled with drugs and crime. Nonetheless, she was able to establish a homelike atmosphere in her small apartment, and her benefactor's church had a "shower" for her in which they provided her with everything she needed to set up housekeeping.

Dorothy was able to get assistance from a transitional living program for the homeless. The program is designed to help individuals who are temporarily homeless get back on their feet. Clients can live there for a year or more. When they first move in, they have thirty days to find a job. Once employed, they begin paying very low rent. They work with a case manager to develop budgeting skills, and they are required to place part of their earnings into a savings account while they are in the program. When they graduate, the case manager helps them locate and obtain housing, and they receive the money they have saved. The program also requires that they remain drug and alcohol free. If they have initial difficulties with that, the case manager may help them find appropriate treatment. Dorothy lived there for over a year, and today she has her own duplex.

Sober living houses such as the Oxford Houses can also provide a safe place for women upon release. Unlike women in the previous chapter, the women who successfully stayed out saw temporary housing and sober living facilities as helpful in transitioning back into the community. Gina was a strong proponent for sober living houses such as Oxford Houses. These provide a safer living environment, support and structure to the women returning home.

> I think that every women going out of prison should probably go into an Oxford House. Because, Oxford Houses are sober living, um, there's accountability, they're all—they have to be—there's fifteen hundred of them across the country—they have to be in nice neighborhoods, they're homes, and they give the woman the chance to stabilize, to not be, um bombarded. Some of them actually are, are women and children's houses, so you could have your kids there, but, I mean, it gives you a chance to still be extracted from and away from that neighborhood [where the woman had lived before prison]. You could even do that without people even knowing you were out of prison.
>
> So, you know, you got like six women in a house, um, they get together and they pay the bills, they pay the rent, they do these things, but they're accountable to not use drugs. They're accountable to go to a set number of meetings a week. And beyond that, they're on their own. So they're not, they don't have to worry about DOC hovering—and most of them are not from DOC, they come out of rehab, but there is an arm of it that's a re-entry, um, that's actually expanding right now, yeah.

Because of the community's attitude toward convicted felons, employment is one of the most difficult problems faced by women returning home. In the 2009 survey of women prisoners, 56 percent of those serving a second or subsequent conviction said that they had trouble finding work. Those who successfully transitioned back into their communities reported employment as one of the biggest struggles. Interestingly, most of the women I interviewed found work almost coincidentally. Misha talked about the problems she originally experienced.

> I got out in November, I started my job January 7. So from—about two months. And the only reason I got the job I have now is because my friend is the manager. Her and her husband own the restaurant. And I just happened to walk in there and she asked me if I was still looking for a job. I told her, "yeah." She called me the next day and told me to come that evening. That I would start the next day.

But I looked for work for—I used my computer, I got bonded. I didn't get to use my bond papers so I don't know if those would have worked or not.

But I got the felon-friendly job list. Some of them don't hire felons. Some of them weren't hiring. Some of them were out of business. But, they say felony friendly, but when you say you're a felon, they still do a background check, and then they won't hire you. Or they give you the run-around telling you to call them. But when you call them . . . I called Burger King, she told me to call back. And when I called back it wasn't even the same manager. You hear what I'm saying? They changed managers within a day. She wasn't even the hiring manager.

Misha noted that women who come out through halfway houses often fare better at finding work. Perhaps the employers see someone living in a more structured and supervised environment as more likely to stay off drugs and out of trouble.

I think a woman is better off finding a job if she starts at the halfway house first. Because you are better off being a felon getting a job if you are at a halfway house. You can transition . . . from the halfway house to the, uh, streets, with a job.

I know people who still have their jobs from the halfway house 'cause it's easier to get a job . . . They'll hire . . . if a woman from a halfway house came, they'll hire her before they hire me. Just because they think she's more reliable because of conditions, she gets the job. They'll give a person incarcerated a job before they'll give me a job. I don't know . . . what it is. It took me a long—I went everywhere. To try to find a job. It's very hard.

That's why I think they should have a halfway house, or like a temp service for felons—only getting released from prison felons—contracts with different—like Wendy's, so when I come home from prison I can go there and I can fill out the paperwork, so when I release they help me get a job. There's no place like that for felons.

Tara found work while she was in a halfway house and kept that job for a number of years. Eventually, her supervisor there went to another organization and took Tara with her. Tara is still at that second job and has been promoted. However, she believes that a key for the newly released woman is to be grateful for whatever type of job she obtains. In her words, "And I was determined to stay on that—to stay on that job, regardless of what."

Gina, as we have seen, did not need to work initially, so she focused on staying in school. Her major was petroleum engineering, and in the summers, she worked internships with major oil companies. During those internships, she earned more than many people earn in a year, so she was able to use that money to live the remainder of each year. It is somewhat amazing that she was able to get the high-paying internship, but her initial employment was partly due to meeting the right person. When Gina interviewed for the internship, the woman doing the hiring was a black woman, like Gina. When the hiring decision was being made, she told the woman about her extensive criminal history. The woman decided to give her a chance, and Gina's performance insured future opportunities with the company. Her criminal background eventually caught up with her, however. The last summer internship she was offered was in a different district. After the contracts were signed, the company ran another background check and invalidated the contract, despite three years of positive experiences with Gina.

Gina's experience is unusual in that she was able to find high-paying work. Most of the women ended up in service industry jobs. Dorothy and Misha work as waitresses. Tara went to work for Goodwill Industries. Kathy worked a series of low-paying jobs before eventually finding work as a Recovery Support Specialist. Mandy works for a friend who has a house-cleaning business. She eventually hopes to start her own cleaning business, but she worries about how her criminal record might affect her ability to get clients on her own.

Transportation is another difficulty faced by women attempting to reintegrate into society. If the woman lives in one of the two largest cities in the state, the public bus system can be used to get to interviews, jobs, and the myriad of appointments she has to keep. Prisoners are often given lists of resources, but Misha reflected that these were often not helpful:

> When you leave prison they give you a resource packet. They give you a little folder. Discharge certificate, your birth certificate and your social security card. And they give you resources. Some people don't use the resources but the ones who really want it, they do. You know, because I see them, you know I went and got my bus pass, tokens . . . those are the ones that want it. You see them riding the bus. They just came home from prison, and got a bus token. Those are the ones who are really out there trying, and uh, that are using their resources.

Most of the communities in Oklahoma, however, have limited public transportation. Those who are released to Tulsa or Oklahoma City can use the bus system, but those in smaller communities have to walk. This can be a barrier to success. The newly released prisoner faces a sometimes baffling number of requirements—parole officers, required treatment, and the immediate need for employment. Not having transportation may contribute to the failure to meet the stipulations of parole and the potential for revocation.

As we saw earlier, Gina had an aunt who immediately provided her with an automobile of her own. Most are not that fortunate, but many of the women I interviewed did have assistance with transportation. One had grand-parents who took her to countless appointments and interviews. She noted they would only take her to those places that were required by her parole, such as reporting to her parole officer, going to treatment or counseling, or to job interviews. However, she recognized that without their assistance, it would have been difficult for her to comply with her parole. After a few months, her mother sold a car to her very cheaply.

> My grandma, she's retired, my grandfather, he gets off work at a certain time. And, if I was looking for a job they'd take me, or pick me up. Take me to work until I got my own car. They're very supportive, taking me places I need to go that—that are beneficial . . . I only got a car like two months ago. My Mom sold me her car. So, I've just lucked upon a car.

Similarly, Tara rode the bus or depended on her family for rides her first few months out. After she had established her own home and kept a job for a while, her grandfather gave her a car. Dorothy was able to save enough money to buy a car while she was in a transitional living program.

Other Issues: Training and Participation in Programs While in Prison

The majority of the women who have remained out of prison either had prior education or sought higher education upon release. Twyla was degreed when she went to prison. Kathy, Gina and Tara all completed bachelor's degrees in the years following their release, and Misha is currently in college. Education, either prior to release or after release, serves a number of purposes. First, it can provide the woman with skills that will help her get work. But, it also helps her gain confidence. According to Gina:

> You know, the people that I encountered really encouraged me. Like I remember, Mr., Mr. O'Dell, uh, and, and, uh, a couple of other people were really encouraging, um, you know, along the way, and they helped me maneuver getting into Vo-Tech. And so I got into Vo-Tech and that was the first time that I learned—you know, things that made me proud of that, that knowledge. And it made me feel worthy. Self-worth, I mean, you know, because up to that point I was feeling pretty worth-less. And then I was a drug addict on top of it, so, making me feel really worthless.

Health and Mental Health Issues

Another way that most of these women differed from those in the previous chapter is that only one had significant health problems, and she had Med-icaid insurance to pay for her prescriptions and doctor's visits. Gina, too, had access to health care as a student. Tara utilized a free clinic in the city when she was sick. This is in stark contrast to the serious health issues faced by the women described in chapter 5. Not only were the women who remained out of prison healthier in general, but they also were more likely to have access to some form of health care.

Overall, these women reported fewer mental health problems than those in the previous chapter. Most had received extensive counseling while incarcerated. Only one reported needing to be on psychotropic medication at the time of her release. Often, their mental health needs were intertwined with their need for substance abuse treatment, and many of the successfully reintegrating women received both mental health and substance abuse services.

The majority of Oklahoma's women prisoners have been assessed with a moderate to high need for substance abuse treatment (Oklahoma Department of Corrections/Division of Female Offenders Operations 2010). Unfortunately, limited budgets mean that a large number leave prison without having received substance abuse treatment. Additionally, those who receive treatment may not be those who most need it, although it may still benefit them. Tara commented:

> I don't have a history of drug abuse or anything like that, but mentally and emotionally, and all those things, I was messed up. I think I'm probably still messed up.
>
> And would always say that I would never do drugs. That was one thing that I would always commit. Never—never did I think that I was going to get a man that—and get caught up in those type of things. I participated in the RDAP[2] Program my judge he ordered me to take that program.

What was even more beneficial to Tara, however, was counseling that she received in prison. Her lifelong decision to not use drugs was based on her mother's addiction. Because her mother was addicted, Tara had been placed in unsafe situations as a child and was molested. She had never dealt with those issues until she was in prison.

> I took a lot of counseling and psych—psychological help. Mmm, my first time experiencing getting to talk to a psychiatrist. I was able to get a lot of things that were on my heart and I was blaming myself for a lot of things that, uh, I should have not been blaming myself for and, uh, I had a lot of childhood trauma that I had—didn't realize that I had.
>
> Once I had started seeing that psychiatrist—which was four years into my incarceration—when my grandmother died—it—it opened up a whole, it was like—it was like a whole new realization that took place in my life. Because I think that I had carried so much, uh, guilt and anger and fear dealing with my mother that I—I closed off so much because I

thought that I wasn't worthy, of anything. You know, those types of things. I think that—so when I started going to see the psychiatrist and was able to talk about—how can a three-year-old or four-year-old know this isn't right? Those types of things that we blame ourselves for—those things that happened in our life.

Additionally, some women who are able to get into treatment while in prison are unable to complete the program because they are either released or transferred to another facility. That was Misha's experience.

I was selected to go to RSAT[3] then in the process of being in RSAT I—I came up for parole. But I took Thinking for a Change, anger management.

I can't say either program helped me because I didn't really graduate from them. But I basically self-helped myself. It just—it really wasn't even a program that helped me. It was just determination.

Because the state has limited resources for providing treatment while in prison, substance abuse treatment is often a stipulation of parole. However, this is usually outpatient treatment and often only one hour a week. This means that the women who successfully stay out of prison must be committed to remaining drug free. In the past, treatment was more obtainable, but because of loss of funding, women in Oklahoma may often have to wait six months to get into a treatment program both while in prison and on the outside.

Several of the women were involved in twelve-step recovery programs or churches that were supportive of their recovery efforts. Kathy has been active for several years in Celebrate Recovery, a Christianity-based support group for those dealing with addictions. Dorothy, Gina, Tasha, and Barbara are all involved with twelve-step programs. Arlena and Misha rely on their churches for support. Tara has never had a problem with drugs or alcohol. However, she is also very involved with her church. All of the women have received counseling of some sort at one time or another. At least two of the women who have stayed out of prison initially had problems with relapsing briefly, but were able to get in-patient treatment to get off drugs and alcohol again.

The Role of Attitude

One of the most significant differences between the women who were reincarcerated and those who successfully stayed out is the attitude towards release. As we saw in chapter 5, many of the women who reentered felt alienated and institutionalized. They tended to view the world as an unfriendly place, and they were frightened and overwhelmed. In contrast, those who have been more successful see their success as a personal responsibility. Virtually all of the women who have successfully stayed out of prison felt that inner motivation was a key element of their success. This intangible, at first glance, seems to be something that the individual must have and that no programs can create. However, programs can help build the sense of self-worth that can help this motivation develop. In Tara's words, counseling helped her immensely:

> I think that when I first had a sense of direction it was that "this is not my home—and I'm not going to get comfortable here. I'm not going to get content here. I will do my part to do what I need to do while I'm incarcerated"—but my main goal was to get home. And what I was going to do to not come back here, to not do this part again. And when I say sense of direction is that you don't have to keep going to jail for drugs. Why would you keep putting yourself in that situation when you can get your high school diploma or those things that are giving you a barrier. I know there's not lots of options in there but you can read. There are things we can do to try to make it better.
>
> So that sense of direction that I'm talking about for me was that I had to start saying to myself—once I had started seeing that psychiatrist—it opened up a whole, it was like—it was like a whole new realization that took place in my life.

The other element all the women believed was necessary was some type of plan for achieving goals. The women who stayed out of prison left there with a clear plan about what they would do. In addition to having a plan, having someone supportive to help them achieve the plan is also essential, according to Tara.

> They have to leave with a plan. And somebody has to be out there to help them work their plan. Everybody is not going to work the plan according to what they feel is right. Because I don't believe—I have met some people that I believe like prison. But I have—I have really met some people that, uh, had what they wanted to do and there was so many roadblocks. So many obstacles. Discouragement. What should I do? You know. I've got these children. And I can't get a job. And when I got my job it was $5.15 an hour. So—and it didn't matter. I was so happy to get a job.
>
> But I think having a plan when you get out. Case managers working with them or whoever. Even if you make your own plan. But having a plan is part of it. Okay, maybe I don't get that job that is paying $15 an hour. Maybe I can look for a $7.35 an hour. But especially when you have low self-esteem. And a lot of us women who have been incarcerated—it's really hard to build your esteem. We put up a front, you know, that everything is all right and all that but it gets really hard.
>
> That's the main thing. Having a plan and being able to work it and sticking to it. And if you do mess up, if you can't accomplish everything in it, if you can accomplish a little of it. Because it builds up our self-esteem.

Financial Obligations

The newly released woman can face an overwhelming amount of money to repay. She may owe fines, court costs, restitution, and child support. Additionally, she has probably lost her driver's license and must pay for reinstatement. In Oklahoma, a drug arrest (not conviction) normally results in immediate revocation of the individual's driver's license. The normal cost for reinstatement is $600 to $750, plus she must obtain automobile liability insurance as well. Parole fees average around $40 per month, and if she is released with an electronic leg monitor, the monitoring fee is normally $140 per month. She also probably is court-ordered to obtain mandatory counseling and drug treatment. Consider the fines, fees, and so forth owed by one individual upon release:

- $28 for clerk fees
- $3 attorney general victim services unit
- $150 sheriff fees
- $9 CLEET penalty assessment
- $50 victim's compensation assessment (VCA)
- $500 fines
- $5 AFIS fund
- $10 sheriff's service and incarceration fee
- $12 law library fee
- $18 court clerk revolving fund
- $3 child abuse multidisciplinary fee
- $5 forensic science improvement assessments
- $10 medical expense liability revolving fund
- $25 DA Council prosecution assessment fee
- $10 Oklahoma Department of Health/trauma care fund
- $150 OCIS revolving fund
- $50 jail fund (bond fee) sheriff or private jail
- $10 sheriff's service fee for courthouse security[4]

The fees just listed add up to more than $1,000 which, disturbingly, does not include all the costs a woman may face. She may owe restitution, court costs, and of course, she will have to pay monthly parole fees. She will also owe child support if the caregivers of her child have sought support from the state (TANF, SNAP, etc.). The women I interviewed did not have overwhelming debt, with the exception of one woman who owed a considerable amount of restitution for checks she had written. However, that woman was able to work out an arrangement for repayment that was not overly burdensome. Given the amount of debt and the fees and other costs, this is the ideal situation for a woman newly released from prison.

Family and Relationships

One of the most important roadblocks for recently released women to overcome is reunification with their children. A majority of women in prison have minor children, and the majority of those with children were living with them prior to imprisonment, often as sole caregivers. When the mother goes to prison, the already fragile family dynamics are further disturbed. Children are often separated not only from their mothers but from their siblings (Sharp and Marcus-Mendoza 2001). The children have often been passed from one relative to another, and so have lacked stable housing and education (Sharp and Marcus-Mendoza 2001). They are often frightened, confused, and angry. Furthermore, even if the mother has received counseling to deal with her problems, her children most likely have not. The family who has been caring for them is worn out and resentful. Now that the mother has been released, they often expect her to immediately retrieve her children. The mother, who has desperately missed her children, struggles to comply, but she is often overwhelmed with a myriad of expectations from others. She must report to her parole officer, begin paying court costs, fines and restitution. She may not have yet found a safe environment for living or stable employment.

Additionally, her children often have been unable to visit her, so they must become reacquainted. Gina pointed out how either not being able to have their children or getting full responsibility too soon could sabotage the chance of successful reintegration.

> Not being able to get her children back may set a woman up for disillusionment and potential relapse. And devastation can happen with women as far as the—So, for instance, they get out and somehow the state/DHS has their kids and they won't return them or DHS has their kids and they return them too quickly.

Most of the women who have successfully stayed out of prison did not have to take over the responsibilities of their children immediately, but they did have contact with those children. For example, Gina's husband, who was in the military, had her children while she was in prison, although the youngest son ended up with his paternal grandmother. She knew her children were safe, and she has spent a number of years rebuilding her relationships with her three sons. However, her contact with her children was very limited while she was incarcerated. For several years, her husband was stationed overseas with her two oldest sons, making telephone calls impossible. Even though the youngest child remained stateside with his paternal grandmother, she ran into a barrier maintaining contact with him.

> So my aunt in DC would call and she would say, you know, "Whatever it costs, if you let her—you know, I can send you some money to it in

advance or you can allow her to call and, you know, let's not make it about the money. Because the price is not an issue, you know, let's keep her connected with the kids." And so, she [the mother-in-law] had to eventually when my family weighed in, you know, kind of comply.

Although Gina has been able to develop good relationships with her sons, she still experiences some distress. Knowing that her actions caused the weakened relationships, she has perhaps tried too hard at times to win back their love.

I felt very guilty about being absent from their life. Because, you know, at the end of the day, despite the fact that the justice system, you know, morphed the situation into something it really wasn't, I initiated the situation. And so, you know, there's a lot of guilt associated with . . . me doing the things I did to land me in prison. And so, in dealing with them, you know, instead of parenting, you know, I, I overcompensated with money, and then they learned how to manipulate that.

Misha's grandparents took care of her daughter while she was in prison. They put effort into maintaining contact with Misha while she was in prison, and they brought her daughter to visit her. When she paroled, she went to live with her grandparents, so she has been able to be around her daughter. However, because she has been gone most of her daughter's life, their relationship is still tenuous.

We really don't have like a close relationship. I went when she was two, basically been gone for ten years, come out when she's 12. So I know she probably has like a resentment toward me. She showed it—when I came out the last time she showed it. She was like, "you've never been there for me." She voiced it. But she hasn't really voiced it this time. But I know that it's still in there. And she's probably, you know, I know she doesn't want anything to happen to me. It would probably hurt her. I think she's protective over me now.

But she's had a very good upbringing. She's been to a private school since she was in pre-school. She went to my church school. She's just now left that school since she's into the seventh grade. She sings in the choir and makes good grades. She's not—she doesn't do anything negative, don't curse, don't . . . She's just a technology kid. Facebook or computer or iPad or something like that. But she's really good.

I thank my grandparents for stepping in and, you know. If I didn't have good family support, you know, the state could have had her. No telling where she'd be. So I had them to step in, give her a good upbringing, taught her moral values, how to respect, and put her in a good school.

Kathy's children were raised by her sister. She did not regain custody after her release, but she has been able to develop relationships with them. Recently, she became a grandmother. As she put it, "Being a grandmother is sort of like a do-over. With my grandchildren, I have the chance to do it right this time."

Some states and many foreign countries recognize the importance of maintaining a strong bond between the woman prisoner and her children, and have developed programs to allow infants to remain with their mothers. In Germany, Preungensheim prison offers one of the most comprehensive mother and child prison programs. This prison accommodates not only mothers with infants but also those with pre-school children. Those women not considered a security risk live in an "open house" that faces out into the larger Frankfurt community. While the mothers work, the children are taken care of by childcare workers, and they participate in various activities including trips to the zoo or to local nature preserves. One of the benefits of this program is that the women are not only able to spend time with their children, but they are responsible for getting them ready in the mornings and taking care of them when they return from work. Assuming this responsibility while still in prison should better prepare the women for taking responsibility for the household once released. Older children may not live in the prison, but again the women are allowed to practice responsibility for their children. Women who are eligible for work-release leave the prison at 5:00 A.M. and go to the households where their children are staying. They are then responsible for getting the children ready for school, delivering them to the school, maintaining their households during the day, including all shopping and household chores. After school lets out, the women are responsible again for the care of their children until bedtime. Once the children have gone to bed, the women return to the prison (Kauffman and Clayton 2001).

Oklahoma does not have programs where women can keep their children with them while in prison. The general attitude is usually that these women are not good mothers and that it would be rewarding bad behavior to allow them to be with their children. However, Misha expressed her belief that those kinds of programs are desperately needed. "I've seen a program where, like, the women do have their newborn kids. In there with them, where they can keep their bonding, you know. Something more like that. More activities with the kids or for women. 'Cause, like Mabel Bassett, it's so locked down, and she doesn't want anything coming in or coming out of there." The Center Point facility for women, a quasi-therapeutic community in Tulsa, does allow those who are on higher levels to have their children stay at the facility on weekends. When I was touring the facility, the director pointed out the child's bed in one of the rooms. A four year old spent weekends there with his mother. However, only a few of the women get to bring their children to the facility, and Center Point only houses 32 women at any given time.

Tara's sister cared for her children during her incarceration. Once she was out and able to establish herself, she eventually was able to get them back. Rebuilding those relationships has taken time. Her relationship with her son has remained difficult, even though she has been out of prison a long period of time. "But Trey is just—he was always like, mm, he was waiting for that day when I mess up. With Mira she was just so happy—it was just—I mean, she was like my everything. [Laughs] He was, too, but it was like two different things. She was like, I don't care, my mom's my mom, always. And then we got to the point where as they got older, Mira became my challenge." Tara's children are now grown, but she remains close to them, especially her daughter, who she sees daily. She laughingly commented that she now sometimes wishes they were at her house a little less often. She married after her release, and she also has a younger child. This is not unusual in former prisoners. Much like Kathy's do-over, the women seem to want the opportunity to try motherhood again, this time more responsibly. Misha expressed a desire to have another child, but she said she probably will not because her daughter does not want her to do so.

In contrast, Arlena lost contact with her children, who lived with their father, for many years. Once released, she had to re-establish relationships with children who had become adults while she was incarcerated. One son was in prison, and the other was very angry at her and at the system. One daughter had followed in her footsteps, becoming addicted and contracting HIV infection. Another daughter, however, developed a long-distance relationship with her through telephone calls and letters. The relationships with her children have been very painful for Arlena, and she has struggled more than most of the women I interviewed.

Social Support

The women who were successfully reintegrating had two things to say about social support. First, having positive social support was essential. They viewed support while in prison as worthwhile but not absolutely necessary. What was necessary was having supportive people on the outside. Tara had support while still in prison that helped build her confidence and self-worth. It also taught her how to have healthy relationships. In particular, she learned that relationships with men did not have to be sexual.

> This couple that I met who were in California that was Caucasian. He started writing me through a Bible study. And they were like 60, 65 years old. And, uh, he's a doctor. And through correspondence, him and his wife started visiting me. And my grandfather, I knew—was always physical. You've got to give to get. You know, growing up in a house where drugs

and all those types of things . . . molestation and all those things are part of. You don't really see what true love is, or . . . so when this couple took me on while I was in prison, mm, it kind of changed somewhat my way of thinking. Not really, not a lot, but as the years went on . . .—because I met them like in '95. '94. I met them like in '94. And from '94 to 2012, they, well Riley had died now but it was always like, uh, a different type. So I learned through them and through people who they brought into my life, it kinda gave me a different look at life.

Tara also developed a relationship with a church that remains supportive in her life today. In particular, one woman helped her in the first few months.

When I first came home, mm—I started going to this one church, but it wasn't, uh . . . I'm trying to think because I—me and my children, this lady Helen was my biggest supporter because I didn't have a car, so she would pick me up and take me where I needed to go. And drop us off. She was a lady from the church. I had met her before I went. But I really didn't know her. But when I came back, I was going to this other church, and I saw one of the old church members at—she invited me to come back to their church, so me and the kids went back there. And, uh, but, I don't— see if they had something like this right here[5] when I came home, or if I had of known about it, this would have been a good place for me. Because I had the tools, and I was afraid I was going to lose them. So having that church foundation when I first came out—there was no healthy family support so that was important.

Misha felt that family support and church support were helping her be successful. While she is unable to attend church regularly, she remains connected to her congregation.

And I just—I have a supportive family, you know. So it's not like I don't have family support.

I normally don't go to church on Sundays 'cause I have to work . . . But uh, I see my pastor because he eats at the restaurant I work at, so I communicate with him and a few other reverends at work that eat there. Talk about a few things I may be going through, so they're supportive.

Dorothy relies on friends she has met in a twelve-step program for her major support. Additionally, she has a close friend that she met while living in transitional housing. Having positive support has been very important to all of these women. However, equally important has been staying away from old friends and non-supportive people. Gina commented that they had not been present for her when she was incarcerated, so she simply had nothing to do with her old crowd once she was released.

I had been gone so long, the thing is, what, what was proven to me was that none of those people were there when I was incarcerated. None of those people wrote letters, none of those people asked my parents how I was or where I was, none of those people cared. They didn't give a damn. So, you know, I just, I knew—there were some things that I came to, that I concluded in prison that were very important. And that was that, you know, I can't be around drugs and that kind of environment AT ALL.

Her comments were echoed by Misha, who also found that her drug-using friends had abandoned her while she was incarcerated, only to seek her out once she was released. Misha felt that the drug users were not real friends, unlike her non-using friends.

I have a few friends that are supportive of me, that wrote me. Not the ones I was smoking PCP with. They didn't write me at all. They're just a turn-off to me. 'Cause I've seen 'em, I've seen 'em high on PCP, and it's like—it disgusts me. But, the other ones, you know, kept in contact. And those are the ones I deal with now. 'Cause in my time of need, they were there.

Summary

The women who have successfully stayed out of prison faced the same problems that those who recidivated faced, but there are certain key differences. First, this was not the first incarceration for many of them. Girshick (2003) talks about planting a seed of rehabilitation during the first incarceration that may come to fruition at a later date. Several of the women spotlighted in this chapter talked about the maturing process that occurred during their second incarceration.

Second, and perhaps more importantly, the women who are able to remain outside generally had strong social support. Many of them had considerable help from families, while a few found assistance from agencies or churches. While there is little the state can do to improve the family situations to which women return, programs such as Oxford Houses or halfway houses can help the newly released prisoner adjust to the outside. Additionally, for those lacking transportation, living in a facility with other women could be very helpful. It would preclude the loneliness that leads some women back into relationships with abusive males or individuals engaging in criminal behavior. The use of mentoring programs that connect women with individuals in the community can also be very important, particularly for those who lack healthy family support.

Jobs are another area that could benefit from intervention. Several of the women in this chapter found jobs through friends. Others reported problems with the "felon-friendly" employer list given to them when they left prison. However, tax breaks and pre-release employment are two tools that could be used to help returning women find stable employment. Increased job training and education could also improve their chances. Certainly, finding jobs that pay living wages is virtually essential to successful reintegration.

It is also very important to keep in mind the overwhelming amount of money the women may need to come up with to repay the legal system. Ideally, the Department of Corrections and the court system should work with each woman to develop a repayment plan that is feasible, taking into account her financial situation. Forbearance on certain fees or court costs for some initial period of time could help. However, revisiting the number of payments and fees would be an even better idea. We are essentially creating a society where a certain segment experiences recurring incarceration simply because of inability to meet all the financial obligations imposed on them, creating a twenty-first century version of debtors' prisons.

The final aspect of successful reentry that these interviews point to is attitudinal. The women who successfully stayed out of prison had developed motivation and saw their success as their own responsibility. Programming to help develop self-esteem and identify personal barriers to success seems could help returning women. Seeing themselves as worthwhile and deserving is likely to improve the likelihood of staying out of prison. It may also help them avoid bonding with an abusive or criminal male upon release. Additionally, assistance in developing a plan for the future is essential to success. The women who successfully stayed out developed both short-term and long-range goals, giving them a blueprint to work towards achieving.

Overall, the keys to success are related to positive social support and inner motivation. While these are factors that cannot be controlled by the state, measures can be taken to improve both. Development of additional mentoring programs with supportive individuals outside of the prison, provision of sufficient counseling and programming to address negative mindsets and low self-worth can help women to overcome many of the barriers faced by those leaving prison. In chapter 7, we will turn to the other half of the equation— the children of incarcerated women. The children experience turmoil, anger, and fear. Without adequate resources and support, they are at high risk of becoming offenders themselves.

CHAPTER 7

The Children and Their Caregivers

BECAUSE OF the poverty of the state, life is not easy for many children in Oklahoma. More than 24 percent were living in poverty in 2010 (Kids Count 2012). Additionally, more than 6,000 children were living in foster care (either familial or nonfamilial), many of them children of women prisoners. The state provides limited resources to those families who have taken on the children of women prisoners. The Temporary Assistance for Needy Families (TANF) Child-Only payment for one child is only $87, and for three children only $241. The foster care payment is $365 per child for those family members who are licensed as foster parents (Kids Count 2012). Approximately 1 in 9 children in the state have no health insurance (Annie E. Casey Foundation 2012; Kids Count 2012). These problems—financial stress and lack of health insurance—are exacerbated among the children of women prisoners. This chapter is based on prisoner surveys and caregiver interviews from 2004 to 2009. Appendix A provides further information on both the prisoner surveys and the caregiver interviews.

When a mother is incarcerated, the effects are often more devastating to the family than when a father is incarcerated, although that can also harm the family. Women prisoners, more often than men, are likely to be single parents, often the only caregivers of their children (Owen 1998; Mumola 2000). The children of prisoners are frequently overlooked by society and are subject to emotional, financial, and developmental problems. This is particularly true when a mother is incarcerated. Those who have a mother in prison are more likely than those with a father in prison to experience poverty, unstable residences, multiple caregivers, or placement in foster care, either with relatives or nonfamilial caregivers. For example, in one year's study, we found that nearly 37 percent of the children had lived in multiple households since the mother's imprisonment began (Sharp 2005a; Sharp 2005b). In several years, we found that approximately 7 percent of the children ended up in foster care (Sharp 2005a; Sharp 2005 b; Sharp 2008a; Sharp and Pain 2010).

Nationally almost 62 percent of women incarcerated in U.S. prisons and jails have minor children, and 55 percent of women prisoners with minor

children are custodial mothers at the time of incarceration (Glaze and Maruschak 2008). In Oklahoma, from about half to two-thirds of the women
surveyed each year were living with minor children (Sharp 2005a; Sharp
2005b; Sharp 2008a; Sharp 2008b; Sharp et al. 2007; Sharp and Pain 2010).
Furthermore, national data indicate that for 35.4 percent of women incarcerated, there was no prior criminal history, and 60.3 percent were incarcerated
for the first time (Glaze and Maruschak 2008), increasing the disruption of
maternal incarceration. This pattern of one-time incarceration holds true for
Oklahoma. According to Oklahoma Department of Corrections officials, the
majority of the women in Oklahoma's prisons are low-level offenders who
probably should never have been incarcerated.[1]

When a father goes to prison, the mother is likely to remain in the home
and care for their children. However, when a mother goes to prison, she may
have been the only adult living in the home. When the mother is arrested,
the children may find themselves not only without their mother but also
without their home (Mumola 2000). Furthermore, children may be separated
from each other (Sharp and Marcus-Mendoza 2001). In 2008, 117 of the 297
women I surveyed reported living with one or more minor children in the
home at the time of incarceration, accounting for 265 children (Sharp and
Pain 2010). Extrapolated, this means that on any given day, more than 2,400
children were living with a woman prisoner immediately prior to her incarceration. Because there is about a 50 percent turnover in women prisoners
each year, the true number of children affected during the year was more
likely over 3,600 (Oklahoma Children of Incarcerated Task Force 2012). Over
a ten-year period, considering the reality that the majority of women are only
incarcerated once, the number of children impacted by maternal incarceration is quite likely over 30,000, a very depressing number. About two-thirds
of these prisoner mothers retained custody of at least one child during their
imprisonment. Furthermore, the majority of the women planned to live with
their children after release, underscoring the importance of maintaining relationships with them (Sharp 2008a).

By 2009, I had developed a clearer picture of the extent of the problem.
In that year's study, 85 percent of the women were mothers, although about
one-third of them reported their children were now grown. About 45 percent
of the women were living with a minor child at the time of they were sent to
prison, averaging just fewer than two children per woman. Most planned
to reunite with their children upon release (Sharp and Pain 2010). Of the 301
women who participated in that year's survey, 257 had children, 148 had children with multiple sex partners, and they reported almost 500 children under
the age of 18, more than half of whom had been living with their mother
when she was incarcerated.

PLACEMENT OF THE CHILDREN

One of the most difficult issues facing a mother who is being sent to prison is where to leave her children. Over the years that I studied incarcerated women and their children, I noticed some changes. Perhaps most strikingly, the caregivers of the children in the early years of my research were most likely to be the prisoners' mothers or other family members, especially grandparents and siblings. By the end of 2009, fathers were almost as likely as grandmothers to have the children while the mother was in prison.

There were distinct racial differences, however. For example, examining the survey data I collected from 2007 through 2009, Hispanics mothers were most likely to report children living with their own mothers (41 percent), 26 percent reported children with the children's fathers, and about 20 percent reported children with other relatives. Slightly more than 31 percent of white mothers who were living with a child prior to incarceration reported the child was now with the other parent, while slightly less reported the child was with the prisoner's mother. Approximately one-third of Native American mothers reported children with the other parent, and another third reported children with their own mothers. More than 10 percent reported children with the prisoners' grandmothers, and 12 percent reported children with other relatives. Another 17 percent reported children with other people. In contrast, less than 14 percent of black mothers reported a child with the child's other parent, 26 percent reported a child with the prisoner's mother, 7 percent reported a child with prisoner's grandmother, and 16 percent reported a child with other relatives.

White mothers were the most likely to report a child in foster care or placed with an agency, and Hispanic mothers were the least likely. In summary, white, Hispanic, and Native American women reported similar rates of placement with their own mothers or the children's fathers. However, black women were far less likely to report that their children were with their children's fathers. That is not surprising considering the high rate of incarceration for Black men.

PROBLEMS OF THE CHILDREN

The problems experienced by the prisoners' children remained similar over time. According to the prisoners, the most common problems experienced by their children were problems with school, problems with caregivers, and depression. School problems often developed after the mother went to prison. For example, 27 percent of the women in 2004 reported a child having difficulty with school, with another 14 percent reporting a child had dropped out, and 10 percent reporting a child had been expelled. Conflicts with caregivers were also common, and several caregivers reported a child had run away.

In 2004, more than one in three prisoners reported that their children were experiencing depression, with one in twelve reporting a child was suicidal. Furthermore, most of these women reported the problem had developed since incarceration (Sharp 2005a). The main problems remained similar throughout the years of research, with depression, school problems, and problems with guardians being the most common issues reported in 2009 (Sharp and Pain 2010).

PROBLEMS WITH PLACEMENT OF THE CHILDREN

Children were sometimes placed with caregivers who had been abusive toward the prisoners themselves as children. Almost 20 percent of the women reported a child in the home with someone who had sexually abused them in childhood, and more than one-third reported children in a home with caregivers who had physically abused the women themselves as children. Additionally in almost one-fourth of the families, the children were with a parent who had been physically abusive toward the prisoner mother in the past. I asked the prisoners to answer a series of open-ended questions at the end of the questionnaire, and their comments in the next few paragraphs are in their own words. Many of the women voiced concerns about the placement of their children. "My mother [son's guardian] is an alcoholic. My son has gotten into a lot of trouble. It seems to be a cycle with her and any children around her (myself and son). He gets no emotional support and little affection." One prisoner went into detail about her concerns for her child, who were with her family in another state. She had a relative who was trying to get the child, but at the time of the survey, there had been no success. She said the child had told her she was being abused by relatives. Because I had no contact information on the family that had the child and the child was in another state, I was unable to alert authorities. I was also unable to verify the situation.

> My 14 year old daughter is being physically and verbally abused by my mother . . . She has been coached and trained on a daily basis what to say to child welfare if they are called. She has threatened to kill my daughter and repeatedly tells her she hates her. She also calls her very, very vulgar names. She also bites her, pulls her hair and just so much more. Then after the abuse she is made to feel sorry for my mother.

Sometimes, the caregiver is viewed by the prisoner as doing the best job possible in a difficult situation. One mother commented, "My child is alright; he's with my mother but she is 74 years old; I pray she lives until I get out." This was echoed by another prisoner, who stated, "My youngest stays with my mother and she's up in age and I'm so scared something will happen to her while I'm gone."

In one family, the prisoner's sister had the child because the prisoner would be eventually paroling to her own mother's home. This prisoner mother could not have contact with the child because a former boyfriend had molested the child when she was about five. The aunt caregiver, however, did not feel that the child needed counseling for her abuse, because "she was so little when it happened and there's a lot she doesn't remember." Yet the caregiver went on to say the child was a problem, running away and using drugs.

Placement with the children's fathers sometimes raised concerns as well about abuse and neglect. Many of these women were with men who were meth cooks, addicts, and criminals. Stated simply, they were not well equipped to take on the sole responsibility of children. One prisoner's mother expressed concerns to me that the children's father was not making the children attend school, and often left them alone. One of her daughter's children was living with her at the time I interviewed her, but she was concerned about the other child. Some of the prisoners themselves expressed concerns about children living with their fathers.

My son's father is using and selling drugs in the presence of our son. DHS has had my son once because of his dad's alcohol and drug problems.

I heard that his grandparents [paternal] gave my son back to his father. Which he just got out of prison, he's 38 living with a 17 year-old little girl. And she is raising my son.

Youngest is with father that is never home. She is 6 years old left with grandfather who is constantly drunk.

I am only concerned because they are with their father who in the past couldn't care for himself let alone his children. His illness has been an issue we have been working on since our second son was born.

Even children in the foster care system may be at risk. The state has a training class for foster parents and makes an attempt to screen them, but on occasion, children end up in bad foster care situations. In one case, a child was made to eat under the house with the dogs because the foster mother said, "No nigger is eating in my kitchen." She later scalded this child, putting him in the hospital. In another family, the mother reported: "They are all separated! 2 of my little girls 6 years and 2 years are with a foster mom that has been abusive to them! I'm very afraid for them!" Many people in the state believe that a mother who uses drugs should not have her children. What they seem unable to grasp is that frequently the mother is one of the healthiest members of the family. The children may be better off with a drug-using mother, particularly if they are getting the needed help. Most of these women come from highly dysfunctional homes, and it is naïve to believe that their families are equipped to take on additional children. The children end up suffering from the loss of their mothers and their siblings, and are placed in dangerous or unstable environments. One woman, who was caring for her great niece, summed up her concerns about the intergenerational issues:

> [The child] is the third generation of her family to go through this, not the second but the third. She is the third generation. My mother's sister went to prison, and my grandmother raised her kids. [The child's] grandmother went to prison, and the same grandparents raised her kids, they were great-grandparents to [the child's] mom, and now [the child]. So this is really the third generation, and if anybody thinks that this doesn't have an impact on families, far, far beyond, just the obvious, then they've got their heads up their butt.

Contact

Research indicates that maintaining contact with the mother while she is in prison predicts better outcomes for the children and the mother (Cecil et al. 2008; Strozier et al. 2011). However, maintaining contact is often difficult and expensive (Bernstein 2005). In 2008, only 29.6 percent of the mothers reported seeing their children at least once a month, and 43.2 percent had no visits. Almost 41 percent spoke to their children once a month or more often, but nearly half had no telephone contact (Sharp 2008a). These numbers are similar to those in other years (Sharp 2004; Sharp 2005a; Sharp 2008b; Sharp et al. 2007; Sharp and Pain 2010).

There are a number of reasons for the low levels of contact. First, Oklahoma's two main women's prisons are located in rural areas not accessible by public transportation. In particular, Dr. Eddie Warrior Correctional Center is in the eastern part of the state in a small community west of Muskogee. The first time I went there, I had difficulty finding the prison. Mabel Bassett Correctional Center is also located in a rural area east of Oklahoma City. Many of these women's families lack reliable transportation to make the drive to the prisons, and there is no public transportation available. Furthermore, while Eddie Warrior is child-friendly, Mabel Bassett is an institutional setting, with a playroom area inside of the visitation room and no outdoor playground.

Those at Eddie Warrior are more likely to have visits from children with transportation difficulties. Quarterly, churches bring children to the campus for a play day that includes games and face-painting. Additionally, Sheila Harbert, director of Girls Scouts Beyond Bars of Eastern Oklahoma, brings girls who are involved in her prisoner mother-child scout troop to the prison. This program has been extended to Mabel Bassett as well, but the primary focus remains at Eddie Warrior.

Mabel Basset has its own program for mothers and children: CAMP (Children and Mothers Program). This program was begun in the late 1990s to promote bonds between women prisoners and their children. However, staffing issues led to the program being conducted during the week, when many caregivers were at work and children were in school. In 2005, I interviewed a young woman who was taking care of her younger brother while their mother was in prison. Her mother had been incarcerated when the caregiver was a child, and she reflected about the change in the program over the years.

> We—we would go spend the weekend with our mom, and we'd spend Friday night and Saturday night and come home Sunday. It was really, really helpful. And, uh, I know the CAMP Program, my mom wants me to bring him up there 'cause she pays for it, but every time—I can't take him out of school. But, that CAMP program, if they even had it like some—it's just during the day and you can't take them out of school. We don't miss school. He does good in school, and that's one of our big pet peeves. You know—not miss a day. I mean, you know, I know it's important for him to see my mom, but I don't feel like it's that important to miss school.

Several of the caregivers interviewed over the years spoke about the difficulties with visitation. For many, age and financial hardship made visitation difficult, but they went as often as they could.

> Right to begin with I was trying to go up once a month. Uh . . . now it's normally . . . now about every other month and uh where she will go and visit with the . . . her visitation is on Saturday and so I'll go up and take [the child] . . . and so she can go see her . . . on Saturday visitation.
>
> And then every other weekend we go and visit her on Sunday so they get to spend time together . . . For a while she was wanting us to come every weekend and I said I can't come every weekend. I got to—I got to do my things to you know I got to wash clothes and get ready for the next week.

Others expressed difficulty making the trip to the prison.

> Well, we haven't gone to visit her yet. That is a major problem. And that is one that someone can do something about. If they would have transportation so that we could go and visit her every Sunday. That would be a great thing.
>
> We don't visit as often. It is a little bit of a trip for us. We visit about once every two months. And then we try to go on, if there is a special holiday or a birthday of hers.
>
> It's a long trip down there [laughter]. The last time it was, it was chaos . . . Well, between that and finances, is the only reason I mean, you know if she was closer certainly we'd visit more often, but it's, it is a long

trip, especially with the baby, I mean . . . and the last one we, I missed my turn so we had to make a really long detour and [laughter] . . . then we ran outta gas cause my gas gauge is messed up.

Now when they're with me, like uh it takes me two-and-a-half hours just one way to drive to take them to see their mother. Uh, the boy has not seen his mother since uh Christmas.

One family found a creative way to maintain contact with the mother:

They put her in a program where, this . . . woman says she's a volunteer but she's licensed by the DOC and drives one of their trucks, buses and she picks up the girls the ones that wants to and takes them to Hillside Baptist Church . . . And ahh, we've been meeting her out there, twice so far and he's enjoyed visiting with her a couple times.

In some cases, the caregivers expressed concerns that visitation was difficult for the child. In some cases, the child was frightened: "I wouldn't take him to the prison. And uhh, he didn't want to go. He was scared and she did not want to put him through that and I didn't either." In other cases, the separation at the end of the visit was traumatic for the child. The caregiver expressed concerns about how the child was being affected by having to leave his mother at the end of each visit. "Whenever we go to see her, he goes and cries whenever we leave—he don't want to leave her and I can tell, boy . . ." Still others talked about the visitation itself being unpleasant and difficult. One young woman who was caring for a younger sibling spoke of the difficulty of taking him to Mabel Bassett. She had a baby of her own, and she found the facility unpleasant.

And they make it so hard for people to go visit. Every little thing. For the first two or three time I went there I had to go out to my car to take something back. Two or three times. "You can't wear this—you can't wear . . ." I mean, I understand a dress code, but I mean, your jewelry, you can't wear no jewelry in, only your wedding ring. Certain things in the baby's diaper bag, like, Gabriel had a diaper rash. I couldn't take in his diaper cream but I couldn't go out to get it to change his diaper, because my visit would be, you know, terminated. And, it was just one thing after another. The guards hassle you—constantly. And they lock the bathroom doors. Where you can't get access to—you have to stand there and wait. And then, half the time they just sit there and look at you like, hold on. Hold on. Okay, like what if I really had to go, you know, really bad. Half the time they're out of paper towels. And last week I had to leave, it was so hot in there. I had my baby. And they didn't turn on the air like they were kind of wanting people to leave. It was so hot in there—my mom, she's a diabetic, and so she was having hot flashes and sweating, and—we were all uncomfortable before we decided to leave.

Age makes a difference in the children's reactions to their mothers. Older children sometimes do not want to see their mother. They are often angry with her for getting into trouble and leaving them. According to one caregiver, "Uh, the 19-year-old refuses to talk to her, or write to her. The 16, in the last year-and-a-half she's talked to her once or twice, and that's it." In a few cases, caregivers did not want the child to have contact with the mother and would not take the child to visit. Another stated, "I don't feel that she deserves a visit. The baby is in the situation he's in because of her decisions."

Telephone calls are also problematic for families (Bernstein 2005). They are expensive and must be made collect by the prisoner. Indeed, the cost is frequently prohibitive for low-income caregivers, and those that have cell phones or low-income telephone service are at a disadvantage.

> I try to keep the phone calls down to twice a week—at four dollars a pop it gets a little steep, but, she calls when she feels like she needs to talk. No problem. It's just real expensive.
>
> GlobalTel handles that for the state and that's very expensive, we spend $350 to $400 a month talking . . . that is some mistake, it should be for dependents, it costs the dependents, it don't cost the incarcerated person and something a little more reasonable, it's like $7 or $8 a call, but uh, for her to call here and uh, of course we've got the money to be able to afford that, but I wonder about people that don't have the money I have, that are not in the financial shape that I'm in . . . how in the world do they afford $200 to $300 a month. I think communication, those that are incarcerated should be able to talk to at least their children, you know? It would be a big benefit, benefit to a child, because that child needs to talk to their parents and that's something . . .
>
> It costs . . . for her to call here and I have to accept a collect call because you know they, when they incarcerated and they call, well the first minute, you know it's like three or four dollars and then, the next minute it goes up and up.
>
> My phone doesn't take collect calls, it's a cell phone so we don't, we don't talk to her unless we're at my brother's and that's hardly ever.
>
> I have to get a debit card because I don't have long distance.

However, other caregivers seemed to be able to put money on their cell phone accounts to allow them to accept calls:

> My husband sends in a check . . . it's called advanced pay service in Colorado . . . Denver, Colorado. It goes to the phone for her so she can

make the calls to the kids. We've got cell phones is all we have, we've done away with our home phone, cause we're never here or was outside working and so we got cell phones, it's easier and uh, she uh, I put money every month at the first of the month.

Because the cost is so prohibitive for those on limited incomes, some families have had to block calls from the prisoner. The sister taking care of her younger brother explained that the family's budget could not handle the cost of telephone calls from her mother. Another sibling caregiver noted, "I had to block calls from my mom. She was calling all the time and the calls are outrageous." This caregiver said she felt bad because her younger sibling could no longer talk to his mother on the telephone. However, before she blocked the calls, if the prison telephone number came up on caller ID, he became very upset if she did not take the call.

Overall, the caregivers agreed that the telephone calls from the prisoners were cost-prohibitive, and this limited the amount of contact possible between the prisoner mothers and their children. The new system, however, seems to be better than what was available a few years ago. While still expensive, it is less expensive. Because it involves placing money on an account for future calls, it should be accessible from any telephone. However, the service charges a $5 fee for each $25 placed on the account.

Not only do many children have limited contact with their mothers, but they also may lose contact with their siblings. Some caregivers talked about children being with other caregivers. In one case, the caregiver was not aware of three siblings of the child she had. Another caregiver noted that the child she cared for was able to see one of his siblings because they played on a sports team together, but that was all the contact the children had. The other child lived in a different town. Others said that the children were only able to see each other infrequently. Given research that indicates poorer outcomes for children whose mothers have been incarcerated (Huebner and Gustafson 2007) and the importance of contact (Poehlmann 2005; Cecil et al. 2008; Shlafer and Poehlmann 2010; Shlafer, Poehlmann and Donnelan-McCall 2012), these difficulties in maintaining contact are cause for concern.

ECONOMICS

Most of the caregivers over the years experienced economic difficulties in caring for prisoners' children. Sometimes they had enough for survival but little left over. Other times, they did not have sufficient income to support the children adequately.

And sometimes I have to go to the food bank to get food, because we don't have enough to last the whole month. You know like, Neighbor for

Neighbor said they were paying utilities. Well I took mine up there Friday. I got a letter today saying they couldn't help me. So now, I got to figure out a way to get my utilities paid before my stuff gets cut off.

You got to feed 'em, get up with 'em, change 'em. So, water gas and electric and stuff like that it's—it's hard. I manage. I try to—there is places where we have to do without . . . Well, my water was turned off; I had to get some money for water.

Other caregivers noted that not only was the child impacted by financial difficulties, but the entire family suffered. This was a common theme:

One of the problems that families have is even if you can get a little bit of money for the kids, you can't get enough for them to—the whole family ends up taking a nose-dive into serious poverty when you take on more kids.

Uh, there's a direct relationship between, between that and the fact that—that we're having a hard time keeping our heads above water right now. And it hurts the child more than you know. It hurts all my kids. I mean, it hurts the entire family. And if we just weren't pig-headed and stubborn, there would really be no option other than to turn her over to the state.

Taking on the responsibility of a young child can be quite expensive as well. A great-aunt who took in her niece's infant found that she had to come up with basic necessities such as car seat, crib, diapers, and clothing, with no warning. Others found the responsibility of caring for the children made it difficult for them to continue working. One grandmother noted: "I was working with my husband and had to quit work and stay home. She was in an in-home daycare. It was a hassle—DHS was paying for it. The woman closed for the whole month of June . . . So, I just gave up. Sometimes my husband's work puts us out of town—I couldn't go because of keeping [the child]." Many of the caregivers did get state assistance, but they felt it was inadequate. One woman was caring for a younger sibling. Her husband was employed, but she did get TANF for the child. However, that was only $87 per month, and in her words, "He can put $87 of food away in a week . . . And the clothes issues, he's still at that stage where they grow so fast." Another noted that their family income made them ineligible for food stamps: "Help with food would be nice, but see, like, they consider our income for the food stamps. Even though you know . . . we're . . . We do okay but there are some grandparents that are out there that have their grandkids that are living on social security and are on retirement are just right over the level to get food stamps. And they really are struggling . . ." In some cases, the programs to help the families seemed too difficult for those with limited transportation to negotiate. One woman mentioned a program to help with school clothes and supplies.

Like they did had one this year, uh, they called it, um, what did they call it, for the first time? Where they give the children a hundred dollars for clothes and fifty dollars for school supplies and I got it, and then, you have to go way across town, to go do the shopping, I have to go like way southwest 74th and Shields, you know. Way out there. And then when I got there, that was so discouraged, um, she, the social worker, didn't, she didn't even sign it like it should have been signed. So then I had to leave a basket of stuff sitting up there to the desk, you know. I need finance (sic) aid with them, you know, and then I's the one has to be driving them back and forth. My car is down, as you can see out there now. It's still moving, but it's poorly moving. I do the best I can.

Another concern was that the prisoner would have to repay the state for any assistance that they received. This is a real and valid concern. Familial caregivers often want the mother to take over the responsibility of her children when she is released. Because she may already be burdened with court costs, fines, restitution, and fees, they fear that having to repay the state for food stamps or other assistance will make it impossible for her to support her children in the future. Even caregivers with middle-class incomes were affected. Stated simply, most families had not planned to take on the expense of raising another child. They had incurred mortgages, car payments, and other debts. Faced suddenly with the need to house, feed, and clothe one or more children, their budgets were strained.

Another caregiver, as grandmother to the child, was a familial foster parent. She said the state had resources for her, such as respite care so that she could have some time to herself. However, she had been unable to find anyone willing to perform respite care who met state approval guidelines. Thus, while the benefit was available, in reality there was no way to make use of it.

One of the most memorable caregivers that I met was a great-grandmother who was raising her granddaughter's four children, one of whom was born while the mother was in custody. This elderly woman (mid-70s) had been living in a senior housing center with a rent subsidy. She was retired, and social security was her sole income. The housing center did not allow children on the premises, so she had to move, which meant coming up with deposits and rent. The children were all quite young, one a newborn who required a special diet because he had been born premature. She had found a small two-bedroom house she could just afford, but heating and cooling bills strained her budget. In spite of all this, the house was immaculate, and she had baked cookies for me the day of the interview. I spent hours with her, looking at the art work of her great-grandchildren. I left convinced that despite the financial strain, the children were in a loving environment. In this case, the prisoner's mother had also been to prison, and the grandmother had raised the prisoner. Now she is raising her third generation of children.

PROBLEMS EXPERIENCED BY THE CHILDREN

Children with incarcerated mothers frequently have difficulty adjusting to not having their mother present. Attachment disorders are common, and children may be fearful, especially young children. This may lead to acting out, and difficulties with guardians and school. One grandmother reported two children who were experiencing considerable emotional problems. The older child, a boy, was very angry about his mother's incarceration. Visitation was difficult, because he was generally angry and distressed upon leaving. The grandmother reported he had even threatened to harm himself after one visit, so she had obtained counseling for him. However, counseling is not always easy to obtain. The majority of the children with mothers in prison have SoonerCare (Medicaid) if they have any insurance. Finding providers willing to take SoonerCare is often difficult, especially for the caregivers and children who live in more rural areas. Several caregivers reported that they had been unable to find any counselors in their communities who would take the state insurance.

Another maternal grandmother reported that her daughter's child, who was living with the grandmother, had lots of emotional problems. The child was only two, but she often threw violent temper tantrums, frequently until she vomited. She had seen her father stab another man and beat her mother. She is now frightened of men, and she is jealous of any other children who get her caregiver's attention. This grandmother wants counseling for the child, but she has been told by the counselors she contacted that the child is too young to benefit from counseling. The child also gets upset because she cannot talk to her mother when she wants, having to wait for the mother's calls.

It is often difficult for the young child to explain why his or her mother is not present. A sibling caring for her younger brother talked about the difficulties he experienced, both with explaining why he is living with his sister and with missing his mother: "My mother being gone is a very big problem. He—at school and stuff people wonder why he lives with me. Sometimes it's hard for me to get him enrolled in school and they all wonder why. I tell them my mom's incarcerated. And they were real close before. She was almost forty-three when she had him and that's her baby. And, he just—he misses her a lot." Missing the mother was a frequent theme. One maternal grandmother reported that her grandson had been expelled from kindergarten because of the tantrums he would throw. They finally figured out that the child was very upset because he did not understand where his mother was. Fortunately, this family was able to get the child into therapy.

Depression and anger were both common in the children. Sometimes this can lead to legal problems for the child:

When he was picked up, before he went to jail, he had to to, go, uh, for psychiatric counseling. When he found out he had ADD, um, they put him on the medication . . . And he went periodically, you know, to see the counselor there . . . They also had him on Zoloft for depression, and um, he was kind of okay as long as he was taking his medicine, but then he stopped taking his medicine because he didn't—that didn't work for him . . . He'd take knives, you know, and kind of tap on his arm, you know . . .

Alex is ah, he gets, he gets very depressed at times. You know, he misses his mother very much. You know and um, the happiest time is whenever we go to see her. That's the happiest time.

He's antisocial. He, uh, he uses, he used the aspect of his mom being in prison as a crutch. You know, "pity, pity me." And he expected everyone to give in to him because he, he felt like everybody owed him.

In another family, the emotional problems were limited to the time of the mother's arrest. One grandparent noted: "Well, the only problem he ever had was when he was, like, three or four was when they came to take her to jail one time. And he, I mean, they actually handcuffed her right in front of him. They even took her out screaming and everything. He was really upset about it then." Another caregiver reported problems the child had at school: "They don't never call me or nothing but he tells me that he got in trouble at school today and I'm like, 'Why?' But, uh, people kind of have the tendency to pick on him a little bit." Similarly, a sister to the prisoner talked about the problems that her niece and nephew had fitting in at their school. Because their mother's crime was sensationalized in the media, the entire family moved to a new community. The children tried to make friends, but when they finally told their new friends where their mother was, they often met rejection. Sometimes playmates were no longer allowed to have the children over or to go to their house to play.

One maternal grandmother showed insight into her grandchildren's emotional state. She commented that even though the children had other family members there to support them, it was not the same as having their mother. "If their parent or mother is incarcerated, it makes them feel like they're all alone. Even though they do have family support, they don't look at it that way. They feel like they have been abandoned." Several caregivers described severe substance abuse problems in teenaged children. In some cases they had received treatment, but in many cases, the family seemed unsure what to do, and hoped the problem would just go away. A maternal grandfather did not see an arrest for theft as serious. The child reported he did not remember what happened because he had taken drugs. The grandfather thought that was funny, not an indication of more serious problems or of a need to intervene. He commented that if the child finished school [a vocational/technical high school] that the problems would end. Similarly, a grandmother talked about her grandson's most recent arrest. Her belief was that her grandson's only problem was having his mother in prison:

> We were out of town, and when we came back, there was a message from a probation officer to call him. That's how we found out. It was really stupid. He broke into a concession stand at the ball field just a few blocks from here and stole money, but there wasn't much so he stole candy. I said, "He hasn't had a rough life, he just hasn't had his mother here."

Finally, caregivers themselves often felt isolated. This was particularly true when a grandparent was raising her grandchildren. One commented that having the small children in the home separated her from other women her own age, whose children were now grown:

> I'm fifty-four, half my friends are grandparents. I, so, I'm not part of, when my kids were, were that age, ya know, part of, I had sibs, and cousins and stuff, we just had the family hand-me-down network. And my friends had kids in this same age range and that kind of thing. Um, and even though a lot of people my age are raising grandkids, not being a part of that. You know, when we go to play day at the park or something like that, everybody thinks I'm a grandma. Um, so that's kinda isolating, it's not uncommon these days to be, to be a grandparent or somebody a grandparent age raising a kid.

Finally, many of these children have health issues, often related to substance abuse by the mother during pregnancy. While the children are eligible for SoonerCare in many cases, if the caregiver does not have legal custody, obtaining insurance and health care can be difficult. Other caregivers have no legal standing to obtain medical care for the child. One man, a minister, had taken in a teenager who had shown up at his church. The boy was very frightened of foster care because he claimed his uncle had been sexually and physically abused in a foster home. So, the caregiver and child were "flying below the radar," in the words of one task force member.[2] However, this became a crisis when the child was diagnosed with a brain tumor. The caregiver had been unable to place the child on his own health insurance plan because he had no legal relationship to the child. The child had Medicaid in the past but did not know the case number, so the caregiver could not get it reinstated. The child developed a brain tumor, making medical care an urgent need.

> That was a big issue with his medical care; we finally went to a lawyer who went before a judge and declared it an emergency and they gave us temporary custody . . . They would not do the surgery until they had the guardian to sign off on it . . . I didn't know how to go about getting Medicaid. They would not give me any feedback because I was not his

guardian. I finally just made enough phone calls that someone felt sorry for me and gave me his case number. Then I could get help—if he were not on Medicaid, I don't know what we would have done.

In other cases, caregivers could not obtain legal guardianship because their family income would make the child ineligible for SoonerCare. In one grandmother's words, the situation was a catch-22.

Many caregivers described health issues face by the children, including poorly developed lungs and asthma as a result of premature birth, underdeveloped intestines, and seizure disorders. Medications were often very expensive and not always covered by Medicaid. Caregivers reported frustration with a system that did not seem to function well for children with incarcerated parents.

Summary

The Adverse Childhood Experiences (ACE) study outlines the ways in which chaotic, neglectful, and abusive childhoods are linked to risky behaviors and other problems during adulthood (Felitti et al. 1998). In an earlier chapter, I outlined how these adversities were linked to female offending. In this chapter, I suggest that the negative experiences faced by their children indicate cause for concern. Clearly, the children of incarcerated mothers are at high risk of experiencing a number of these adversities, including abuse, neglect, and of course, having a parent in prison. Thus, without effective interventions, there is a significant risk that children whose mothers are in prison will develop emotional problems, substance abuse problems, and ultimately end up in legal trouble. Without intervention and support for these children, if laws remain as they currently stand, the prison population will increase significantly over the next decade, at a time when the rest of the country is moving towards reduction of incarceration. Furthermore, these children are poised to experience mental health difficulties and educational problems.

While many caregivers are doing the best they can to take care of the children of women prisoners, taking on an additional child or children adds strain to any household. Few of these families are equipped to take on the additional financial burdens. Many of the children are eligible for state assistance, but the families are very hesitant to access those resources because of the additional financial stress it will place on the prisoners upon release. For aging caregivers, raising small children can be very difficult. At a time when they have finished bringing up their own children, they find themselves in the role of raising another generation. This can lead to depression and exhaustion, especially among grandmothers who are raising grandchildren.

Most women prisoners come from families with histories of dysfunction. Placing children in those homes puts them at potential risk of neglect and abuse (Sharp and Marcus-Mendoza 2001). In addition, placement with the father of many of the children is not always the best solution. While many of these men do not have criminal and drug histories, others do. Many prisoners as well as caregivers reported children living with fathers who were using and even selling drugs, often leaving the children with other people for long periods of time. Some caregivers who had one child of the prisoner shared concerns about the prisoner's other children, whom they could not care for but felt were in risky situations.

While the situation is bleak for many of the children of mothers in prison, there are also glimmers of hope. Recent awareness of the problem has led to many positive responses. In chapter 8, I will describe a few of the efforts being made to mitigate the harm done by the high incarceration rate of Oklahoma women.

CHAPTER 8

Winds of Change

OKLAHOMA IS a state of contradictions. Viewed by much of the nation as one of the most conservative states in the country due to its voting record in national elections, it is also a state with a populist history and a strong distrust of elitism. At the same time, it is a state whose major income comes from the oil and gas industry. Those two characteristics may appear to be in conflict, but often they are complementary, with contributions from leaders in the petroleum industry being the largest source of philanthropy in the state. The conservatism and punitive stance of the state legislature is counterbalanced by the restorative justice approach of leaders in state agencies as well as industry. That leadership has taken on the issue of female incarceration in the state and its impact on families as a major social issue.

Some legislative leaders such as former Speaker of the House Kris Steele have become outspoken advocates for new policies to reverse some of the damage done by past laws. While Oklahoma remains one of the most punitive states in the nation, especially where women are concerned, there is evidence of change. New programs are being developed to divert women from prison, and one of the larger county jails has developed a special program to help women in the jail develop the skills and support necessary for success in the community.

When I first began research on incarcerated women in the early 1990s few people were interested in the subject. That has changed over time. In late 2003, the state set up a task force to study the problem of incarceration of women. Many recommendations were made, but the main one enacted was the ongoing data collection that resulted in my partnership with the Oklahoma Commission on Children and Youth (OCCY). Shortly thereafter, I was asked to present my research to the Board of Corrections. Board members were intently focused on what the research showed, and they began investigating options for the treatment of women who offended, recognizing the role of addiction in the high female incarceration rate. They grilled me for a couple of hours about specific problems created by the mass incarceration of women, who were mainly mothers. They then visited innovative programs around the country searching for models to implement in Oklahoma.

One of the first innovations was Center Point, which opened in 2007. Center Point is an intensive program for women in the custody of the Department of Corrections (DOC) who have substance abuse problems. The program is a therapeutic community model, and participants are selected by the program director from interested women with substance abuse issues who are already sentenced to time in the prison system. While the women are still technically prisoners, they are addressed by names, not numbers. They live in a dormitory-style setting rather than in cells. Most importantly, the women earn the right to have their children with them for overnight or weekend visits. In a few cases, the child may actually get to live with the mother. The program only has 32 beds, however, meaning that only a few of the women who need the program can actually get into it. Still, it has definitely been a step in the right direction, and the success rate is very high.

Oklahoma has exceptional leadership in many key positions. The former director of the Department of Corrections had a clear grasp on the issues of incarcerated women and worked with lawmakers and others to develop diversionary programs and to acknowledge the need for woman-centered corrections. Furthermore, a separate division focusing on female offenders was created within the DOC in 2008. This was followed by the selection of a deputy director over that division whose training was as a psychologist with a focus on working with women with substance abuse issues. These are just two examples of the commitment of the Oklahoma DOC to the problems faced by Oklahoma's women prisoners. Many of those in upper management have also been strong advocates for diversionary programs. Additionally, one of the more important changes in the past few years has been the separation of female assessment from male assessment and the removal of the female offender assessment unit to Mabel Bassett Correctional Center. This has had a twofold impact on women prisoners. First, the women are no longer temporarily housed in a male facility. Second and more importantly, the assessments of women prisoners now utilize gender-sensitive instruments and result in gender-appropriate plans for those women.

Facing budget shortfalls and immense cuts, the policies of the DOC have often been constrained in providing programming. As a result, the women's facilities have developed strong working relationships with volunteer organizations to maximize the programming with limited resources. Since around 2006, the DOC has acknowledged the importance of focusing on trauma in the treatment of women offenders and has strived to provide trauma-informed care and other gender-sensitive programs to women prisoners, combining volunteer efforts with other programs. A life-coaching program is one example of a volunteer effort that some of the women have reported to me as beneficial. This program helps the women identify their personal thought patterns that have interfered with their abilities to be successful. The goal is to help the women identify their values, get their behaviors in consonance with those values, and empower them to do so.

Lisa Smith, director of OCCY, is another state leader who has helped focus attention not only on the plight of women in the state's prison but also on how their children are affected. Lisa was assistant director of the agency when I began partnering with OCCY. She was later promoted, and she has made these issues a major focus of the agency. She is joined by dedicated staff, including Treasa Lansdowne, Jack Chapman, Michael Walsh, Dan Ingram, and Doris Simms, all of whom work tirelessly on problems related to children of incarcerated parents. OCCY is the state agency that has become the leader in efforts to improve the lives of incarcerated women and their children.

Over the past few years, a number of groups have put significant resources into policy changes and public education. In January 2010, policy makers, corrections officials, service providers, academics, and community leaders from around the state met at the Complex Dialogues Summit at Oklahoma Christian University in Edmond, Oklahoma. The focus of the meeting was development of policy to reduce the high female incarceration rate. The keynote speaker was a representative from another state who had authored legislation that had been successful in reducing recidivism. One piece of legislation that resulted from this summit was HB 2998 (2010), which authorized a pilot diversionary program for female offenders in Oklahoma County, which will be discussed in greater depth later in this chapter. Another positive outcome came from the judicial subcommittee of the summit. In the words of one of the summit organizers:

> The committee worked with organizers of the judicial conference, district attorneys conference and Oklahoma Bar Association annual conference to include a session on female incarceration as part of their 2010 conferences, which were held in November. The judicial conference held a session on female incarceration and invited district attorneys to attend. The Oklahoma Bar Association also hosted a session focused on incarceration during their conference. There is more work to be done, and this committee played an important role by identifying current and proposed statutes and practices that are having a significant impact on the female incarceration rate in our state and discussed these with the legislative committee. (Bush 2010)

Additional efforts were made by service agencies and providers to identify resources already in place, resources still needed to improve opportunities for at-risk women as well as those already involved in the criminal justice system. During the 2011 legislative session, a bill was passed that ordered a task force on children of incarcerated parents to further study the problem. The task force was composed of representatives from state agencies, law enforcement, treatment providers from throughout the state, those affected by parental incarceration, various arms of the court system and researchers (see Appendix B). I was asked to co-chair this task force. After more than six months developing data and recommendations, the task force published a report with seven major recommendations:

- Support activities that serve to maintain contact between an incarcerated parent and a minor child.
- Eliminate any barriers that prevent children of incarcerated parents from accessing quality health care, regardless of their ability to pay. Children have a right to have access to quality health care despite their living situation.
- Develop a consistent statewide training curriculum which serves to educate participants on the sweeping effects that parental involvement in the criminal justice system has on children.
- Provide parent education programs (including child development) to incarcerated parents to help support a healthy and strong parent-child relationship.
- Provide information to incarcerated non-custodial parents who have court-ordered child support obligations on how to responsibly address those financial obligations while incarcerated.
- Expand the use of community-based sentencing options in conjunction with evidence-based intervention programs and services targeted to reduce criminal risk factors.
- Designate the Oklahoma Commission on Children and Youth as the official state agency responsible for coordinating research, the collection of data, and creating a resource clearinghouse; developing an educational toolkit describing available services to children of incarcerated parents; and coordination of an advisory committee to continue to work collaboratively with agencies and service providers to better meet the needs and improve the quality of life for children of incarcerated parents. (Children of Incarcerated Parents Task Force 2012)

Two of the recommendations were particularly important in addressing the needs of Oklahoma's women offenders. First, the Task Force recommended expanding the use of community sentencing and interventions. Second, the OCCY was designated as a data repository and clearinghouse. As well, the commission was tasked with forming an advisory committee to continue working on the issues. That committee is currently meeting regularly and working on continued data collection, legislative recommendations, and toolkits for consumers.

The recommendation for expanding community sentencing and interventions had several secondary recommendations. First, prior to recommending sentencing, a thorough assessment of risks and problems should be undertaken. Second, when there were minor children involved, determination should be made that children would be appropriately placed, and treatment programs should be expanded to allow custodial parents to remain with their children. Treatment and intervention should be able to address trauma issues. Where possible, offenders should be diverted to community-based programs, not only for drug offenders but for those whose crimes were drug related. Acceptance into court diversion programs should be made more accessible. Procedures for expunging records should be made affordable. Savings gained through use of community-based options should be utilized in early intervention programs such as substance abuse and mental health treatment and parenting skills programs. These recommendations are clear evidence of the willingness and desire to move away from incarceration as the primary response to offending, especially drug offending.

Subcommittees of the Children of Incarcerated Parents (CIP) Advisory Committee have also been working on projects to include educating incarcerated parents on their rights to defer court-ordered child support while in prison, putting together a toolkit for caregivers of children of incarcerated parents, and a comprehensive online system for those who provide services to allow them to link cases so that all the needs of these families and children can be met. Committee members include researchers, state agencies leaders, nonprofit organizations, and formerly incarcerated individuals.

In addition to Kris Steele, a number of other state legislators have also focused on the problem of female incarceration. While there are too many to enumerate, several stand out: State Senator Constance Johnson, State Representative Jeannie McDaniel, State Senator Brian Bingman, State Senator Patrick Anderson and State Representative Jabar Shumate. All have played a role in focusing state attention on resolving the over-incarceration of women.

Private philanthropy has played a key role in some of the changes in the state, too. The George Kaiser Family Foundation, based in Tulsa, Oklahoma, has led the way in concentrating on the need for change. Their focus is on interrupting the cycle of intergenerational poverty, and they have specifically taken on helping incarcerated women and their children over the past several years. They support a number of programs that specifically focus on female offenders and their children.[1]

One program funded by the foundation focuses on reentry for women returning to Tulsa County, working with the Community Service Council and the Resonance Center for Women. Resonance provides both rehabilitation services and job skills training to women involved with the criminal justice system. Extensive reentry planning is done prior to release, and support is offered to the women when they return to the community.

The most exciting programs are those designed as diversionary programs, or alternatives to incarceration. In 2009 the George Kaiser Family Foundation launched Women in Recovery. The Women in Recovery program serves women in the Tulsa area who might otherwise be sent to prison. The program is an intensive outpatient program that takes a holistic approach to women offenders, providing assistance with varied issues such as housing, mental health needs, and substance abuse treatment. In addition to substance abuse counseling, the Women in Recovery program offers women tools ranging from anger management and stress reduction to job placement. The program operates in cooperation with the DOC. The women may live in halfway houses or sober living facilities and be under intensive supervision.

The Inasmuch Foundation of the Gaylord family has also been a major contributor to programs for women offenders in Oklahoma. The foundation has been a major supporter of the ReMerge program in particular. While Women in Recovery was designed for women in the Tulsa area, little existed until recently for other women in the state. Representative Steele and other legislators authored HB 2998 in 2010. This innovative bill created a plan for the DOC to create pilot programs funded by both state dollars and private contributions. These pilot programs will create programs for both diversionary programs and reentry services for nonviolent offenders who are also the primary caregivers of minor children. The first diversion program is ReMerge of Oklahoma County . . . Moms Breaking the Cycle. The target group is women who are either caregivers of small children or pregnant, who would have otherwise been sent to prison for a nonviolent offense. The District Attorney's office, the office of the Public Defender, private attorneys, the Oklahoma County judicial system and the DOC are all involved in the program. Using a wraparound model, the program addresses women's needs for food, shelter, clothing, transportation, education, job training and placement, behavioral health and domestic violence interventions, parenting skills training, and spiritual support. The women remain in the community, often placed in a sober-living house or transitional living program but are under close supervision from the Department of Corrections. They are assisted with health care, education, training and employment placement. Finally, they can receive assistance with developing spiritual support, while under close supervision in the community. The program is designed to serve up to fifty women each year. Currently more than thirty women have entered the program.

While the George Kaiser Family Foundation and the Inasmuch Foundation have been major contributors to innovative programs for Oklahoma's women offenders, they are not the only ones. Several of the major energy companies such as Chesapeake and SandRidge have also supported efforts around the state.

Another piece of legislation, HB 2131, was signed into law on May 12, 2011. Kris Steele worked tirelessly while he was in office to enact sensible policies that would address the incarceration issues of the state. In HB 2131, the goal was to use community sentencing and electronic monitoring more often and incarceration less often. Touted as the state's first efforts in decades to return to alternative sentencing, the goal is to help offenders stay out of prison and become productive members of society.

At the county level, Cleveland County Sheriff's Department has launched S-CAP (Second Chance Act Program). S-CAP was founded in 2009 and works with women in the Cleveland County jail. When the women are released, the program provides them with housing and food assistance, job readiness training, and its own unique form of case management. Trained navigators work with each woman, helping her find safe housing, preparing her for work, and helping her face problems on the outside. A navigator is more than a case manager, though. A navigator also serves as both mentor and friend. The navigator not only helps the woman locate resources but actually takes her around to various appointments and agencies to ensure she is able to get the help she needs. Women participating in S-CAP may be taken for a makeover at a local beauty college, or they and their children may get a day at the museum.

Because of the bonding between inmates and navigators, participation has been high in the program. Initial contact and planning begins while the women are still in the county jail. Upon release, their navigator helps them reestablish their lives, often taking them to get driver's licenses reinstated, to apply for jobs, and—when funding is available—helping them get into safe housing. The program operated a drop-in facility for a while, but due to loss of funding, they are now located in the sheriff's office. Approximately 300 women have entered the program, and currently more than 100 remain active. The program is currently seeking additional funding to enable it to move back into its own separate location, and they are working with a junior college to establish on-site courses. One of the more exciting plans is to incorporate a training program for water technicians into the on-site program. This program will train women to be able to test water for municipalities. From what the program director and undersheriff have said, it appears that state municipalities are willing to hire convicted felons for these jobs.

Programs for Children

There are a number of innovative and effective programs available for children with mothers in prison in Oklahoma. A number of faith-based programs are available to help children and their mothers. New Day Camp, administered by Criminal Justice and Mercy Ministries of the United Methodist Church, is one of several programs that this denomination administers statewide. Any child with an incarcerated parent is eligible for membership. One of the strengths of the program is that it uses small groups that foster a bond between leaders and members. The camp features water sports and typical camp activities. The camp is free for the child, and children who do not have appropriate clothing can get free items at the camp store.

Operation Hope Prison Ministries works to maintain contact between incarcerated mothers and their children, among other things. In cooperation with Dr. Eddie Warrior Correctional Center, their volunteers take children to the prison for a four-hour playday three times a year, and around 100 children are served annually. While this is a small number, it nonetheless is helping to improve contact between women prisoners and their children. Not only are the children allowed to visit with their mothers (or in some cases, grandmothers) for hours, but they also participate in healthy and fun activities while at the prison. Face-painting, games, picture-taking, and other activities are all designed to foster bonding between mother and child.

Angel Tree Ministry ensures that children of prisoners are not forgotten at Christmas. Prisoners are allowed to submit the name and contact information to the program, and caregivers are contacted to ensure that they want the children to participate.[2] Using donations, volunteers then put together gifts for all children and deliver them, along with gift cards to help purchase Christmas dinners.

The most unique program I found is Little Light Christian School, which serves the children of prisoners. Director Robin Khoury had years of experience with ministry to women prisoners at Mabel Bassett. In 2012, she expanded her ministry to the children, opening an elementary school. Robin is passionate about helping, and she spent considerable time educating herself and her staff about the problems these children have experienced. When looking for a location, she visited a decrepit building in the northern part of Oklahoma City. While at the site, she was approached by a minister who said that building was not really safe but that he would let them use his church for the school. The school uses a core academic curriculum and adds art and music classes, as well as some religious teachings. Each child not only has instruction from a teacher, but volunteer learning coaches work with them individually. Many of the volunteers are experienced educators who are now retired. The school even has a therapy dog and a garden the children have helped plant. While the initial enrollment is small, Robin is a visionary who hopes to expand the program.

There are also two important secular programs that are having an impact on the children. The Big Brothers Big Sisters Amachi Program in Oklahoma received a $1.6 million grant to support the program. However, funding to the program was cut. Big Brothers Big Sisters of Oklahoma had been awarded the grant for three years beginning in fiscal year 2011. In 2011, the U.S. Department of Health and Human Services eliminated all funding for its Mentoring Children of Prisoners Program. Thus, funding from October 1, 2011 through September 30, 2013 was no longer available. Most readers are familiar, no doubt, with Big Brothers Big Sisters, a national mentoring program. The Amachi Program is a special program for children with an incarcerated parent. Older mentors are matched with these children, helping to foster healthy bonds and provide good role models. The Amachi Program recently was awarded a grant through the OCCY, which received funds to support a statewide mentoring program. The Amachi Program was the only mentoring program that met the requirement of being statewide and was therefore funded.

The other program that is having considerable impact is the Girl Scouts Beyond Bars Program (Moses 1995). Sheila Harbert, the charismatic leader of Oklahoma's Girl Scouts Beyond Bars program, has worked diligently to ensure that Project MEND (Mothers Encouraging and Nurturing Their Daughters) reaches girls (and now boys) throughout the state. Originally launched at Turley Center in Tulsa and partly funded by the George Kaiser Family Foundation, the program now exists in six correctional facilities. The focus is on building strong and healthy relationships between women prisoners and their daughters through the Girl Scouts program.

> Together, they participate in a unique Girl Scout troop with curriculum that includes drug and alcohol prevention, conflict resolution, and other valuable life skills. Guest speakers discuss self-esteem, healthy eating and exercise, dealing with stress, and anger management. Animosity between daughters and mothers is tackled head on. Girls also go on trips together and participate in community service, as they would in any other traditional Girl Scout troop. Once the mothers return home, many choose to continue in the program with their daughters in a special troop for bridged MEND participants. (Girl Scouts of Eastern Oklahoma n.d.)

The program has been highly successful, with literally hundreds of participants since it was started in 2002. According to Sheila Harbert, none of "her girls" have gone to prison. The program received widespread attention when a University of Oklahoma student, Amina Benalioulhaj, produced a video about Oklahoma's women prisoners (2010). Amina, who was my student, had done an internship with me early in her college career, helping me organize contact lists of caregivers for potential interviews. She then took my Women, Girls, and Crime course, and she made the film her senior project for her major in Women's and Gender Studies. The documentary, which lasts about forty minutes, includes not only footage of the women and their children and interviews with prisoners, but also interviews with corrections officials and service providers such as Sheila Harbert. The film has received considerable attention around the state and has been shown in a wide range of venues to help educate the public. According to Amina:

> I've studied domestic violence, the gender wage gap, the feminization of poverty, divorce, single motherhood, abortion, reproductive rights, and sexual health education. All these issues that touch women in particular touch incarcerated women disproportionately . . . The most important thing that I've learned interacting with these women and their children is that they're human. (Larson 2010)

Girls Scouts Beyond Bars of Eastern Oklahoma has widened its focus in recent years, adding two important programs. Boys 2 MENd extends programming to the sons of incarcerated mothers. Project Reconnect has added a reentry program for the prisoner mothers. This program builds on the relationships begun in Project MEND and offers a variety of supports and services to women returning home from prison. To become a participant, the woman must have participated in the in-prison program and be willing to undergo training and evaluation. Services offered include:

- Vocational training
- Transportation to training
- Drug counseling
- Housing assistance
- Clothing assistance
- Job placement after graduation
- Meals during training
- Life-changing workshops
- Transportation for children for enrichment activities
- Tutoring for children
- Fun outings for children
- Free Girl Scout registration

The women enrolled in this program participate in a twelve-week training program and must pass a workforce skills test. In 2010, the services of the Girls Scouts of Eastern Oklahoma were further expanded to incorporate a one-on-one mentoring program (Girl Scouts of Eastern Oklahoma n.d.). This program is designed to help mothers navigate the problems they face upon release in order to facilitate reintegration into the community.

SUMMARY

Oklahoma appears to be heading in a more positive direction, although there is strong resistance in the state to what is often seen as being "soft on crime." Countless individuals and leaders are working tirelessly to develop programs and to educate the public about the causes of female incarceration as well as how to respond to female crime. I began studying the problems in this state in early 1997. At that time, few were interested in why Oklahoma had such a high female incarceration rate. The general attitude was that we should harshly punish anyone who violated the law.

Fifteen years later, although the incarceration rate remains high, it is rare to go a week without reading or viewing a major news story about the issues. Furthermore, the majority of those stories focus on the triangulated relationship between abuse, mental health problems, and addiction. They also generally acknowledge the negative impact on the children of these women. Today, it would surprise me to hear a public figure or academic state that, "Oklahoma has mean women." While there is still some disagreement about the best way to address the problem, the movement is towards earlier intervention.

Because the state is relatively small, leaders in the public sector, the private sector and the academy all seem to know each other and are working together to change the legal system and revive needed social services such as substance abuse and mental health treatment. However, while there are many people in the state legislature who are part of this, there are still those who want to enact ever tougher laws. Thus change happens slowly. Even so, I remain encouraged that change is happening.

While there have been many positive changes and countless individuals working on resolving the problems of incarcerated women in the state, not all of the changes have been quite so positive. The director of the Oklahoma Department of Corrections has recently announced his intention to retire, and there is no guarantee that all the changes there will continue. Nonetheless, overall the movement in the state has been towards not only reducing the rate of incarceration but also addressing the problems that lead women into drug addiction and crime.

CHAPTER 9

Lessons Learned and Moving Forward

THE LIVES of women prisoners in Oklahoma are bleak: before, during, and after their imprisonment. The research reported in this book documents their lives of poverty, abuse, mental illness, and substance abuse, and the women's voices help contextualize their lives and their struggles. These struggles occur in an environment that is harsh and punitive, with laws that tend to put offenders away and out of sight for extended periods of time rather than intervening to help those with mental health and substance abuse problems. While there are definitely changes occurring in some parts of the state's leadership, the laws have not changed enough to reverse the high incarceration rate. Furthermore, little is being done to intervene in the lives of girls and women *before* they are caught up in the criminal justice system. Drug treatment is scarce for those who do not have insurance, and most programs for those without insurance primarily treat criminal justice-referred clients. The woman who has a drug problem and no criminal record may be unable to secure one of the limited treatment slots and must wait until she gets into legal trouble to get help. Furthermore, because so many of the women who end up in prison are single mothers, they are even less likely than men to be able to get treatment for a drug problem. They usually have no one to care for their children while they are getting help. Thus, they struggle with addiction, often for years, until they end up in prison.

The high incarceration rate of women in Oklahoma can be explained by two things: mean lives and mean laws. These women tend to come from highly dysfunctional families. Many grew up in households characterized by divorce, sexual abuse, physical abuse, addiction, and criminal behavior. They have then replicated the abusive conditions of their childhoods in their adult lives. Their children are now growing up in similar situations, ensuring the cycle of drug use, crime, and incarceration will continue if effective interventions do not occur.

This book was framed in feminist strain theory, informed by both general strain theory and feminist pathways approaches. In chapter 1, I outlined three pathways common to the women in this study, drawing on earlier feminist approaches. Poverty and perceived disadvantage characterized the first pathway. These were women who came from families that had experienced multigenerational crime and addiction. The second pathway involved women who linked themselves with criminal men, often being arrested for minimal participation in crimes perpetrated by those men and sometimes taking the fall for crimes committed by the men in their lives. The third pathway involved the extensive abuse histories of the women, both in childhood and adulthood. In many of the women, abuse led to mental health issues, especially post-traumatic stress disorder, anxiety and depression. Many began using drugs to cope with their negative emotions, and the drugs led them either directly or indirectly to prison. The Adverse Childhood Experiences (ACE) study provided an additional framework for examining the often chaotic backgrounds of these women, providing further evidence that childhood strains are linked to mental health problems and addiction in adulthood. These three pathways are similar to what other researchers have found. For example, Salisbury and Van Voorhis described three main pathways to incarceration for women. The first pathway started with childhood victimization leading to mental illness and substance abuse. In the second path described by Salisbury and Van Voorhis, relationships that further victimized the women were linked to offending. Finally, the third pathway was a result of limited social and human capital (2009).

However, emphasis should be placed on the reality that these three pathways are not necessarily separate and discrete. While some women fell neatly into only one category, most were found in all three or at least some combination of two or more pathways. Women raised in poverty and criminogenic environments also frequently experienced abuse, chaotic family lives, and childhood maltreatment. Many of these women used drugs both as a learned behavior from their families and partners and to cope with their extensive histories of strain and abuse. Finally, their choices in male partners were constrained by both the environments in which they were raised and their substance abuse. Their pool of potential mates was limited primarily to drug-using, criminal men who were often abusive. Women who use drugs or engage in crime are far less likely than men who engage in the same behaviors to find mates who are well-integrated into society, because they are seen as doubly deviant, and therefore in some way not worthy of the opportunity to improve their situations (Schur 1984).

Clearly the lives of the women described in this book are characterized by multifaceted problems that at least partially explain their offending. What is clear is that women's offending often results from mean lives. Childhood abuse, poverty, low educational attainment, and a limited pool of intimate partners contribute to not only their initial offending but also their persistent offending (Salisbury and Van Voorhis 2009).

A merging of general strain theory with feminist pathways approaches can help us understand why women offend, why they continue to offend, and also why some women with the same backgrounds do not offend. Feminist strain theory helps fill in a gap that exists in feminist pathways approaches. Pathways approaches rightly pinpoint how women's social positions in a patriarchal society lead to victimization, which in turn leads to offending, especially drug use. However, most pathways approaches do not have the capacity to explain why some women who have those experiences do not offend. Integrating Agnew's (1999; 2006) general strain theory into a pathways approach provides a mechanism to explain why not all strain leads to drug use and crime.

The knowledge gained from examining the lives of women prisoners through this framework can then be used to help develop programs for these women. Helping the women resolve emotional and psychological issues that result from the poverty and abuse they have experienced, and teaching them how to develop their personal resources and alternative coping strategies, could empower those women who have experienced mean lives, allowing them to develop new ways to respond to trauma. This suggestion ties in with recommendations made by Salisbury and Van Voorhis (2009) and others recommending effective interventions designed to enhance personal and social resources. By knowing what characteristics help prevent some stressed and abused women from turning to drugs and criminal activity as a coping strategy, programs can be developed to help those who are involved in the system change their trajectories and become successful.

The second half of the equation explaining the high rate of female imprisonment is the presence of mean laws. Oklahoma is a microcosm that reflects the punitive laws and policies that have led to the massive rise in the imprisonment of women in the United States since the 1980s. Because Oklahoma has very harsh and repressive laws, this draconian response to women's drug use is carried to an extreme. However, the policies and laws that drive the incarceration rate in Oklahoma are different from those in other parts of the country primarily in degree, not in kind. Harsh sentences for drug possession and less use of probation increase the number of women who end up in Oklahoma prisons. Other damaging policies include life without parole sentences for drug charges, or having to serve 85 percent of an already long sentence before accruing credits for time served. Additionally, defining drug delivery offenses by quantity possessed rather than any actual drug sales or delivery means that some women who were addicted or involved with criminal men are now serving sentences for drug trafficking.

The popular belief of the general public continues to be that the high incarceration rate is due to a high crime rate. With about half the women serving time on drug offenses and most of the rest for drug-related offenses, this is clearly not the only explanation. However, effective drug treatment for women without insurance is very limited, especially for those with children. There is a strong need to increase the availability of resources such as drug treatment, mental health treatment, and job training. And yet there is very little funding available to do this. Clearly, this needs to change. The prison system has become one of the largest providers for mental health care and substance abuse treatment. This is more costly, not only financially but in the harm done to those caught up in the system. Irreparable damage is done to those who are unable to secure needed treatment and ultimately end up in prison. Not only are those individuals damaged, but their families, especially their children, are also harmed. Under current policies, each year thousands of children in Oklahoma experience losing their mothers to prison. Since the recidivism rate is quite low, each year a new group of a thousand or more women enter the prison system for the first time, many of them leaving behind small children. The disastrous impact this has on Oklahoma families is clear. And that impact disproportionately affects those with the fewest resources—the poor and members of minority groups.

While Oklahoma may have more punitive laws than most other states, the similarity of Oklahoma prisoners to those in other jurisdictions is strong enough to make the findings in this book applicable to women prisoners in the United States in general, and even to women prisoners in other countries. The majority of the women are mothers, and they are single (Kruttschnitt et al. 2013). Many of the women are incarcerated for low-level drug offenses or probation and parole violations. Furthermore, one of the biggest problems women experience while in prison is finding ways to fill their time. Kruttschnitt and her colleagues found that women who were able to be involved in programs felt that they had more control over their lives. The Oklahoma women often faced difficulty getting into programs because of limited availability and long waiting lists. This brings to light one of the greatest paradoxes resulting from the increased incarceration of women. While we have been locking up more of them for a number of years, we are at the same time putting less funding into the prisons for education, vocational training, and mental health services. Department of Corrections officials have tried to counterbalance this through creative use of volunteers to provide needed services, but more funding is needed.

As noted above, the majority of women incarcerated in Oklahoma's prisons are mothers, and their children suffer. Numerous programs have been developed to assist these children, but as we have shown, those most in need of intervention are those least likely to participate in programs. The advisory group working on this issue is trying to find a way to get the school systems involved in order to reach more children. The group is also working on helping service providers coordinate their services to the children of prisoners and their caregivers. To that end, a screening questionnaire has been developed to assist service providers and is in the testing stage. The goal of the screening instrument is to identify how many of those seeking services with housing, food, and health care have the children of an incarcerated parent in their household. This will be used to modify outreach efforts to more effectively reach this population with all the services the children need. Without intervention, these children are the prisoners of the future.

Some states have recognized the need to revisit their statutes, taking measures to reduce the populations in their overflowing prisons. Oklahoma has taken steps to both decrease and increase the prison population, so things have remained roughly the same. Diversionary programs for women are being put into place, but stricter probation and parole violation consequences are probably offsetting some of the changes. To have a real impact on the high incarceration rate, there are a number of problems that should be addressed.

First, the state needs more easily accessible mental health and substance abuse treatment for those without insurance. Second, more work needs to be done to reduce the abuse of children. Intervening prior to any criminal justice involvement is ultimately the best solution. Third, for those who are arrested, more diversionary programs with wraparound services are needed. To be most effective, these programs should be individualized, gender-responsive, and include strong social support programs, such as the navigation program of the Cleveland County Sheriff's office. While these types of interventions are costly, in the long run they are far less expensive than mass incarceration, both financially and socially. Fourth, for those women who do end up in prison, more services are needed. While the state has a number of excellent programs and services, funding to provide these services to more women is sorely needed. Finally, those women leaving prison have a number of needs that must be met if we are to reduce the number returning to prison and reduce the possibility that their children will end up in the criminal justice system. Supportive reentry services are needed, but that is only part of the solution. The returning women find that they are faced with a society that does not want to help them rejoin the fold. Finding jobs and safe housing are both very difficult. And even though they may eventually find some type of work, they are often caught up in paying fines and fees that ensure that they will remain marginalized, even if they are able to avoid having their parole revoked for noncompliance. They are both legally and socially barred from improving their situations in many ways. Legally, they can no longer get some types of housing assistance and are also barred from many jobs. Socially, landlords and employers often do not want these women. Financially, they often must pay out hundreds of dollars each month just to comply with the terms of their parole. Parole costs include mandatory services they must obtain and parole fees they must pay. They also have to pay fines, restitution, and court costs. Additionally, some of the institutions of higher learning restrict their enrollment, requiring the woman with a felony conviction to convince an admissions board that she should not be automatically barred from enrolling. Finally, it is very difficult for the women to ever escape their pasts. It is quite difficult for them to have their records expunged. Generally, unless they have deferred adjudication, a governor's pardon is the only option. This requires that they hire legal assistance to petition the governor. Since most of the women are struggling to survive financially, few have the resources to pursue a pardon. A few legislators have tried authoring legislation to allow nonviolent offenders to more routinely have their records expunged, but to date these efforts have been unsuccessful. Efforts continue to try to educate the state's residents about how this would ultimately benefit them, by allowing former offenders to integrate into the society and become productive members.

While the situation is dire, there are also bright spots. Currently, there are numerous individuals, advisory groups, researchers and legislators educating the public and the state legislature on the need to revise state laws, which have become increasingly harsh over the past three decades, particularly in regards to drug offenses. Reform is needed. The women who are serving life without parole sentences for drug offenses have the potential to be rehabilitated and succeed in society.

One of the leaders in the reform movement reached his term limit and is no longer able to introduce bills. Fortunately, he remains committed to enacting change, working now from outside the legislative system. Others continue to address the problem from within. In the current political climate in Oklahoma, change comes slowly, and with much resistance, so real meaningful change will not occur quickly. The situation has taken a few decades to develop, and it will take time to improve the situation. The research in this book has highlighted the need for diversionary programs, drug treatment, and prison programs for Oklahoma's women offenders, as well as the need for changes in the statutes. Hopefully, the success of the current diversionary programs will convince the public and lawmakers of the need to increase funding for programs, while also changing the laws that make incarceration the first choice.

The story of Oklahoma's women prisoners and their children is a sad story, but there are reasons to be hopeful. Although public awareness of the problem is still somewhat limited, it has improved significantly. In 1997, when

I first began studying the problem, there were very few people who were interested or willing to engage in efforts to bring about change. Indeed, some even objected to research on the problems of incarcerated women and their children. More than fifteen years later, it is one of the primary issues on which both the public and private sectors have focused attention. Hopefully, in the foreseeable future, Oklahoma will not rank first in the incarceration of women. Until that occurs, however, efforts to provide women with the services they need to successfully reenter society are of paramount importance.

APPENDIX A: RESEARCH METHODS

THIS BOOK is based on several research projects, including surveys of prisoners, interviews with caregivers of the children of women prisoners, in-depth interviews with women released from prison who subsequently returned, and interviews of women who have successfully stayed out of prison after release. In addition, some information has been drawn from personal correspondence with prisoners and former prisoners. In those cases, I have obtained permission from the correspondent to use her words in this book.

The initial research was conducted in 1997 and 1998, on both male and female drug offenders. The instrument used contained questions about families, including economic changes, placement of children, problems with children, domestic violence, and the effects of incarceration on the family, as well as questions about demographics, criminal records, and drug use. Questions from existing measures as well as questions constructed by the research team were included. Some questions were drawn from the National Youth Survey, Wave VI (Elliot 1983), Men's Relationship Study (Umberson 1995), Inmate Population Survey (Marcus-Mendoza and Briody 1996), and the AIDS Initial Assessment (National Institute on Drug Abuse 1993). We added questions about changes in family income, problems that children might have faced, and more open-ended questions concerning perceptions of the positive and negative effects of their incarceration on their families (Sharp et al. 1997).

As a result of Oklahoma SJR 48 (2004), I conducted the Oklahoma Study on Incarcerated Women and their children from 2004 through 2009, and the majority of the data for this book comes from that work. Most years, I surveyed about 11 percent of the women housed in the Oklahoma Department of Corrections (DOC) and also interviewed the caregivers of their children.

The questionnaires included extensive questions about the women's histories, both during childhood and in adulthood. Additionally, they were asked about their mental health histories and treatment, and their substance abuse and treatment. They also were administered standardized instruments on self-esteem, self-efficacy, coping strategies, and emotional responses to strain. From 2004 forward, questions from the Adverse Childhood Experiences (ACE) study were incorporated. The second half of each questionnaire focused on the children of the incarcerated women, including placement both before and after the mother's imprisonment, problems experienced by the children, resources available to them, and so forth. Each year, a series of open-ended questions at the end of the instrument allowed the women to put into their own words their concerns, as well as what they thought they needed to help them succeed.

In 2004, 203 women prisoners were administered the questionnaire, of whom 119 participated in the more in-depth second phase that focused on questions about children. As in the 1997 research, I again ran into issues related to conducting research in correctional institutions. The women themselves were suspicious and hostile when we administered the survey. Our response rates varied significantly from one institution to the next. For example, at the Turley Halfway House in Tulsa, despite making prior arrangements with staff and sending a list of the sample that was being asked to participate, I drove all the way across the state only to discover that the majority of the women in my sample were away from the facility on passes. In contrast, at Hillside Correctional Center, more than three-fourths of the women who were in the proposed sample were present and willing to participate, and at Dr. Eddie Warrior Correctional Center, almost 90 percent of the women on the list chose to complete the questionnaire.

However, fewer than half of the women in the sample drawn for Mabel Bassett Correctional Center participated. There were a number of reasons for this. Some of the women drawn in that sample were incarcerated for harming their children, making them inappropriate subjects for the study, according to the DOC. Others were simply not available, while others were simply unwilling. It was during this project that I discovered several dynamics that could impact my research. One was that if one or two inmates were negatively vocal about the research, others would follow them and leave the room. Another was that staff had an enormous impact on the participation level. At Eddie Warrior, staff stayed out of the room and let the women make their own decision about participation. At Mabel Bassett, staff stayed in the room, watching the prisoners complete the questionnaires. Prisoners who asked questions of the research team were sometimes reprimanded. This, of course, could be in part due to the different security levels. Eddie Warrior is minimum security, whereas Mabel Bassett, at that time, was primarily medium- and maximum-security level.

The survey was repeated in 2005 with women who had not participated in the 2004 research. No new data were collected in 2006. However, in 2007 I again administered the survey to women who had not participated in 2004 or 2005. In this study, 234 women were surveyed. A representative sample was again drawn, stratified by facility, race, and time in the DOC system. We again ran into problems with one facility when a prisoner led a number of prisoners out of the room, stating she did not want the DOC to know anything more about her.

The 2008 study went more smoothly and resulted in 297 completed questionnaires. In fact, at Eddie Warrior, the women gave me a standing ovation because they were so pleased that I was continuing the research. Some policy changes and programmatic changes had started occurring, in part as a result of my annual reports on incarcerated women in the state. That year, the response rate was 75 percent; it would have been even higher but for two reasons. First, a number of women had been transferred or were in segregated housing. Second, the day that we went there, the women and their children were participating in a playday, and some understandably chose not to participate in the study so that they could maximize their time with their children.

The final study was conducted in 2009, with 301 subjects. The overall response rate was 60 percent, somewhat lower than the prior year. However, this was primarily due to problems at Mabel Bassett. Some on the list had been transferred out already, while others were unable to participate due to physical or mental health problems because all women with serious health issues are imprisoned at Mabel Bassett. However, we were able for the first time to survey women just admitted to the DOC in the sample because of the new assessment center at Mabel Bassett. Nonetheless, 56 percent of the names drawn for that facility did participate. Close to two-thirds at the other three facilities also participated.

METHODS FOR THE CAREGIVER STUDY

In several of the years (2004, 2007, and 2009), I conducted a study of the caregivers of incarcerated women in order to provide more information about what happens to the children when a mother goes to prison. At the time we administered the survey to the women prisoners, we asked those who were willing to provide contact information for the caregivers of their children. The last page of the questionnaire asked for contact information and permission to contact the caregivers. We used the contact information provided by the prisoners to contact caregivers and request permission to interview them. Each year, only a small percentage of the names provided to us could be located and were willing to participate. Some expressed concern that any information they provided could be harmful to the prisoners' attempts to parole, despite assurances about confidentiality. It became painfully clear that caregivers, like the prisoners themselves, had very limited trust in anything that appeared to be in any way associated with governmental agencies. Even those who did participate expressed similar concerns.

The sample of the 2004 caregivers study was limited in size to twenty respondents. The contact information given by many of the women for the caregivers was often inaccurate, thus I was unable to contact many of them. And as mentioned above, some of the caregivers I did contact were distrustful of any research that was even tangentially related to the DOC or other state agencies. Therefore, only twenty caregivers were interviewed in depth about the children in their care. In 2007, I also had difficulty finding caregivers willing to participate, and only thirteen were interviewed. In 2008, no caregiver study was carried out due to lack of funding. In 2009, twenty caregivers were also interviewed.

FORMER PRISONERS

Chapter 5 is based on in-depth interviews of women who were released and then returned to prison. Interviews were conducted by my doctoral student at the time, Dr. Juanita Ortiz, with twenty-one women who were serving a second or subsequent incarceration at the time of the interview. A description of these women is provided in Table A.1.

TABLE A.1

Subject Demographics, Women Returning to Prison

Code Name	Age	Race	Days Out of Prison
Amanda	42	White	981
Amos	56	Native American	818
Angel	28	Native American	352
Anne	35	Black	783
Bad Girl	47	Black	321
B-Dog	35	White	531
Beth	38	White	575
Beverly	32	Black	550
Bree	34	Black	530
Cody	37	Black	370
Dirty Lucy	49	White	656
Laci	46	White	916
Lone Wolf	34	Native American	859
Missy	30	Black	605
Pooty	29	Native American	1084
Shoshone	55	Native American	867
Sweet	35	Black	900
Tamara	25	White	686
Vanda	39	White	279
Vivian	49	White	760
Young	35	Black	1006
Average	38.6 years		687.1

In comparison, chapter 6 focuses on interviews with twelve women who have successfully stayed out of prison. Subjects for this chapter were drawn primarily from women who had contacted me after their release and women they then referred for interviews. The material for this chapter was drawn from in-depth interviews, illuminating how they handled some of the problems faced by all women who have been released, hoping to shed some light on how we can best prepare women for success. Table A.2 provides a description of these women.

TABLE A.2
Subject Demographics, Women Staying Out of Prison

Code Name	Age	Race	Years Out of Prison
Arlena	54	Black	1–1/2
Barbara	41	Native American	4
Dorothy	28	White	11
Gina	46	Black	8
Jonetta	39	Black	9
Kathy	45	White	10
Mandy	39	White	4
Misha	31	Black	1
Nelda	32	White	3
Tara	40	Black	12
Tasha	35	Black	3
Twyla	47	White	5
Average	39.8 years		Approximately 6

Appendix B: Oklahoma Children of Incarcerated Parents

Task Force Members

Reverend Dr. Stan Basler, Faith Community Criminal Justice and Mercy Ministries

Alice Blue, Community Service Council

Jeanne Burruss, Oklahoma Department of Commerce

Detective Darren Carlock, City of Tulsa, Oklahoma

Gene Christian, Executive Director, Office of Juvenile Affairs

Tre Clark, Parent

Gwen Downing, Department of Mental Health and Substance Abuse Services

Rebecca Frazier, Office of the Governor

Sheila Harbert, Girl Scouts of Tulsa, Oklahoma

Kenny Holloway, Oklahoma Department of Corrections

Robin Jones, Oklahoma Department of Human Services

Jay Keel, Chickasaw Nation

Beth Martin, Oklahoma State Department of Health

Laura NesSmith, Parent

Dr. Laura Pitman, Oklahoma Department of Corrections

Dr. Susan Sharp, University of Oklahoma

Lisa Smith, Executive Director, Oklahoma Commission on Children and Youth

Richard Smothermon, District Attorney's Council

Dr. Ron Thrasher, Oklahoma State University

Cynthia Valenzuela, Oklahoma State Department of Education

The Honorable Judge April Sellers White, Post Adjudication Review Board

The Honorable Judge Richard Woolery

Task Force Staff

Karen Waddell, Facilitator

Linda Terrell, Oklahoma Institute for Child Advocacy

Julie Bisbee, Oklahoma Institute for Child Advocacy

Jack Chapman, Oklahoma Commission on Children and Youth

Treasa Lansdowne, Oklahoma Commission on Children and Youth

Notes

Chapter 2 Mean Laws

1. Personal conversation with Justin Jones, Director of Oklahoma Department of Corrections.
2. Conversation with Justin Jones.
3. Thanks to Andrew Spivak, who tracked these numbers down for me for 1982 through 1991. The remaining years were obtained from the *Prisoner Series* of the Bureau of Justice Statistics.
4. In November 2012, a state resolution was passed to remove the governor from the parole process for nonviolent crimes. While this is definitely a start, Oklahoma's classification of trafficking charges as violent crimes—and the draconian definition of trafficking by amount possessed—will continue to place women in this political dilemma.

Chapter 3 Mean Women or Mean Lives?

1. In the prisoner surveys, women were asked how often they used a number of different drugs. I defined heavy drug use as using any of the following drugs more often than once per week or daily: crack, cocaine, methamphetamines, heroin, speedballs, other opiates such as prescription painkillers, barbiturates, or tranquilizers. Heavy marijuana use was defined as daily use, and heavy alcohol use was defined as daily use.

Chapter 4 The Prison Experience

1. Because of limited funding, those with life or life without parole sentences are frequently at the end of long lists of those wanting to enroll in various programs. The logic is that since they will not be returning to society, they do not need rehabilitation.

Chapter 6 Coming Home and Staying Out

1. Oklahoma State Bureau of Investigation
2. Residential Drug and Alcohol Program
3. Residential Substance Abuse Treatment
4. This was drawn from a case pulled at random from the Oklahoma Supreme Court Network.
5. Here, she is referring to the organization where she is employed. It is a transitional living program that provides case management and other services to women who are or are in danger of becoming homeless. The programming takes women who are involved in the criminal justice system.

CHAPTER 7   THE CHILDREN AND THEIR CAREGIVERS

1. Private conversations with high-ranking Oklahoma Department of Corrections officials who asked to remain anonymous.
2. In 2004, after SJR 48 was passed, making research a requirement, we formed a task force with representatives from multiple state agencies such as Department of Human Services, Department of Corrections, Oklahoma Commission on Children and Youth, Oklahoma Juvenile Authority, Department of Mental Health and Substance abuse Services and myself to formulate our research agenda on the issue of incarcerated women and their children. When I made a report to the group on the research, I noted that many caregivers were very hesitant to obtain any state assistance because they had concerns that the child would be taken away and placed in the foster care system, or the mother would have to repay any assistance once she was released. This was dubbed "flying below the radar" by one group member, and we frequently refer to this issue when trying to develop plans for getting services to the children.

CHAPTER 8   THE WINDS OF CHANGE

1. The George Kaiser Family Foundation was founded in 1999 by George Kaiser, CEO of the Kaiser-Francis Oil Company and Chairman of the Board for the Bank of Oklahoma. Kaiser and his children have used the foundation money to tackle social issues in the state such as low educational achievement and lack of social services. For more information on the foundation, visit http://gkff.org.
2. In some cases, children's names may be submitted by a prisoner who is legally denied contact with a child because of crimes against that child or other family members. This is why caregivers are contacted to determine the appropriateness.

References

ACE Reporter. 2003a. "Growing Up with Alcoholism." *ACE Reporter* 1 (2): 1–3.

———. 2003b. "Highlights: ACEs and Alcoholism." *ACE Reporter* 1 (2): 1–4.

———. 2006. "The ACE Study: Depression and Suicide." *ACE Reporter* 1 (3): 1–2.

———. 2007. "Adverse Childhood Experiences and Stress: Paying the Piper." *ACE Reporter* 1 (4): 1–2.

Acoca, Leslie. 1998. "Outside/Inside: The Violation of American Girls at Home, on the Streets, and in the Juvenile Justice System." *Crime & Delinquency* 44: 561–589.

Adler, Freda. 1975. *Sisters in Crime*. New York: McGraw-Hill.

Agnew Robert. 1985. "A Revised Strain Theory of Delinquency." *Social Forces* 64: 151–167.

———. 1992. "Foundation for a General Strain Theory of Crime and Delinquency." *Criminology* 30: 30–47.

———. 2005. *Why Do Criminals Offend?: A General Theory of Crime and Delinquency*. Los Angeles: Roxbury Publishing Company.

———. 2006. *Pressured into Crime: An Overview of General Strain Theory*. Los Angeles: Roxbury Publishing Company.

Agnew, Robert, and Helene Raskin White. 1992. An Empirical Test of General Strain Theory. *Criminology* 32: 475–499.

Aizer, Anna, and Jospeh H. Doyle, Jr. 2013. "Juvenile Incarceration, Human Capital and Future Crime: Evidence from Randomly-Assigned Judges." NBER Working Paper No. 19102, June 2013. Retrieved August 8, 2013, from http://www.nber.org/papers/w19102.pdf?new_window=1.

Alexander, Michelle. 2010. *The New Jim Crow: Mass Incarceration in the Age of Color-Blindness*. New York: The New Press.

Altheide, David. 2002. *Creating Fear: News and the Construction of Crisis*. New York: Aldine De Gruyter.

Amicus Brief. 2007. Theresa Lee Hernandez. Retrieved December 1, 2010, from http://advocatesforpregnantwomen.org/FINAL%20HERNANDEZ%20AMICUS.pdf.

Anda, Robert F. n.d. "The Health and Social Impact of Growing Up with Adverse Childhood Experiences: The Human and Economic Costs of the Status Quo." Retrieved October 1, 2010, from http://www.acestudy.org/files/Review_of_ACE_Study_with_references_summary_table_2_.pdf.

Anda, Robert F., Janet B. Croft, Vincent J. Felitti, Dale Nordenberg, Wayne H. Giles, David F. Williamson, and Gary A. Giovino. 1999. "Adverse Childhood Experiences and Smoking during Adolescence and Adulthood." *Journal of the American Medical Association*. 282: 1652–1658.

Anda, Robert F., Charles L. Whitfield, Vincent J. Felitti, Daniel Chapman, Valerie J. Edwards, Shanta R. Dube, and David F. Williamson. 2002. "Adverse Childhood

Experiences, Alcoholic Parents, and Later Risk of Alcoholism and Depression." *Psychiatric Services* 53 (8): 1001–1009.

Anderson, Tammy L. 2003. "Issues in the Availability of Health Care for Women Prisoners." In *The Incarcerated Woman: Rehabilitative Programming in Women's Prisons*, edited by Susan F. Sharp, 49–60. Upper Saddle River, NJ: Pearson Education, Inc.

Anderson, Tammy L., Andre B. Rosay, and Christine Saum. 2002. "The Impact of Drug Use and Crime Involvement on Health Problems among Female Drug Offenders." *The Prison Journal* 82 (1): 50–68

Annie E. Casey Foundation—KIDS COUNT. *Stepping Up for Kids: What Government and Communities Should Do to Support Kinship Families.* Baltimore, MD: Annie E. Casey Foundation. Retrieved June 18, 2012, from http://www.aecf.org/~/media/Pubs/Initiatives/KIDS%20COUNT/S/SteppingUpforKids2012PolicyReport/SteppingUpForKidsPolicyReport2012.pdf.

Annie E. Casey Foundation. 2012. Kids Count Data Center. Retrieved June 18, 2012, from http://datacenter.kidscount.org/data/bystate/StateLanding.aspx?state=OK.

Arditti, Joyce A., and April L. Few. 2006. "Mothers' Reentry into Family Life Following Incarceration." *Criminal Justice Policy Review* 17 (1): 103–123.

Austin, James, and John Irwin. 2001. *It's About Time: America's Imprisonment Binge.* Belmont, CA: Wadsworth.

Austin, James, John Irwin, and Patricia Hardyman. 2002. "Exploring the Needs and Risks of the Returning Prisoner Population." Presented at the U.S. Department of Health and Human Services From Prison To Home Conference, January 30–31, 2002.

Baer, Demelza, Avinash Bhati, Lisa Brooks, Jennifer Castro, Nancy La Vigne, Kamala Mallik-Kane, Rebecca Naser, Jenny Osborne, Caterina Roman, John Roman, Shelli Rossman, Amy Solomon, Christy Visher, and Laura Winterfield. 2006. *Understanding the Challenges of Prisoner Reentry: Research Findings from the Urban Institute's Prisoner Reentry Portfolio.* Urban Institute Justice Policy Center.

Beattie, Robb. 2005. "Putting the Crack Baby Myth to Bed." *National Review of Medicine,* 2 (13). Retrieved December 1, 2010, from http://www.nationalreviewofmedicine.com/issue/2005/07_30/2_feature04_13.html.

Beck, Allen J. 2000. *Prisoners in 1999,* NCJ-183476. Washington, DC. National Institute of Justice. Retrieved October 10, 2010, from http://bjs.ojp.usdoj.gov/index.cfm?ty=pbdetail&iid=928.

———. 2001. *Recidivism: A Fruit Salad Concept in the Criminal Justice World.* Justice Concepts, Inc. Retrieved September 3, 2008, from http://www.justiceconcepts.com/recidivism.pdf

Beck, Allen J., and Darrell K. Gilliard. 1995. *Prisoners in 1994,* NCJ-151654. Washington, DC. National Institute of Justice. Retrieved October 10, 2010, from http://bjs.ojp.usdoj.gov/index.cfm?ty=pbdetail&iid=1280.

———. 1996. *Prison and Jail Inmates, 1995,* NCJ-161132. Washington, DC. National Institute of Justice. Retrieved October 10, 2010, from http://bjs.ojp.usdoj.gov/index.cfm?ty=pbdetail&iid=838.

———. 1998. *Prisoners in 1997,* NCJ-170014. Washington, DC. National Institute of Justice. Retrieved October 10, 2010, from http://bjs.ojp.usdoj.gov/index.cfm?ty=pbdetail&iid=930.

Beck, Allen J., and Paige M. Harrison. 2001. *Prisoners in 2000,* NCJ-188207. Washington, DC. National Institute of Justice. Retrieved October 10, 2010, from http://bjs.ojp.usdoj.gov/index.cfm?ty=pbdetail&iid=927.

———. 2002. *Prisoners in 2001*, NCJ-195189. Washington, DC. National Institute of Justice. Retrieved October 10, 2010, from http://bjs.ojp.usdoj.gov/index.cfm?ty =pbdetail&iid=926.

———. 2003. *Prisoners in 2002*, NCJ-200248. Washington, DC. National Institute of Justice. Retrieved October 10, 2010, from http://bjs.ojp.usdoj.gov/index.cfm?ty =pbdetail&iid=921.

———. 2004. *Prisoners in 2003*, NCJ-205335. Washington, DC. National Institute of Justice. Retrieved October 10, 2010, from http://bjs.ojp.usdoj.gov/index.cfm?ty =pbdetail&iid=918.

———. 2005. *Prisoners in 2004*, NCJ-210677. Washington, DC. National Institute of Justice. Retrieved October 10, 2010, from http://bjs.ojp.usdoj.gov/index.cfm?ty =pbdetail&iid=915.

———. 2006. *Prisoners in 2005*, NCJ-215092. Washington, DC. National Institute of Justice. Retrieved October 10, 2010, from http://bjs.ojp.usdoj.gov/index.cfm?ty =pbdetail&iid=912.

Beck, Allen J., and Christopher Mumola. 1997. *Prisoners in 1996*, NCJ-164619. Washington, DC. National Institute of Justice. Retrieved October 10, 1996, from http://bjs .ojp.usdoj.gov/index.cfm?ty=pbdetail&iid=934.

———. 1999. *Prisoners in 1998*, NCJ-175687. Washington, DC. National Institute of Justice. Retrieved October 10, 2010, from http://bjs.ojp.usdoj.gov/index.cfm?ty =pbdetail&iid=929.

Beck, Allen J., and Bernard E. Shipley. 1989. *Recidivism of Prisoners Released in 1983*. Bureau of Justice Statistics Special Report No. NCJ-116261. Washington, DC: U.S. Department of Justice.

Belknap, Joanne. 2004. "Meda Cheney-Lind: The Mother of Feminist Criminology." *Women & Criminal Justice* 15: 1–23

———. 2007. *The Invisible Woman: Gender, Crime and Justice*, 3rd ed. Belmont, CA: Wadsworth.

Belknap, Joanne, and Kristi Holsinger. 2006. "The Gendered Nature of Risk Factors for Delinquency." *Feminist Criminology* 1: 48–71.

Benalioulhaj, Amina. 2010. Women Behind Bars. (Self-produced documentary at the University of Oklahoma.)

Bernstein, Nell. 2005. *All Alone in the World: Children of the Incarcerated*. New York: The New Press.

Bloom, Barbara. 1995. "Imprisoned Mothers." In *Children of Incarcerated Parents*, edited by Katherine Gabel and Denise Johnston, 271–284. New York: Lexington.

Bloom, Barbara, Barbara Owen, and Stephanie Covington. 2003. *Gender-Responsive Strategies: Research, Practice, and Guiding Principles for Women Offenders*. National Institute of Corrections. Washington, DC. Retrieved May 28, 2008, from http://www.nicic.org/pubs/2003/018017.pdf

Brame, Robert, Doris Layton MacKenzie, Arnold R. Waggoner, and Kenneth D. Robinson. 1996. "Moral Reconation Therapy and Problem Behavior in the Oklahoma Department of Corrections." *Journal of the Oklahoma Criminal Justice Research Consortium*. Retrieved March 16, 2011, from http://www.doc.state.ok.us/offenders/ocjrc/96/Moral%20Reconation%20Therapy%20and%20Problem%20Behavior.pdf.

Brennan, Tim, Markus Breitenbach, William Dieterich, Emily J. Salisbury, and Patricia Van Voorhis. 2012. "Women's Pathways to Serious and Habitual Crime: A Person-Centered Analysis Incorporating Gender Responsive Factors." *Criminal Justice and Behavior* 39: 1481–1508.

Britton, Dana M. 2000. "Feminism in Criminology: Engendering the Outlaw." *Annals of the American Academy of Political and Social Science* 57: 57–76.

Broidy, Lisa M. 2001. "A Test of General Strain Theory." *Criminology* 39: 9–35.

Broidy, Lisa, and Robert Agnew. 1997. "Gender and Crime: A General Strain Theory Perspective." *Journal of Research in Crime and Delinquency* 34: 275–306.

Browne, Angela, Brenda Miller, and Eugene Maguin. 1999. "Prevalence and Severity of Life-time Physical and Sexual Victimization among Incarcerated Women." *International Journal of Law and Psychology* 2: 301–322.

Bureau of Justice Statistics. 2010. National Archive of Criminal Justice Data: Data Online. Retrieved August 30, 2010, from http://bjs.ojp.usdoj.gov/.

Burgess-Proctor, A. 2012. "Pathways of Victimization and Resistance: Toward a Feminist Theory of Battered Women's Help-Seeking." *Justice Quarterly* 29: 309–346.

Bush, Brian. 2010. "Addressing Our High Incarceration Rates." *Oklahoma Watch*. Retrieved December 28, 2012, from http://oklahomawatch.org/voices.php?vid=4.

Bush-Baskette, Stephanie R. 1998. "The War on Drugs as a War against Black Women." In *Crime Control and Women: Feminist Implications of Criminal Justice Policy*, edited by Susan Miller, 113–129. Thousand Oaks, CA: Sage Publications. Reprinted in Meda Chesney-Lind and Lisa Pasko, eds.. 2004. *Girls, Women and Crime: Selected Readings*, 185–194. Thousand Oaks, CA: Sage Publications.

Cain, Maureen. 1990. "Towards Transgression: New Directions in Feminist Criminology." *International Journal of the Sociology of Law* 1: 1–18.

Camp, Camille Graham, and George M. Camp. 1982. *The Corrections Yearbook*. Middletown, CT: Criminal Justice Institute.

———. 1983. *The Corrections Yearbook*. Middletown, CT: Criminal Justice Institute.

———. 1984. *The Corrections Yearbook*. Middletown, CT: Criminal Justice Institute.

———. 1985. *The Corrections Yearbook*. Middletown, CT: Criminal Justice Institute.

———. 1986. *The Corrections Yearbook*. Middletown, CT: Criminal Justice Institute.

———. 1987. *The Corrections Yearbook*. Middletown, CT: Criminal Justice Institute.

———. 1988. *The Corrections Yearbook*. Middletown, CT: Criminal Justice Institute.

———. 1989. *The Corrections Yearbook*. Middletown, CT: Criminal Justice Institute.

———. 1990. *The Corrections Yearbook*. Middletown, CT: Criminal Justice Institute.

———. 2000. *The Corrections Yearbook*. Middletown, CT: Criminal Justice Institute.

Carlen, Pat. 1983. *Women's Imprisonment: A Study in Social Control*. London: Routledge & Kegan Paul.

———. ed. 1985. *Criminal Women: Autobiographical Accounts*. Cambridge: Polity Press.

Carson, E. Ann, and William J. Sabol. 2012. *Prisoners in 2011*, NCJ-239808. Washington, DC: U.S. Department of Justice/Bureau of Justice Statistics.

Cecil, Dawn K., James McHale, Anne L. Strozeir, and Joel Pietsch. 2008: "Female Inmates, Family Caregivers, and Young Children's Adjustment: A Research Agenda and Implications for Corrections Programming." *Journal of Criminal Justice* 36: 513–521.

CED Division of Research. n.d. Crime Rates Ranked by State Total: 2008. Retrieved August 30, 2010, from http://www.ced.ky.gov/edis/Deskbook/files/CrimeRatesSt.pdf.

Chasnoff, Ira J., William J. Burns, Sidney H. Schnoll, and Kayreen A. Burns. 1985. "Cocaine Use in Pregnancy." *New England Journal of Medicine* 313: 666–669.

Chavkin, Wendy. 2001. "Cocaine and Pregnancy: Time to Look at the Evidence." *Journal of the American Medical Association* 285 (12): 1626–1628.

Chesney-Lind, Meda. 1973. "Judicial Enforcement of the Female Sex Role: The Family Court and the Female Delinquent." *Issues in Criminology* 8 (2): 51–70.

————. 1974. "Juvenile Delinquency: The Sexualization of Female Crime." *Psychology Today* (July): 43–46.

————. 1977. "Judicial Paternalism and the Female Status Offender: Training Women to Know Their Place." *Crime and Delinquency* 23 (2): 121–130.

————. 1986. "Women and Crime: The Female Offender." *Signs* 12:78–96.

————. 1989. "Girls' Crime and Woman's Place: Toward a Feminist Model of Female Delinquency." *Crime & Delinquency* 35: 5–29.

————. 1991. "Patriarchy, Prisons, and Jails: A Critical Look at Trends in Women's Incarceration." *Prison Journal* 71: 51–67.

————. 1997. *The Female Offender: Girls, Women, and Crime.* Thousand Oaks, CA: Sage Publications.

————. 2003. "Reinventing Women's Corrections." In *The Incarcerated Woman*, edited by Susan F. Sharp, 3–113. Upper Saddle River, NJ: Prentice-Hall.

————. 2006. "Patriarchy, Crime, and Justice: Feminist Criminology in an Era of Backlash." *Feminist Criminology* 1 (1): 6–26.

Chesney-Lind, Meda, and Katherine Irwin. 2007. *Beyond Bad Girls: Gender, Media, and Hype.* Florence, KY: Routledge

Chesney-Lind, Meda, and Joycelyn Pollock-Byrne. 1995. "Women's Prisons: Equality with a Vengeance." In *Women, Law, and Social Control*, edited by Joycelyn Pollock-Byrne and Alida Merlo, 155–175. Boston: Allyn & Bacon.

Chesney-Lind, Meda, and Noelie Rodriguez. 1983. "Women Under Lock and Key: A View from the Inside." *The Prison Journal* 63: 47–65.

Chesney-Lind, Meda, and Randall G. Shelden. 2004. *Girls, Delinquency, and Juvenile Justice.* 3rd ed. Belmont, CA: Wadsworth.

Children of Incarcerated Parents Task Force. 2012. Final Report, January 1, 2012. Oklahoma City: Oklahoma Commission on Children and Youth.

Christian, Johnna. 2005. "Riding the Bus: Barriers to Prison Visitation and Family Management Strategies." *Journal of Contemporary Criminal Justice* 21 (1), 31–48.

Cooper, Cynthia. 2002. "Medical Treatment in Women's Prisons Ranges from Brutal to Nonexistent." *The Nation*, May 6. Retrieved December 1, 2007, at http://www.thenation.com

Cooper, Matthew, William J. Sabol, and Heather C. West. 2009. *Prisoners in 2008*, NCJ-228417. Washington, DC. National Institute of Justice. Retrieved October 10, 2010, from http://bjs.ojp.usdoj.gov/index.cfm?ty=pbdetail&iid=1763.

Couture, Heather, Paige M. Harrison and William J. Sabol. 2007. *Prisoners in 2006*, NCJ-219416. Washington, DC. National Institute of Justice. Retrieved October 10, 2010, from http://bjs.ojp.usdoj.gov/index.cfm?ty=pbdetail&iid=908.

Covington, Stephanie. 2002a. *A Woman's Journey Home: Challenges for Female Offenders and Their Children.* Working papers prepared from the From Prison to Home National Policy Conference of the Urban Institute, U.S. Department of Human Services, Jan. 30–31, 2002.

————. 2002b. "Helping Women Recover: Creating Gender-Responsive Treatment." In *The Handbook of Addiction Treatment for Women: Theory and Practice*, edited by S.L.A. Straussner and S. Brown. San Francisco: Jossey-Bass. Retrieved February 17, 2012, from http://www.stephaniecovington.com/pdfs/5.pdf.

Daly, Kathleen. 1992. "Women's Pathways to Felony Court: Feminist Theories of Lawbreaking and Problems of Representation." *Southern California Review of Law & Women's Studies* 2: 11–52.

————. 1997. "Different Ways of Conceptualizing Sex/Gender in Feminist Theory and Their Implications for Criminology." *Theoretical Criminology* 1: 25–51.

Daly, Kathleen, and Meda Chesney-Lind. 1988. "Feminism and Criminology." *Justice Quarterly* 5: 497–538.

Damphousse, Kelly R. 2003. "Review of the Oklahoma Incarceration Rate/Crime Rate and Offenders: Appendix C." Prepared for the Oklahoma Alliance for Public Policy Research, Inc., and the Oklahoma Criminal Justice Resource Center.

Darcy, R. 2010. "Oklahoma Women's County Status: Baseline Statistical Report, 2010." Retrieved October 9, 2010, from http://women.library.okstate.edu/countyreport/docs/fullreport.pdf.

Davis, Tiffany Ann. 2010. "The Impact of Drug, Habitual Offender and Truth-in-Sentencing Statutes on the Distribution of State Funds in Oklahoma from 1980 to 2009" (master's thesis, University of Oklahoma).

Delcour, Julie. 2009. "Prison Numbers." *Tulsa World*, November 29, 2009. Retrieved October 7, 2010, from http://www.allbusiness.com/crime-law-enforcement-corrections/corrections-prisons/13475053–1.html.

Deschenes, Elizabeth P., Barbara Owen, and Jason Crow. 2006. *Recidivism among Female Prisoners: Secondary Analysis of the 1994 BJS Recidivism Data Set*. Report submitted to the U.S. Department of Justice.

Dietrich, Sharon. 2002. "Criminal Records and Employment: Ex-Offenders Thwarted in Attempts to Earn a Living for Their Families." In *Every Door Closed: Barriers Facing Parents with Criminal Records*, edited by A. Hirsch, S. Dietrich, R. Langau, P. Schneider, I. Ackelsberg, J. Bernstein-Baker, and J. Hohenstein. Philadelphia: Center for Law and Social Policy and Community Legal Services, Inc.

Dirks, Danielle. 2004. "Sexual Revictimization and Retraumatization of Women in Prison." *Women's Studies Quarterly* 32: 102–115.

Dodge, Mary, and Pogrebin, Mark R. 2001. "Collateral Costs of Imprisonment for Women: Complications of Reintegration." *The Prison Journal* 81 (1): 42–54.

Dong, Maxia, Robert F. Anda, Vincent J. Felitti, Shanta R. Dube, David F. Williamson, T. J. Thompson, C.M. Loo, and Wayne H. Giles. 2004. "The Interrelatedness of Multiple Forms of Childhood Abuse, Neglect, and Household Dysfunction." *Child Abuse and Neglect* 28 (7): 771–784.

Dube, Shanta R., Robert F. Anda, Vincent J. Felitti, Valerie Edwards, and Janet B. Croft. 2002. "Adverse Childhood Experiences and Personal Alcohol Abuse as an Adult." *Addictive Behavior* 27: 713–725.

Dube, Shanta R., Vincent J. Felitti, Maxia Dong, Daniel P. Chapman, Wayne H. Giles and Robert F. Anda. 2003. "Childhood Abuse, Neglect, and Household Dysfunction and the Risk of Illicit Drug Use: The Adverse Childhood Experience Study." *Pediatrics* 111 (3): 564–572.

Eaton, Mary. 1986. *Justice for Women? Family, Court, and Social Control*. Milton Keynes, UK: Open University Press.

———. 2000. "A Woman in Her Own Time." *Women & Criminal Justice* 12 (2–3): 9–28.

Elliott, Delbert. 1983. National Youth Survey: Wave VI, 1983. ICPSR 9948. Retrieved November 29, 2013, from http://www.icpsr.umich.edu/icpsrweb/ICPSR/series/88/studies/9948?archive=ICPSR&sortBy=7

Engle, Richard. 2008. "Defining Oklahoma's Conservatism." *Tulsa Beacon*. Retrieved December 1, 2010, from http://www.tulsabeacon.com/?p=319.

Faludi, Susan. 1991. *Backlash: The Undeclared War against American Women*. New York: Anchor/Doubleday.

Families Against Mandatory Minimums (FAMM). n.d. "Sheila Devereux." Retrieved December 13, 2010, from http://www.famm.org/ProfilesofInjustice/StateProfiles/SheilaDevereuxOklahoma.aspx.

Federal Bureau of Investigation. 2009. *Crime in the United States,* Table 5. Retrieved, September 15, 2010, from http://www.fbi.gov/about-us/cjis/ucr/crime-in-the-u.s/2008.

Felitti, Vincent J. 2003. "The Origins of Addiction: Evidence from the Adverse Childhood Experiences Study." Originally published in German as "Ursprünge des Suchtverhaltens— Evidenzen aus einer Studie zu belastenden Kindheitserfahrungen." *Praxis der Kinderpsychologie und Kinderpsychiatrie* 52: 547–559. Retrieved January 11, 2011, from http://www.jumpstarttulsa.com/images/ACE%20Addiction_final_ASF2.pdf.

Felitti, Vincent J., and Robert F. Anda. 2010. "The Relationship of Adverse Childhood Experiences to Adult Medical Disease, Psychiatric Disorders, and Sexual Behavior: Implications for Healthcare." In *The Hidden Epidemic: The Impact of Early Life Trauma on Health and Disease,* edited by R. Lanius and E. Vermetten, 77–87. Cambridge: Cambridge University Press

Felitti, Vincent J., Robert F. Anda, Dale Nordenberg, David F. Williamson, Alison M. Spitz, Valerie Edwards, Mary P. Koss, and James S. Marks. 1998. "Relationship of Childhood Abuse and Household Dysfunction to Many of the Leading Causes of Death in Adults." *American Journal of Preventive Medicine* 14: 245–258.

Fentiman, Linda C. 2008. "Pursuing the Perfect Mother: Why America's Criminalization of Maternal Substance Abuse Is Not the Answer." Pace Law Faculty Publications. Retrieved December 1, 2010, from http://digitalcommons.pace.edu/cgi/viewcontent.cgi?article=1487&context=lawfaculty.

Finkelhor, David, and Angela Browne. 1985. "The Traumatic Impact of Child Sexual Abuse: A Conceptualization." *American Journal of Orthopsychiatry* 5: 530–541.

Flavin, Jeanne. 2001. "Feminism for the Mainstream Criminologist: An Invitation." *Journal of Criminal Justice* 29: 271–285.

Fogel, Catherine I., and Michael Belyea. 1999. "The Lives of Incarcerated Women: Violence, Substance Abuse, and at Risk for HIV." *Journal of the Association of Nurses in AIDS Care* 10 (6), 66–74.

Forsyth, Craig J. 2003. "Pondering the Discourse of Prison Mamas: A Research Note." *Deviant Behavior* 24: 269–380.

Fox, Aubrey, ed. 2004. *Bridging the Gap: Researchers, Practitioners, and the Future of Drug Courts.* New York: Center for Court Innovation.

Gaarder, Emily, and Joanne Belknap. 2002. "Tenuous Borders: Girls Transferred to Adult Court." *Criminology* 40: 481–518.

Gelsthorpe, Lorraine, and Allison Morris. 1990. "Introduction: Transforming and Transgressing Criminology." In *Feminist Perspectives in Criminology,* edited by Lorrain Gelsthorpe and Allison Morris. Milton Keynes, UK: Open University Press.

Gilfus, Mary E. 1992. "From Victims to Survivors to Offenders: Women's Routes of Entry and Immersion into Street Crime." *Women & Criminal Justice* 4: 63–90.

Gilliard, Darrell K., and Allen J. Beck. 1994. *Prisoners in 1993.* Washington, DC: National Institute of Justice

Girl Scouts of Eastern Oklahoma. Project MEND. Retrieved June 27, 2013, from http://www.girlscoutseastok.org/mecgs/Project_MEND2.asp.

Girshick, Lori. 1999. *No Safe Haven: Stories from Women in Prison.* Boston: Northeastern University Press.

———. 2003. "Leaving Stronger: Programming for Release." In *The Incarcerated Woman: Rehabilitative Programming in Women's Prisons,* edited by Susan F. Sharp. Upper Saddle River, NJ: Prentice-Hall.

Glaze, Lauren. 2002. *Parole and Probation in the United States, 2001.* Washington, DC: Bureau of Justice Statistics.

Glaze, Lauren and Laura M. Maruschak. 2008. Parents in Prison and Their Children. NCJ-22984. Washington, DC. National Institute of Justice. Retrieved October 10, 2010, from http://www.bjs.gov/content/pub/pdf/pptmc.pdf.

Gomez, Laura E. 1997. *Misconceiving Mothers: Legislators, Prosecutors and the Politics of Prenatal Drug Exposure.* Philadelphia: Temple University Press.

Goode, Eric, and Nachman Ben-Yehuda. 1994. "Moral Panics: Culture, Politics, and Social Construction." *Annual Reviews of Sociology* 20: 149–171.

Greene, Judith. 2007. "Banking on the Prison Boom." In *Prison Profiteers: Who Makes Money from Mass Incarceration,* edited by T. Herivel and P. Wright, 3–26. New York: New Press.

Greene, Judith and Kevin Pranis. 2012. "The Punitiveness Report." The Women's Prison Association. Retrieved December 27, 2012, from http://www.wpaonline.org/institute/hardhit/part1.htm#sv.

Guerino, Paul, Paige M. Harrison, and William J. Sabol. 2011. *Prisoners in 2010* (NCJ-236096). Washington, DC: Office of Justice Programs/Bureau of Justice Statistics.

Hagan, John, A. R. Gillis, and John H Simpson. 1987. "Class in the Household: A Power-Control Theory of Gender and Delinquency." *American Journal of Sociology* 92: 788–816.

———. 1993. "The Power of Control in Sociological Theories of Delinquency." In *Advances in Criminological Theory* 4, edited by Freda Adler and William Laufer. New Brunswick, NJ: Transaction Press.

Hahn, Jeffrey M. 1991. "Pre-Employment Information Services: Employers Beware." *Employee Relations Law Journal* 17, 45–69.

Harding, Sandra. 1991. *Whose Science? Whose Knowledge?* Ithaca, NY: Cornell University Press.

Harer, Miles D. 1994. *Recidivism among Federal Prisoners Released in 1987.* Federal Bureau of Prisons/Office of Research and Evaluation. Washington, DC.

Harris, Patricia M., and Kimberly S. Keller. 2005. "Ex-Offenders Need Not Apply: The Criminal Background Check in Hiring Decisions." *Journal of Contemporary Criminal Justice* 21 (1): 6–30.

Harrison, Lana D. 2001. "The Revolving Prison Door for Drug-Involved Offenders: Challenges and Opportunities." *Crime & Delinquency* 47 (3): 462–485.

Harrison, Paige M. 2000. Females under Local, State, or Federal Correctional Supervision, 1993 and 1988 (corpop35.csv). Washington, DC: Bureau of Justice Statistics. Retrieved August 30, 2010, from http://bjs.ojp.usdoj.gov/content/dtdata.cfm#persons.

Harrison, Paige M., and Allen J. Beck. 2005. *Prisoners in 2004* (NCJ-210677). Washington, DC: U.S. Department of Justice, Office of Justice Programs/Bureau of Justice Statistics.

Harrison, Paige M., and Allen J. Beck. 2006. *Prison and Jail Inmates at Midyear 2005.* NCJ-213133. Washington, DC: U.S. Department of Justice, Office of Justice Programs/Bureau of Justice Statistics.

Heidensohn, Frances. 1968. "The Deviance of Women: A Critique and an Enquiry." *British Journal of Sociology* 19 (2): 160–175.

———. 1985. *Women and Crime.* London: Macmillan.

Heimer, Karen. 1997. "Socioeconomic Status, Subcultural Definitions, and Violent Delinquency." *Social Forces* 75 (3): 799–833

Heney, Jan, and Connie M. Kristiansen. 1998. "An Analysis of the Impact of Prison on Women Survivors of Childhood Sexual Abuse." *Women & Therapy* 20: 29–44.

Henry, Jessica S., and James B. Jacobs. 2007. "Ban the Box to Promote Ex-Offender Employment." *Criminology and Public Policy* 6 (4): 755–762.

Hinton, Mick. 2010. "Sorry, No Help." *The Norman Transcript*, March 24, 2010.

Hirsch, Amy. 2002. "Parents with Criminal Records and Public Benefits: 'Welfare Helps Us Stay in Touch with Society.'" In *Every Door Closed: Barriers Facing Parents with Criminal Records*, edited by Hirsch, A., Dietrich, S., Landau, R., Schneider, P., Ackelsberg, I., Bernstein-Baker, J., and Hohenstein, J., 27–40. Washington, DC: Center for Law and Social Policy and Community Legal Services.

Holsinger, Kristi, and Alex M. Holsinger. 2005. "Differential Pathways to Violence and Self-Injurious Behavior: African American and White Girls in the Juvenile Justice System." *Journal of Research in Crime and Delinquency* 42 (2): 211–242.

Holtfreter, Kristi, Michael D. Reisig, and Merry Morash. 2004. "Poverty, State Capital, and Recidivism among Women Offenders." *Criminology & Public Policy* 3 (2): 185–208.

Hope, Trina L., Esther Isabelle Wilder and Toni Terling-Watt. 2003. "The Relationships among Adolescent Pregnancy, Pregnancy Resolution, and Adolescent Delinquency." *Sociological Quarterly* 44: 555–576.

Huddleston, C. West III, Douglas B. Marlowe, and Rachel Casebolt. 2008. "Painting the Current Picture: A National Report-Card on Drug Courts and Other Problem-Solving Court Programs in the United States." Alexandria, VA: National Drug Court Institute, Col II, No. 1.

Huebner, Beth M., Christina Dejong, and Jennifer Cobbina. 2010. "Women Coming Home: Long-Term Patterns of Recidivism." *Justice Quarterly* 27 (2): 225–254.

Huebner, Beth M., and Regan Gustafson. 2007. "The Effect of Maternal Incarceration on Adult Offspring Involvement in the Criminal Justice System." *Journal of Criminal Justice* 35: 283–296.

Humphries, Drew. 1999. *Crack Mothers: Pregnancy, Drugs and the Media*. Columbus: Ohio State University Press.

Institute for Women's Policy Research. 2004. *Status of Women in Oklahoma*. Washington, DC: Institute for Women's Policy Research.

———. 2010. Data from "Status of Women in the States." Retrieved March 16, 2011, from http://www.iwpr.org/publications/resources/femstats/status-of-women-in-the-states.

Irwin, John. 2005. *The Warehouse Prison: Disposal of the New Dangerous Class*. Los Angeles: Roxbury Press.

Jacobs, Ann. 2000. "Give 'Em a Fighting Chance: The Challenges for Women Offenders Trying to Succeed in the Community." Women's Prison Association. Retrieved November 1, 2007, from http://www.WPAonline.org/pdf/WPA_Fightingchance.pdf.

Jacobson, Michael. 2005. *Downsizing Prisons: How to Reduce Crime and End Mass Incarceration*. New York: NYU Press.

Jang, Sung Joon, and Byron R. Jonson. 2003. "Strain, Negative Emotions, and Deviant Coping among African Americans: A Test of General Strain Theory." *Journal of Quantitative Criminology* 19: 79–105.

Johnson, Holly. 2004. "Key Findings from the Drug Use Careers of Female Offenders Study." *Trends and Issues in Crime and Criminal Justice*, 289. Retrieved January 4, 2011, from http://www.aic.gov.au/documents/6/8/E/%7B68E7AB0D-9818-4C68-8162-C61FFE620153%7Dtandi289.pdf.

Jones, Justin. 2012. "Welcome to Inside Corrections." *Inside Corrections*, July/August: 4. Retrieved December 9, 2012, from http://www.doc.state.ok.us/newsroom/insidec/08_12/julyaugust.pdf.

Journal of the Oklahoma Criminal Justice Research Consortium. 1996. Retrieved December 14, 2010, from http://www.doc.state.ok.us/offenders/ocjrc/96.htm.

Kappeler, Victor E., Mark Blumberg, and Gary W. Potter. 2000. *The Mythology of Crime and Criminal Justice.* Lone Grove, IL: Waveland Press.

Katz, Rebecca S. 2000. "Explaining Girls' and Women's Crime and Desistance in the Context of Their Victimization Experiences." *Violence Against Women* 6 (6): 633–660

Kaufmann, Jeanne G., and Cathy Spatz Widom. 1999. "Childhood Victimization, Running Away, and Delinquency." *Journal of Research in Crime & Delinquency* 36: 347–370.

Kauffman, Kelsey, and Susan L. Clayton. 2001. "Mothers in Prison." *Corrections Today* 63 (1): 62–65.

Kearney, Margaret H., Sheigla Murphy, and Marsha Rosenbaum. 1994. "Mothering on Crack Cocaine: A Grounded Theory Analysis." *Social Science & Medicine* 8 (2): 351–361.

Kempf-Leonard, Kimberley, and Pernilla Johansson. 2007. "Gender and Runaways: Risk Factors, Delinquency, and Juvenile Justice Experiences." *Youth Violence and Juvenile Justice* 5: 308–327.

Kids Count Data Center. 2012. Retrieved June 18, 2012, from http://datacenter .kidscount.org/data/bystate/StateLanding.aspx?state=OK.

Klein, Dorie. 1995. "The Etiology of Female Crime: A Review of the Literature." In *The Criminal Justice System and Women*, edited by Barbara R. Price and Natalie Sokoloff, 30–53. New York: McGraw-Hill.

Kruttschnitt, Candace. 1982. "Women, Crime, and Dependency: An Application of a Theory of Law." *Criminology* 19: 495–513.

Kruttschnitt, Candace, Anne-Marie Slotboom, Anja Dirkzwager, and Catrien Bijleveld. 2013. "Bringing Women's Carceral Experiences into the 'New Punitiveness' Fray." *Justice Quarterly* 30: 18–43.

Langan, Patrick A., and David J. Levin. 2002. *Recidivism of Prisoners Released in 1994.* Bureau of Justice Statistics Special Report No. NCJ 193427, Washington, DC, U.S Department of Justice.

Lappin, Harley G., Thomas R. Kane, William G. Saylor, and Scott D. Camp. 2005. *Evaluation of the Taft Demonstration Project: Performance of a Private-Sector Prison and the BOP.* Washington, DC: U.S. Department of Justice, Federal Bureau of Prisons. Retrieved May 15, 2006, from http://www.bop.gov/news/research_projects/published_reports/ pub_vs_priv/orelappin2005.pdf.

Larson, Annika. 2010. "Student's Documentary Explores Incarceration of Women." *Oklahoma Daily*, October 26, 2010, 1. Retrieved December 28, 2012, from http://oudaily .com/news/2010/oct/26/students-documentary-explores-states-incarceration/.

Laub, John H., Daniel S. Nagin, and Robert J. Sampson. 1998. "Trajectories of Change in Criminal Offending: Good Marriages and the Desistance Process." *American Sociological Review* 68: 225–238.

Laub, John H., and Robert J. Sampson. 1993. "Turning Points in the Life Course: Why Change Matters to the Study of Crime." *Criminology* 31: 301–325.

———. 2006. *Shared Beginnings, Divergent Lives: Delinquent Boys to Age 70.* Cambridge, MA: Harvard University Press.

Lester, Barry M. 2007. "Substance-Exposed Newborns: Time for Policy to Catch Up with Research." PowerPoint presentation, Brown Medical School: The Brown Center for the Study of Children at Risk. Retrieved December 1, 2010, from http://www .brown.edu/Departments/Children_at_Risk/Presentations.htm.

Leverentz, Andrea M. 2006a. "The Love of a Good Man? Romantic Relationships as a Source of Support or Hindrance for Female Ex-Offenders." *Journal of Research in Crime and Delinquency* 43 (4): 459–488.

———. 2006b. "People, Places, and Things: The Social Process of Reentry for Female Ex-Offenders (Final Report)." National Criminal Justice Reference Service. Retrieved June 2008 at http://www.ncjrs.gov/pdffiles1/nij/grants/215178.pdf.

Levy, Robin, and Ayelet Waldman, eds. 2011. *In This Place Not of It: Narratives from Women's Prisons.* San Francisco: McSweeney Books.

Lombroso, Cesare, and Guglielmo Ferrero. 2004. *Criminal Woman, the Prostitute, and the Normal Woman.* A new translation with an introduction and annotations by Nicole Hahn Rafter and Mary Gibson. Durham, NC: Duke University Press.

Lurigio, Arthur J., and Joan Petersilia. 1992. "The Emergence of Intensive Probation Supervision Programs in the United States." In *Smart Sentencing: The Emergence of Intermediate Sanctions*, edited by James M. Byrne, Arthur J. Lurigio, and Joan Petersilia, 3–17. Newbury Park, CA: Sage Publications.

Marcus-Mendoza, Susan, and Robert Briody. 1996. "Inmate Population Study." Unpublished paper.

Marcus-Mendoza, Susan T., and Susan F. Sharp. 1998. "The Impact of Incarceration on Families in Oklahoma: Implications for Policymakers." Report to the Oklahoma Sentencing Commission.

Mazerolle, Paul, Robert Brame, Ray Paternoster, Alex Piquero, and Charles Dean. 2002. "Onset Age, Persistence, and Offending Versatility: Comparisons Across Gender." *Criminology* 38:,1143–1172.

McCorkle, Richard C., and Terance D. Miethe. 2002. *Panic: The Social Construction of the Street Gang Problem.* Upper Saddle River, NJ: Prentice-Hall.

McDevitt, Jack, and Robyn Miliano. 1992. "Day Reporting Centers: An Innovative Concept in Intermediate Sanctions." In *Smart Sentencing: The Emergence of Intermediate Sanctions*, edited by James M. Byrne, Arthur J. Lurigio, and Joan Petersilia, 152–165. Newbury Park, CA: Sage Publications.

Messina, Nena P., and Christine E. Grella. 2006. "Childhood Trauma and Women's Health Outcomes in a California Prison Population." *American Journal of Public Health* 96 (10): 1842–1848.

MGT of America, Inc. 2007. Performance Audit of the Oklahoma Department of Corrections for the Legislative Service Bureau of the Oklahoma Legislature: Final Report. Retrieved October 26, 2010, from http://www.okhouse.gov/Documents/OKRVSDFinalReport080103.pdf.

Moffitt, Terrie E., Avalom Caspi, Michael Rutter, and Phil A. Silva. 2001. *Sex Differences in Antisocial Behavior: Conduct Disorder, Delinquency, and Violence in the Dunedin Longitudinal Study.* Cambridge: Cambridge University Press.

Morash, Merry, and Pamela J. Schram. 2002. *The Prison Experience: Special Issues of Women in Prison.* Long Grove, IL: Waveland Press

Moses, Marilyn. 1995. *Keeping Incarcerated Mothers and Their Daughters Together: Girl Scouts Beyond Bars*, NCJ-156217. Washington, DC: National Institute of Justice.

Mukamal, Debbie. 2001. *From Hard Time to Full Time: Strategies to Help Move Ex-Offenders from Welfare to Work.* U.S. Department of Labor, Employment and Training Administration.

Mumola, Christopher J. 1999. *Substance Abuse and Treatment, State and Federal Prisoners, 1997.* Bureau of Justice Statistics Special Report No. NCJ-172871. Washington, DC: U.S. Department of Justice.

———. 2000. *Incarcerated Parents and Their Children.* Bureau of Justice Statistics Special Report No. NCJ-182335. Washington, DC: U.S. Department of Justice.

Naffine, Ngaire. 1996. *Feminism and Criminology.* Philadelphia: Temple University Press.

National Commission on Correctional Health Care. 2002. *The Health Status of Soon-to-Be-Released Inmates: A Report to Congress,* Vol. 1. Retrieved November 15, 2007, from http://www.ncchc.org/stbr/Volume1/Health%20Status%20(vol%201).pdf

O'Brien, Patricia. 2001. *Making It in the Free World.* Albany: State University of New York Press.

Oklahoma Academy. 2009. Oklahoma Academy 2008 Report: "Oklahoma's Criminal Justice System: Can We Be Just as Tough But Twice as Smart?"

Oklahoma Alliance for Public Policy Research, Inc. (OAPPR). 2003. *Rational Justice Policy: Findings and Recommendations.* A report to the Oklahoma State Senate pursuant to SR 61.

Oklahoma Department of Corrections. 2010. *Facts at a Glance, July 30, 2010.* Oklahoma City: Oklahoma Department of Corrections. Retrieved August 30, 2010, from http://www.doc.state.ok.us/newsroom/facts/July%202010%20Facts%20at%20a%20Glance.pdf.

Oklahoma Department of Corrections Division of Female Offender Operations. 2009. *Fiscal Year 2009 Annual Report.* Retrieved May 10, 2009, from http://www.doc.state.ok.us/field/female/FY%202009%20Female%20Offender%20Operations%20Annual%20Report.pdf

———. 2010. *Fiscal Year 2010 Annual Report.* Oklahoma City: Oklahoma Department of Corrections. Retrieved January 31, 2011, from http://www.doc.state.ok.us/field/female/Fiscal%20Year%202010%20Annual%20Report%20Final.pdf.

Oklahoma Department of Corrections Female Offender Management Group. 2008. *Work Summary for Fiscal Year 2007.* Retrieved January 5, 2009, from http://www.Doc.State.Ok.Us/Field/Female/FOM%20Work%20Summary%20Fy2007%20PlAin.Txt.

Oklahoma Governor's and Attorney General's Blue Ribbon Task Force on Mental Health, Substance Abuse and Domestic Violence. 2005. *Oklahoma Criminal Justice System: Costs of Mental Health, Substance Abuse and Domestic Violence.* Oklahoma City.

Oklahoman Editorial. 2010. "Teen Pregnancy, Incarceration Rates Major Issue for Oklahoma." *Daily Oklahoman.* Retrieved October 8, 2010, from http://newsok.com/teen-pregnancy-incarceration-rates-major-issues-for-oklahoma/article/3496825.

Oklahoma State Auditor and Inspector. 2008. *Oklahoma County Drug Court and Community Sentencing Performance Audit July 1, 2005 through May 31, 2007.* Retrieved November 30, 2010, from http://www.sai.state.ok.us/Search%20Reports/database/drugcourt07.pdf.

Olson, David E., Arthur J. Lurigio, and Magnus Seng. 2000. "A Comparison of Female and Male Probationers: Characteristics and Case Outcomes." *Women & Criminal Justice* 11 (4): 65–79.

Owen, Barbara. 1998. *In the Mix: Struggle and Survival in a Women's Prison.* Albany: State University of New York Press.

Palumbo, Dennis J., Mary Clifford, and Zoann K. Snyder-Joy. 1992. "From Net-Widening to Intermediate Sanctions: The Transformation of Alternatives to Incarceration from Benevolence to Malevolence." In *Smart Sentencing: The Emergence of Intermediate Sanctions,* edited by James M. Byrne, Arthur J. Lurigio, and Joan Petersilia, 229–244. Newbury Park, CA: Sage Publications.

Petersilia, Joan. 2003. *When Prisoners Come Home: Parole and Prisoner Reentry.* New York: Oxford University Press.

Petersilia, Joan, Susan Turner, and Elizabeth Piper Deschenes. 1992. "Intensive Supervision Programs for Drug Offenders." In *Smart Sentencing: The Emergence of Intermediate Sanctions*, edited by James M. Byrne, Arthur J. Lurigio, and Joan Petersilia, 18–37. Newbury Park, CA: Sage Publications.

Piehl, Anne. 2003. "Crime, Work, and Reentry." Presented at the Urban Institute Reentry Roundtable, Employment Dimensions of Reentry: Understanding the Nexus Between Prison Reentry and Work, May 19–20, 2003, New York.

Poehlmann, Julie. 2005. "Incarcerated Mothers' Contact with Children, Perceived Family Relationships, and Depressive Symptoms." *Journal of Family Psychology* 19: 350–357.

Pollak, Otto. 1950. *The Criminality of Women*. Philadelphia: University of Pennsylvania Press.

Radosh, Polly F. 2002. "Reflections on Women's Crime and Mothers in Prison: A Peacemaking Approach." *Crime & Delinquency* 48: 300–315.

Rafter, Nicole. 2005. "Cesare Lombroso and the Origins of Criminology: Rethinking Criminological Traditions." In *The Essential Criminology Reader*, edited by Stuart Henry and Mark Lanier. Westview/Basic Books. Retrieved September 3, 2010, from http://www.farum.it/publifarumv/n/01/pdf/Rafter.pdf.

Real Cost of Prisons blog. 2008. "OK: Good News Theresa Hernandez." Retrieved December 1, 2010, from http://realcostofprisons.org/blog/archives/2008/11/ok _good_news_ab.html.

Reisig, Michael D., Kristy Holtfreter, and Merry Morash. 2002. "Social Capital and Women Offenders: Examining the Distribution of Social Networks and Resources." *Journal of Contemporary Criminal Justice* 18 (2): 167–187.

———. 2006. "Assessing Recidivism Risk across Female Pathways to Crime." *Justice Quarterly* 23: 354–405.

Richie, Beth E. 1996. *Compelled to Crime: The Gender Entrapment of Battered Black Women*. New York: Routledge.

———. 2001. "Challenges Incarcerated Women Face as They Return to Their Communities: Findings from Life History Interviews." *Crime & Delinquency* 47: 368–389.

Riggs, Angel. 2008. "Prison Intake Facility Is for Women Only." *Tulsa World* online. Retrieved April 2, 2012, from http://www.tulsaworld.com/news/article .aspx?articleID=20080218_1_A1_SWor124500.

Rivera, Beverly, and Cathy S. Widom. 1990. "Childhood Victimization and Violent Offending." *Violence and Victims* 5: 19–35

Rose, Dina R., Venezia Michaelsen, Dawn R. Wiest, and Anupia Fabian. 2008. "Women, Reentry, and Everyday Life: Time to Work?" The Women's Prison Association. Retrieved May 25, 2008, from http://66.29.139.159/pdf/Women%20Reentry%20 and%20Everyday%20Life%20%20Final%20Report.pdf.

Rosenbaum, Marsha. 1979. "Difficulties in Taking Care of Business: Women Addicts as Mothers." *American Journal of Drug and Alcohol Abuse* 6: 431–446.

———. 1981. *Women on Heroin*. New Brunswick, NJ: Rutgers University Press.

———. 1997. "Women: Research and Policy: Part I." In *Substance Abuse: A Comprehensive Textbook*, 3rd ed., 654–665. Baltimore: Williams & Wilkins.

Sabol, William J., and Heather C. West. 2008. *Prisoners in 2007*, NCJ-224280. Washington, DC. US Department of Justice/Bureau of Justice Statistics. Retrieved October 10, 2010, from http://bjs.ojp.usdoj.gov/index.cfm?ty=pbdetail&iid=903.

Sabol, William J., Heather C. West, and Matthew Cooper. 2009. *Prisoners in 2008*, NCJ-228417. Washington, DC: US Department of Justice/Bureau of Justice Statistics. Retrieved August 30, 2010, from http://bjs.ojp.usdoj.gov/content/pub/pdf/p08.pdf.

Salisbury, Emily J., and Patricia Van Voorhis. 2009. "Gendered Pathways: A Quantitative Investigation of Women Probationers' Paths to Incarceration." *Criminal Justice and Behavior* 36: 541–566.

Salisbury, Emily J., Patricia Van Voorhis, and Georgia V. Spiropoulos. 2009. "The Predictive Validity of a Gender-Responsive Needs Assessment: An Exploratory Study." *Crime & Delinquency* 55: 550–585.

Sampson Robert, J., and John H. Laub. 1993. *Crime in the Making: Pathways and Turning Points Through Life.* Cambridge, MA: Harvard University Press.

Sandhu, Harjit S., Salem Al-Mosleh Hmoud, and Bill Chown. 1994. *Journal of the Oklahoma Criminal Justice Research Consortium.* Retrieved December 2, 2010, from http://www.doc.state.ok.us/offenders/ocjrc/94/940650c.htm.

Schur, Edwin. 1984. *Labeling Women Deviant: Gender, Stigma and Social Control.* New York: Random House.

Schram, Pamela J. 2003. "Stereotypes and Vocational Programming for Women Prisoners." In *The Incarcerated Woman: Rehabilitative Programming in Women's Prisons*, edited by Susan F. Sharp. Upper Saddle River, NJ: Prentice Hall.

Seiter, Richard P. and Karen R. Kadela. 2003. "Prisoner Reentry: What Works, What Doesn't, and What's Promising." *Crime & Delinquency* 49 (3): 360–388.

Sentencing Project. 2005. "New Incarceration Figures: Thirty-Three Years of Consecutive Growth." Retrieved October 26, 2010, from http://www.sentencingproject.org/doc/publications/inc_newfigures.pdf.

———. 2010. "Crack Reform." Retrieved October 19, 2010, from http://www.sentencingproject.org/crackreform/index.cfm.

———. n.d. "Crack Cocaine Sentencing Policy: Unjustified and Unreasonable." Retrieved October 19, 2010, from http://www.prisonpolicy.org/scans/sp/1003.pdf.

Severance, T. 2004. "Concerns and Coping Strategies of Women Inmates Concerning Release: 'It's Going to Take Somebody in My Corner.'" *Journal of Offender Rehabilitation* 38 (4): 73–97.

Sharp, Susan F. 1996. "Not for Men Only: Women, Injecting Drug Use, and AIDS." PhD diss., University of Texas at Austin.

———. 1998. "Relationships with Children and Needle-Risk Behaviors among Female IDUs." *Deviant Behavior* 19: 3–28.

———. 2004/2005. Oklahoma Study of Incarcerated Women and Their Children: Phase I data.

———. 2004. "Incarcerated Mothers and Their Children, Phase I." Report to the Oklahoma Commission on Children and Youth and the Oklahoma State Legislature. Oklahoma City: Oklahoma Commission on Children and Youth.

———. 2005a. "Incarcerated Mothers and Their Children, Phase II." Report to the Oklahoma Commission on Children and Youth and the Oklahoma State Legislature. Oklahoma City: Oklahoma Commission on Children and Youth.

———. 2005b. "Incarcerated Mothers and Their Children, Phase III." Report to the Oklahoma Commission on Children and Youth and the Oklahoma State Legislature. Oklahoma City: Oklahoma Commission on Children and Youth.

———. 2006. "Incarcerated Mothers and Their Children, 2006." Report to the Oklahoma Commission on Children and Youth and the Oklahoma State Legislature. Oklahoma City: Oklahoma Commission on Children and Youth.

———. 2007. Oklahoma Study of Incarcerated Women and Their Children: Phase I data.

———. 2008. Oklahoma Study of Incarcerated Women and Their Children: Phase I data.

———. 2008a. "The Real Cost of Incarcerating Mothers: Study of Incarcerated Women and Their Children." Report to the Oklahoma Commission on Children and Youth and the Oklahoma State Legislature. Oklahoma City: Oklahoma Commission on Children and Youth.

———. 2008b. "Breaking the Cycle of Violence: Study of Incarcerated Women and Their Children." Report to the Oklahoma Commission on Children and Youth and the Oklahoma State Legislature. Oklahoma City: Oklahoma Commission on Children and Youth.

———. 2009. Oklahoma Study of Incarcerated Women and Their Children: Phase I data.

Sharp, Susan F., ed. 2003. *The Incarcerated Woman: Rehabilitative Programming in Women's Prisons.* Upper Saddle River, NJ: Prentice-Hall.

Sharp, Susan F., Jennifer Hartsfield, Sonya Conner, and Marcus Wolf. 2007. "Incarcerated Mothers and Their Children, 2007." Report to the Oklahoma Commission on Children and Youth and the Oklahoma State Legislature. Oklahoma City: Oklahoma Commission on Children and Youth.

Sharp, Susan F., and Susan Marcus-Mendoza. 1997. *A Preliminary Analysis of Gender Differences in the Effects of Parental Incarceration.* Report to Oklahoma Department of Corrections.

———. 1997-1998. Oklahoma Study of Gender Differences in the Impact of Incarceration on the Families of Drug Offenders data.

———. 2001. "It's a Family Affair: Incarcerated Women and Their Families." *Women & Criminal Justice* 12: 21–49.

Sharp, Susan F., Susan T. Marcus-Mendoza, Robert G. Bentley, Debra B. Simpson, and Sharon R. Love. 1998. "Gender Differences in the Impact of Incarceration and Children and Families of Drug Offenders." *Journal of the Oklahoma Criminal Justice Research Consortium* 4, http://www.doc.state.ok.us/offenders/ocjrc/97_98/gdiffrnc .pdfOffenders. Reprinted in K. Train and M. Corsianos, eds. *Interrogating Social Justice: Politics, Culture and Identity.* Toronto: Canadian Scholars' Press Inc.

Sharp, Susan F., and Emily Pain. 2010. *No Sympathy.* Oklahoma City: Oklahoma Commission on Children and Youth.

Shelden, Randall G. 2001. *Controlling the Dangerous Classes: A Critical Introduction to the History of Criminal Justice.* Needham Heights, MA: Allyn and Bacon.

———. 2010. *The Prison Industry.* San Francisco: Center on Juvenile and Criminal Justice. Retrieved December 10, 2010, from http://www.cjcj.org/files/The_Prison _Industry.pdf.

Shlafer, Rebecca J., and Julie Poehlmann. 2010. "Attachment and Caregiving Relationships in Families Affected by Parental Incarceration." *Attachment & Human Development* 12: 395–415.

Shlafer, Rebecca J., Julie Poehlmann, and Nancy Donnelan-McCall. 2012. "Maternal Jail Time, Conviction, and Arrest as Predictors of Children's 15-Year Antisocial Outcomes in the Context of a Nurse Home Visiting Program." *Journal of Child and Adolescent Psychology* 41: 38–52.

Siegel, Jane A., and Williams, Linda M. 2003. "The Relationship between Child Sexual Abuse and Female Delinquency and Crime: A Prospective Study." *Journal of Research in Crime and Delinquency* 40: 71–94.

Simon, Rita. 1975. *The Contemporary Woman and Crime.* Washington, DC: National Institute of Mental Health.

Simpson, Sally. 1989. "Feminist Theory, Crime, and Justice." *Criminology* 27: 605–631.

Simpson, Sally S., Jennifer L. Yahner, and Laura Dugan. 2008. "Understanding Women's Pathways to Jail: Analysing the Lives of Incarcerated Women." *Australian and New Zealand Journal of Criminology* 41: 84–108.

Smart, Carol. 1976. *Women, Crime and Criminology: A Feminist Critique*. London: Routledge and Kegan Paul.

Spivak, Andrew, and Kelly R. Damphousse. 2006. "Who Returns to Prison? A Survival Analysis of Recidivism among Adult Offenders Released in Oklahoma, 1985–2004." *Justice Research & Policy* 8: 57–88.

Spivak, Andrew, and Susan F. Sharp. 2008. "Inmate Recidivism as a Measure of Private Prison Performance." *Crime & Delinquency* 54: 482–508.

Steffensmeier, Darrell, and Emilie Allan. 1996. "Gender and Crime: Toward a Gendered Theory of Female Offending." *Annual Review of Sociology* 22: 459–487.

Strozier, Anne L., Mary Armstrong, Stella Skuza, Dawn Cecil, and James McHale. 2011. "Co-Parenting in Kinship Families with Incarcerated Mothers: A Qualitative Study." *PubMed*. Retrieved January 7, 2012, from http://www.ncbi.nlm.nih.gov/pmc/articles/PMC3124244/.

Talley, Tim. 1998. "'Truth-in-Sentencing' Debate Continues." *The Journal Record*, February 17, 1998. Retrieved October 26, 2010, from http://findarticles.com/p/articles/mi_qn4182/is_19980217/ai_n10116671/pg_2/?tag=content;c011.

Thomas, W. I. 1923. *The Unadjusted Girl*. Boston: Little, Brown and Company.

Travis, Jeremy. 2005. *But They All Come Back: Facing the Challenges of Prisoner Reentry*. Washington, DC: Urban Institute Press.

Travis, Jeremy, Solomon, Amy L., and Michelle Waul. 2001. *From Prison to Home: The Dimensions and Consequences of Prisoner Reentry*. Washington, DC: Urban Institute, Justice Policy Center.

Travis, Jeremy, and Christine Visher, eds. 2005. *Prisoner Reentry and Crime in America*. Cambridge: Cambridge University Press.

Tulsa World. Crime Watch. 2010. "Review Asked in Case Involving Accused Tulsa Officers." Retrieved December 13, 2010, from http://www.tulsaworld.com/webextra/content/2010/crimesite/article.aspx?subjectid=450&articleid=20101030_298_0_Awoman960383.

Tupper, Michael. 2007. "Oklahoma Drug Courts: Fighting Addictions and Changing Behaviors." *Oklahoma Bar Journal* 78. Retrieved November 30, 2010, from http://www.okbar.org/obj/articles07/110307tupper.htm.

Umberson, Debra, Kristin Anderson, and Susan F. Sharp. 1996. "Mern's Relationship Study."

U.S. Census. 2006. State Ranking—Statistical Abstract of the United States: Violent Crime. Retrieved August 30, 2010, from http://www.census.gov/statab/ranks/rank21.html.

———. 2010. Oklahoma Quick Facts. Retrieved January 3, 2010, from http://quickfacts.census.gov/qfd/states/40000.html.

U.S. Department of Justice. 1994. "Record Number of Prisoners Reached Again Last Year." Press Release, June 1, 1994. Retrieved October 15, 2010, from http://bjs.ojp.usdoj.gov/content/pub/press/PI93.PR.

U.S. Department of Justice. 1995. "State and Federal Prisons Report Record Growth During Last 12 Months." Press Release, December 5, 1995. Washington, DC: U. S. Department of Justice. Retrieved August 30, 2010, from http://bjs.ojp.usdoj.gov/content/pub/pdf/pam95.pdf.

United States Sentencing Commission. 1995. Report on Cocaine and Federal Sentencing Policy. Retrieved October 19, 2010, from http://www.ussc.gov/

Vera Justice Institute. 1996. *The Unintended Consequences of Incarceration: Papers from a Conference Organized by Vera Institute of Justice, January 1996*. Retrieved December 14, 2010, from http://www.vera.org/download?file=231/uci.pdf.

Visher, Christine A., and Jeremy Travis. 2003. "Transitions from Prison to Community: Understanding Individual Pathways." *Annual Review of Sociology* 29: 89–113.

West, Heather C. 2010. *Prisoners at Year End 2009—Statistical Tables.* NCJ-230113. Washington, DC: U.S. Department of Justice: Bureau of Justice Statistics. Retrieved August 30, 2010, from http://bjs.ojp.usdoj.gov/content/pub/pdf/pim09st.pdf.

West, Heather C., and William J. Sabol. 2010. *Bulletin: Prisoners in 2009.* NCJ-231675. Washington, DC: U.S. Department of Justice: Bureau of Justice Statistics. Retrieved August 30, 2010, from http://bjs.ojp.usdoj.gov/content/pub/pdf/pim09st.pdf.

Western, Bruce. 2002. "The Impact of Incarceration on Wage Mobility and Inequality." *American Sociological Review* 67 (4), 526–546.

Widom, Cathy S. 1989. "The Cycle of Violence." *Science* 244: 160–166.

———. 1995. *Victims of Childhood Sexual Abuse—Later Criminal Consequences.* Research in Brief/National Institute of Justice. Washington, DC: U.S. Department of Justice.

Widom, Cathy Spatz, and Michael G. Maxfield. 2001. *An Update on the "Cycle of Violence."* Research in Brief/National Institute of Justice. Washington, DC: U.S. Department of Justice.

Wildeman, Christopher, Jason Schnittker, and Kristin Turney. 2012. "Those They Leave Behind: Paternal Incarceration and Maternal Instrumental Support." *Journal of Marriage and the Family* 73: 1149–1165.

Wilson, William Julius. 1987. *The Truly Disadvantaged.* Chicago: University of Chicago Press.

———. 1996. *When Work Disappears: The World of the New Urban Poor.* New York: Random House.

Women's Advocacy Project. 2005. "Making Family Reunification a Reality for Criminal Justice-Involved Women." Retrieved December 27, 2012, from http://www.wpaonline.org/pdf/Recommendations_2005.pdf.

Yaniv, Oren. 2012. "WEED OUT: More Than a Dozen City Maternity Ward Regularly Test New Moms for Marijuana and Other Drugs." *Daily News*, December 25, 2012. Retrieved December 27, 2012, from http://www.nydailynews.com/new-york/weed-dozen-city-maternity-wards-regularly-test-new-mothers-marijuana-drugs-article-1.1227292#ixzz2GAyg5w54.

Index

About the Authors

SUSAN F. SHARP is the David Ross Boyd and presidential professor of sociology and women's and gender studies at the University of Oklahoma, where she has taught since 1996. She received her doctorate in sociology from the University of Texas at Austin in 1996. Dr. Sharp has conducted research on the impact of criminal justice policies on families of offenders since 1997 and co-chaired the Oklahoma Legislative Task Force on Children of Incarcerated Parents. She is the author of over thirty articles on gender, crime, and the criminal justice system, as well as the book *Hidden Victims: Effects of the Death Penalty on Families of the Accused*.

JUANITA ORTIZ, author of chapter 5, is an assistant professor in the criminal justice department at the University of Illinois–Springfield. She received her doctorate from the University of Oklahoma. Her chapter is based on her 2008 dissertation research, which focused on interviews with women who had returned to prison after being released.

Michael Welch, *Crimes of Power & States of Impunity: The U.S. Response to Terror*

Michael Welch, *Scapegoats of September 11th: Hate Crimes and State Crimes in the War on Terror*

Saundra D. Westervelt and Kimberly J. Cook, *Life after Death Row: Exonerees' Search for Community and Identity*

Laura S. Abrams and Ben Anderson-Nathe, *Compassionate Confinement: A Year in the Life of Unit C*

Jamie J. Fader, Falling Back: Incarceration and Transitions to Adulthood among Urban Youth

Andrea M. Leverentz, *The Ex-Prisoner's Dilemma: How Women Negotiate Competing Narratives of Reentry and Desistance*